Villainy Often Goes Unpunished

Indian Records from the North Carolina General Assembly Sessions

1675-1789

William L. Byrd, III

HERITAGE BOOKS
2012

HERITAGE BOOKS
AN IMPRINT OF HERITAGE BOOKS, INC.

Books, CDs, and more—Worldwide

For our listing of thousands of titles see our website
at
www.HeritageBooks.com

Published 2012 by
HERITAGE BOOKS, INC.
Publishing Division
100 Railroad Ave. #104
Westminster, Maryland 21157

Copyright © 2002 William L. Byrd, III

All rights reserved. No part of this book may be reproduced or transmitted in any form or by any means, electronic or mechanical, including photocopying, recording or by any information storage and retrieval system without written permission from the author, except for the inclusion of brief quotations in a review.

International Standard Book Numbers
Paperbound: 978-0-7884-2046-7
Clothbound: 978-0-7884-9454-3

"Certaine Indian Captives belongen to ye Town of Bare River should be Exposed to Sale: to such persons as Should bid Highest for them..." *Bare River Indians captured during the Tuscarora War, 1711.*

"Capt Luton Came & undertook ye Sd Survey by Various Courses did Lay out a tract of Land for ye sd Indians but wholy Contrary to ye Intent & Meaneing of ye sd Order for ye Petitioners are very Confident that ye Intent of ye Councill was that such Land should be layd out for them as would produce Corn." *Mattamuskeet Indian Petition to the Colonial Government of North Carolina.*

"That each of the said Indians who shall be taken captive during the Present War by any Person as aforesaid, shall and is hereby declared to be a slave and the absolute right and Property of him who shall be the Captor of Such Indian" *North Carolina Laws, 1760*

"Brothers here is One thing You Your Selves are to Blame Very much in, That in You Rot Your grain in Tubs out of which You take and make Strong Spirits You Sell it to our Young men And give it them, many times; they got Very Drunk with it this is the Very Cause that they Often times Commit those Crimes that is offensive to You and we and all thro' the Effect of that Drink it is all Very bad for our people, for it Rots their guts and Causes our men to get Very Sick and Many of our people has Lately Died by the Effect of that Strong Drink." *King Hagler, Chief of the Catawba Indians, 1754*

Whereas it has been represented to this Assembly that divers Persons under pretence of dealing with the Cherokee & Catawba Indians have committed many Frauds and irregularities to the great disturbance of those People. *The North Carolina General Assembly, 1757.*

Your Committee recommend to the House that a proper Allowance be made for the taking of an Indian Scalp Produced by Mr. John Frohock: taken by Henry Harmon who went with a partie under the Command of Captn. Tage[?] Allowed by the House. *Committee of Claims, North Carolina General Assembly, 1760.*

Contents

Introduction .... *vii*
Acknowledgements .... *xi*
Chapter One *1*
   Colonial Court Records *1*
     1675 - 1775 .... *1*
Chapter Two *31*
   General Assembly Sessions records *31*
     1709 - 1776 .... *31*
Chapter Three *99*
   General Assembly Sessions Records *99*
     1777 - 1789 .... *99*
Appendix A *259*
   North Carolina Law *259*
Appendix B *279*
Index *281*

Introduction

The General Assembly Sessions Records are comprised of a vast collection of manuscripts bulging with a wealth of historical documents. They consist of 624.4 cu. ft. of records stored in 1,561 fibredex boxes. The records are arranged chronologically, and by record type.[1]

Some of the documents in this collection are torn, faded, or unreadable. Occasionally, in document groups, a few pages are missing. For the most part, they have remained intact since the Colonial era, and loss of records appears to be minimal.

---

[1] *Guide to Research Materials in the North Carolina State Archives: State Agency Records* (Raleigh: Division of Archives and History, Department of Cultural Resources, 1992), 738.

North Carolina's legislature most likely met for the first time in 1665, as the General Assembly of Albemarle County.[2] The transcriptions published in this volume span the years from 1709 to 1789, and represent a wide variety of documents.

North Carolina's General Assembly Sessions records are filled with intrigue of every description. This particular volume contains Indian records, and records indirectly relating to Indians. In addition, documents relating to Indians from the University of North Carolina, the University of Virginia, and Duke University are also been included. The records are filled with warfare, murder, massacres, revenge, deceit, first person narratives, petitions, Indian traders, lists of people killed, Indian slavery, Indian narratives, and hundreds and hundreds of names. The documents in this book are complete and full transcriptions of the records so far as they could be read.

Chapter One begins with colonial records of North Carolina's early tribes.[3] Westward expansion and unfair trade practices soon cause tensions to rise between the Indians and colonists. The grievances between the two eventually erupt in 1712, and culminate in the Tuscarora War. There were massacres on both sides, and the Colony of North Carolina appealed to South Carolina for help. In the end, the Indians were defeated, and a treaty was signed.

By the time of the French and Indian War in 1756 the colonists were settled as far west as the Catawba River. Nestled in the Appalachian Mountains farther west was the home of the Cherokees. Beyond the Cherokees to the west and southwest were the tribes of the Creeks, Choctaws and Chickasaws; all standing in the path of the inevitable tide of immigrants and settlers who would change their way of life forever.

The attempts by whites to control Indians by using cruel and violent methods is similar to the cruel treatment of the Moors by the Spaniards in seventeenth century Spain.[4] Indian slavery was also not uncommon in North Carolina. The large number of captive Indians taken during the Tuscarora War spurred Governor Hyde to exploit "...the great

---

[2] Ibid, 734.
[3] See **Appendix B** at the back of this book for a list of North Carolina's early tribes
[4] David R. Wrone and Russell S. Nelson, Jr., eds., *Who's the Savage? A Documentary History of the Mistreatment of the Native North Americans* (Connecticut: Fawcett Publications, 1973) 22.

advantage that may be made of slaves, there being many hundreds of them; women and children; May we not believe three or four thousand."[5] The practice of enslaving Indians in "Just Wars," was endorsed by North Carolina law into the late 1700s.[6]

It has been estimated that before European arrival there were five million Indians living in what would become the United States. By the year 1800, the estimate dropped to around 500,000.[7] In eastern North and South Carolina the decline in Indian population between 1685 and 1790 was near 97%. This decline was preceded by two earlier centuries that brought disease and devastation. The result of this was that at the end of the 18th century less than 5,000 Native people were left alive in all of eastern Virginia, North Carolina, South Carolina and Louisiana combined.[8] Other than the Cherokees and Catawbas, only remnant tribes of North Carolina's earlier Indian population remain today. The majority of these tribes are recognized by the State of North Carolina.

A word about the Tuscaroras: There is such a voluminous amount of original and secondary documents that have surfaced in relation to the Tuscarora Indians, that they will be published in a separate book. Some of the papers unearthed by this author have never been published or referenced (or at least not as far as this author is aware.)

---

[5] Almon Wheeler Lauber, *Indian Slavery in Colonial Times within the Present Limits of the United States* (1913; reprint, Massachusetts: Corner House Publisher, 1979) 133.

[6] Douglas L. Rights, *The American Indian in North Carolina* (Winston-Salem: John F. Blair, Publisher, 1957) 180-181.

[7] Russell Thornton, *American Indian Holocaust and Survival: A Population History Since 1492* (Oklahoma: University of Oklahoma Press, 1987) xvii, Figure P-1

[8] David E. Stannard, *American Holocaust: The Conquest of the New World* (New York: Oxford University Press, 1992) 121.

Acknowledgements

The publishing of this book would not have been possible without the courteous help and knowledge of the staff of the North Carolina State Archives. It is a sometimes frustrating job, but they always seem to know how to deal with problems in a helpful and diplomatic manner.

Credit is also due to the staff of the Manuscript Reading Room of the *Southern Historical Collection* at the University of North Carolina. They guided me to the appropriate collections related to Colonial North Carolina Indians. They were always helpful and courteous.

Acknowledgment is also due to Sheila Stover. She worked with me early on trying to ferret out what became of North Carolina's early Indian Tribes. Most of my interest in the early tribes stems from her.

Colonial Court Records
1675 - 1775

Chapter One
Colonial Court Records
1675 - 1775

North Carolina State Archives
Colonial Court Records, CCR - 192
Miscellaneous Papers, 1677-1775
File Named: Indians - 1697-1758

In the name of our Lord God Everlasting Amen We that have under written Viz. James Bennet Thomas Hiter Charles Beasley Jemiah Pushing Send greeting to all Christian People Know ye that for & in Consideration of one hundred pounds Currant Bills of North Carolina to us in hand paid or Secured to be paid by James Hinton the Receipt whereof we the Sd Indians do hereby acquitt Exonerate & Discharge the sd James Hinton his heirs and assignes for ever have given granted Bargained & Sold & Do by these presents give grant bargain & Sell all that part and parcell of Land Lying and being in Chowan Precinct Beginning at the fork where Wm Axon Lives and Runing up along Jacob Hintens Line to his Corner Tree & So to the Syprus Tree and from thence to the main Road to the Maple Branch & Down the Maple Branch to the first Station Containing by Estimation five hundred Acres be the same more or less, To have & to hold the sd Land Bargained & Sold as aforesaid unto James Hinton his he[irs] and assignes forever with all rights & appurtenances thereof with all Clear Land Wood Land & all other Liberties and privileges thereunto or thereon Contained and wee the Sd Indians Viz. James Bennett Thomas Hiter Charles Beasley Jeremiah Pushing all & every of us do promise & warrant that att the Ensealing & Delivery hereof we have a good right Lawful athority to Sell

Colonial Court Records
_1675 - 1775_

the Same to James Hinten as Being given to us by an Instrument of Writing frome the Honourable Governor & Counsell of the Province aforesd Bearing Date 1734 and we the Indians all & every of us Do warrant the sd premises Bargained and Sold as aforsd to James Hinten his heirs and assignes for ever free from all Claims and Demands of us the Sd Indians our heirs Extors & admrs or any other person or persons Whatsoever Laying Lawfull Claim Thereunto or any part or parcell thereof & for the Acknowledgment of the Same before the Honourable Governor & Counsel when thereunto Reasonably Req[Torn] Wee do bind our Selves our heirs Extors admrs in the full Sum of two hundred Pounds Bill moneys for witness Whereof we have hereunto Sett our hands & Seal this 9th day of January 1733
Signed Seald & Delivered
In Presents of us

John Ashton	James Bennett
Thomas Garrett	Thomas Hiter
John Thomas	Charles Beasley
Thos. Carman	Jeremiah Pushing
May ye 20th 1734	Nuce Will

     This Day Came before James Bennet and acknowledged that he executes the above deed in due forme of law as did also Thos Carman who made oath that he Said Thos. Hiter acknowledged the same forme. Let it be Registered
               Wm. Smith CJ

****

In The name of our Lord God Everlasting and Wee that have under written Stand greeting to all Christian People know ye that wee James Bennett Thos. Hiter Charles Beazley Jeremiah Pushen John Robins John Reding Nuce Will Indians of Chowan precinct in the County of Albemarle and Province of north Carolina of the one Part & Thos. Garrett of the Precinct & Province afsd Witnesseth that wee James Bennett Thos. Hitter and Charles Beazley Jeremiah Pushin John Robins John Reding Nuce Will for & in Consideration of one hundred & fifty Pounds Currant Bills of north Carolina to them in hand paid on [?] to be Paid by Thomas Garrett aforsd whereof wee the sd Indians doth hereby acquit Exonerate and Discharge the Sd Thomas Garrett his heirs & assignes for ever have given Granted

Colonial Court Records
1675 - 1775

bargained & Sold and do by these Presents fully Clearly absolutely give grant bargain aline & Sell all that Part & Parcell of Land lying & being in Chowan Prect aforsd and being part of a pattent bearing Date one thousand Seven hundred & twenty four the Sd Land beginning at the mouth of a branch Known by the name of Gum Branch So up the Swamp to a branch to Capt. Aron Blansherds line So along his line to a branch by his Plantation at a bridge then from The Bridge by a line of markt trees the Course runing to the head of the Tarkill Branch by a pond along to the jeneper Branch then Down the Jeneper branch to a bridge Called the Jeneper Bridge then from the bridge along the Path to the Gum Branch then down the gum branch to the first Station Containing by Estimation four hundred Acres be it more or less to have & to hold the Sd Land bargained & Sold as aforsd unto Thomas Garrett his heirs & Assignes for ever with all timbers Lite wood & all Pro[Torn] Belonging thereunto & thereon Contained and wee the Sd Indians James Bennett Thos. Hiter Charles Beazley Jeremiah Pushing John Robins Jno. Reding Nuce Will all & every of us our heirs Extors admitors & assignes Do promise & warrant at the Ensealing & delivery hereof wee have a good right and Lawfull authority to Bargain and Sell the Same to the Sd Thomas Garrett his heirs and assignes forever and by these Presents doth Warrant the sd Premises free from all Claims and Demands and Incumbrances that may incurr hereafter of us the Sd Indians of any or either of us our heirs Extors or admitors and that the land & primisses now are and so Shall and may for ever hereafter Remain Continue & be unto the Sd Thomas Garrett his heirs or assignes for ever & for the acknowledgment of the Same before the Governor & his Counsell or any other Person appointed for that Purpose when theirunto Required wee do bind ourselves our heirs Extors & admitors assignes all & every of us in the Sum of one thousand pounds Currant money of this Province Given under our hands and Seales this seventh day of april 1734

Signed Sealed & Delivered	James Bennett
In the Presents of us	Thomas Hitter
Michael Ward	Charles Beazley
Henry Hill	Jeremiah Pushing
May ye 20th 1733	John Robins
	John Reding
	Nuce Will

Colonial Court Records
1675 - 1775

This day Came before me James Bennett Jeremiah Pushing & Jno. Robins Indians & acknowledged that they Executed the above Deed in due form of Law & was ordered to be Registered
                      William Smith   C.J.

****

North Carolina State Archives
Colonial Court Records
CCR - 192
Miscellaneous Papers, 1675-1775
File Named: Indians - 1697-1758
Treaties, Petitions, Agreements, and Court Cases

        William Frys Deposition Relative to the Indians

The deposition of William Fry aged about Eighteen Years on oath Saith

That on the 24th day of May 1757 he was travelling on the Road leading from Bonners Bridge to Cashy after passing Bonner Bridge about one Mile and Some better I saw a woman lying dead on the Road With a great deal of blood lying at the place where She lay being in a Small Branch over which was a pole Caus way I Run with My might till I heard Somebody Call Who Asked me if I saw Ever a woman I told there was one dead a little way of and further Saith not
        Examined before Me Jos. Hardy
        Coroner   William [?]

****

      The Deposition of John Liscomb Matter Concerning the Indian

The Deposition of John Liscomb a man Aged about 36 years on oath Saith

That on the 24th day of May 1757 he was Travilling with Elizabeth Knott to go to Virginia and Between Cashy Bridg and Bonners Bridg They Came to the house of John Wyatts who told them that the Indians Came into his house that day and Behaved Themselves in Very Ill Manner Wyatt told them to Call at the Next house and they would hear a great deal more but when we Come there was nobody at home Mrs: Knott then Missing a

Colonial Court Records
1675 - 1775

handkercheif desired I would goe Back and pick it up she Likewise Said She had it in Sight of the plantation where we then Was She further Said She would walk slowly on till I overtook her again I went and found the Handkercheif in Sight of the plantation as She Said & returning I Mett two Men Near the Spot I parted from her at then I saw the Beast she Rode Coming back full Speed I desired they would assist Me to cetch her then I Taking the beast and went on to look the woman thinking the beast had flung her in Rideing Some better than a Quarter of a mile I called her three times and looking forward I Saw an Indian Rise from the Earth which put me in a Surprise the Indian hallered three times Waugh and stamped I Saw him dart to one side the road Supposing he was going for his gun I turned My horse about and Called to the two men I had left: for to help: one of the men coming to me I told him I wanted assistance which he refused as having no Arms: we all three turned out of the Road to Gitt Arms: then Seeing a lad Running up the Road I turned about and called to him and he coming to us as Quick as he could I asked him Whether he had Seen any Woman on the road he Replyed for god Sake what Woman is that lyes dead there: I asking where he said there was one dead in a bottom Lying upon Some poles Which Was the place I Saw the Indian Rise from and that it was not Six Minutes from the time I Saw the Indian Rise to the time the lad told Me that he Saw the woman dead and further this deponent Saith not

Taken before Me Jos Hardy Coroner John Liscomb

****

North Carolina

At a Supreme Court of Justice Oyer and Terminer and General Goal Delivery began and held at Edenton on the Second Tuesday in October in the thirtieth year of the Reign of our Sovereign Lord George the Second now King of Great Brittain (and so forth) for the Countys of Currituck, Pasquotank, Perquimans, Chowan, Bertie and Tyrell before the Honourable Peter Henly Esquire Cheif Justice of the Province aforsd.

The Jurors for our Lord the King upon their oath present that James Strawberry an Indian late of society parish in the County of Bertie not having the fear of God before his Eyes but being Moved and Seduced by the Instigation of the Devil on the Twenty Fourty day of May in the

Colonial Court Records
1675 - 1775

Thirtieth Year of the Reign of our Sovereign Lord George now King of Great Brittain (and so forth) about the hour of three in the afternoon of the same Day at Society Parish aforesaid in the Province aforesaid with force and Arms made an Assault in and upon Elizabeth Knott then and there being in the Peace of God and of our said Lord the King and that the said James Strawberry at Society Parish aforesaid in the County aforesaid did feloniously wilfully and of his Malice aforethought Strike and Wound the said Elizabeth Knott with a Light Wood Knott which the said James Strawberry had and held then and there in his Right Hand and did feloniously and of his Malice aforethought at Society parish aforesaid in the County aforesaid Give to the said Elizabeth Knott three Mortal Wounds with a Light Wood Knott aforesaid in and upon the Back part of her Head off the length of one Inch and off the Depth of one Inch of which said Mortal Wounds the said Elizabeth Knot at Society Parish aforesaid in the County aforesaid Instantly Died and so the said Jurors upon their Oath aforesaid Say that the said James Strawberry on the said Twenty fourth day of May in the Year above Mentioned at Society Parish aforesaid in the County aforesaid did feloniously Wilfully and of his Malice forethought, hitt and Murder the said Elizabeth Knott in Manner and form aforesaid against the Peace of our said Lord the King his Crown and Dignity

Ewd [?]　　　　　　　J P Mr. [?]
Thos Kimsey[?]
John Liscomb
Willm. Fry

****

Dom Rex
Vs.
James Strawberry
Recognizance Concerning the Indian

North Carolina
Bertie County

The Twenty [?] day of May in the year of Our Lord One thousand seven hundred and Fifty seven came before me Joseph Hardy Coroner John Liscomb And william Fry and Acknowledged Each of themselves To be Indebted To our sovereign Lord the King in the sum of Ten Pound sterling

Colonial Court Records
1675 - 1775

Lawful money of Great Brittain the condition of this recognizance is such that if the above bound John Liscomb & William Fry doth Personally appear before our Cheif Justice at the next asize to be holden at Edenton on the second Tuesday of October next For the said County then and there two deliver and set Forth their Knowledge touching the death of Elizabeth Knott and do not Depart thence without License of the said Court. That non effect or else to be and Remain In full Force and Virtue Acknowledged before me the day and year above Written

Jos. Hardy Coroner

****

Colonial Court Records
North Carolina State Archives
CCR - 192
Miscellaneous Papers, 1675-1775
File Named: Indians - 1697-1758
Treaties, Petitions, Agreements, and Court Cases

Indian Deed in ye Cause
Taylor
Vs
Blanchard
Dd. Copy the Version

This indenture made this 10th: day of September 1733 Betweene James Bennett and Charles Beasley and Thomas hittor Jereme pushen and Thomas pushen and John Reding of Jowan precinct of the one part and Thomas tailor of Jowan aforesaid as witnesseth that the Said indians for and under the rents and Covenants hear after expressed hath and here by doth demise grant Let and to farm let unto the Said Thomas Tailler his Executives Administrators or assignes one hundred acres of Land lying between the myrey branch and the poplar branch upon the pocoson side lying **[Torn]** Chowan presinct belonging to the Jowan indians Called the Rain gras neck with land with all the profetes and preveledges there unto belonging to have and to hold all the above demised and granted premisses unto the Said Thomas Taillor his Executors Administrators or assignes from the 10th: day of September the 10 day unto the full term 13 years Two yeares went free firm and fully Completed and ended yealding and

Colonial Court Records
1675 - 1775

paying therefore unto the Said indians In Jowan aforesaid the rent or Sum of Two hundred 50[?] pound of Tobacko To Them there are and asinges To be paid yearly after 2 yers rent free now to the performance of these artickles above written [Faded] jointly and severly that is To [Torn] The fore Said Indins or [?] and asigns in The Sum of 2[?] hundred pounds Corent money of North Carolina to be payed upon The Nonperformances of this grement In witnos here of the Sed partes to these presens have heare unto Changeably Set there hands the day and year first above written Sinned Selled and delivered in the presents of us And if Sold the Sd Thomas taillor To have the Refuse of ye Sd Land

John ffreeman	James bennet
Walter Droughan	Charles besly
William [?]	Jereme Pushing
John Reading	

****

North Carolina State Archives
Colonial Court Records
CCR - 192
Miscellaneous papers, 1675-1775
File Named: Indians - 1697-1758
Treaties, Petitions, Agreements, and Court Cases

Broughton Vs Glover

North Carolina Ss   March General Court 1736

Andrew Broughton Esqr complains of John Glover of Bertie prect. planter in custody of ye marshall & for that to witt Whereas the said Andrew on or about ye tenth day of June in ye year of our Lord one thousand seven hundred and thirty five in the province of South Carolina was possessed of an Indian man Slave called Cyrus aged about thirty Seven years by trade a Carpenter of the price of One hundred pounds proclamation mony being the Slave and property of the said Andrew and being so possessed he the said Andrew afterwards that is to say on the aforesaid tenth day of June in the year aforsd and in the province of South Carolina aforesaid out of his hands and possession the aforesaid Indian Slave called Cyrus did casually loose which said Indian Slave so lost afterwards that is to say on or about

Colonial Court Records
1675 - 1775

the tenth day of September in the year aforesaid in the Prect. of Bertie in the aforesaid province of North Carolina into the hands and possession of the aforesaid John Glover by finding same and notwithstanding he the said John well knew the said Indian Slave Cyrus to be the property and slave of the said Andrew and that of right he then belongs to him yet he the said John continuing and intending him the Sd Andrew of the said Indian Slave to [**Torn**] and the Said Indian Slave to him ye sd. Andrew hath not as yet delivered altho often since in the precinct of Bertie aforesaid by him the sd. Andrew he the said John was so to do required But he ye said John the said Indian Slave afterwards to witt on or about the twentieth day of September in the year and prect. aforesaid for his own proper use and J[**Torn**]ns & did convert and dispose of to the said Andrews damage of five hundred pounds currt. mony of the aforesaid province of North Carolina and thereupon he Brings this Suit &c
J Montgomery Att:

****

North Carolina State Archives
Colonial Court Records
CCR - 192
Miscellaneous Papers, 1675-1775
File Named: Indians - 1697-1758
Treaties, Petitions, Agreements, and Court Cases

No. Carolina
Genl. Court

Nath: Chevin Esqr. is pl agt the sd
Wm: Reed Esqr [?] in a plea of the Case:

And ye: Said Plt Demands of ye Deft. ye Sum of Twenty nine pounds: five Shillings wch. to have Sheweth for that whereas at a Committy of both: Houses of assembly: holden at ye house of Capt: John Hecklefield in Little River on ye 20th of march Anno: 1711 in [?] into [?] Consideration [?] Certaine Indian Captives belongen to ye Town of Bare River should be Exposed to Sale: to such persons as Should bid Highest for them and that ye: money: thereby arising upon ye Sale of ye Said Indians Should be paid into ye hands of ye sd: Plt: on or before ye: tenth of march then next

Colonial Court Records
1675 - 1775

Ensuing, at wch. time & place ye afsd [?] for and in Consideration of ye five of ye: afsd: Indians Slaves upon: himself Did assume and then & there Did faithfully promise: That he: ye. afsd. Sum of Twenty nine pounds & five Shillings: would [?] Truely pay to ye sd plt: on or before: ye: Deft. ye: afsd. Sum: of Twenty nine pounds five Shillings to pay hath & Doth Still refuse the often? thereunto required whereby ye. plt: is [?] & hath Damage to ye value of five pounds & therefor he Bring this Suite
         Chevin Plt

Coll: Wm: Reed is Deft. by E: Moseley his Attorney comes and defends for & Inquiry when [?] And Saith that he did not Assume in manner & forme [?] And of this he putt himself upon ye Country
        Moseley for ye Deft.
and the plt. in Like Manner
Bonwicke Ag Deft.

Wee of the Jury find for The pltf:

****

North Carolina State Archives
Colonial Court Records
CCR - 192
Miscellaneous Papers, 1675-1775
File Named: Indians - 1697-1758
Treaties, Petitions, Agreements, and Court Cases

North Carolina

    To Mr. Anthony Hatch March 1 Late [?] Recei[?]
In Little River

  you are hereby directed and Required for the use of the Hatteras Indyans that they may not be unprovided to serve the publick if occasion requires to delivr unto Captn John Oneale Commands on the banks and of the Indyans aforesd twenty pound of powdr & forty pounds of shott with one hundred flints if so mutch be in store if not delivr as mutch of Eatch Kinde as you have by you taking his receipte for the same and for so doeing this shall be ye warrt Given under My hand in Chowan this 5th day of Septembr 1720

Colonial Court Records
1675 - 1775

Charles Eden

sepbr: 7th 1720

Received by Order of ye Governor twenty pounds: of powder and twenty Six pounds of Shott and one hundred gun flints by me

       his
    John [?] Oneale
       Mark

****

North Carolina State Archives
Colonial Court Records
CCR - 192
Miscellaneous Papers, 1675-1775
File Named: Indians - 1697-1758
Treaties, Petitions, Agreements, and Court Cases

The Honble. Landgrave Robert Daniell Esq
Govrnr of No. Carolina

The Humbl. Petition of Nicolas Dawe Sheweth

  Whereas yr Honrs. Petitionr. having Receaved Dammages to ye Value of five pound by Tom King of the Woccon Ind: Most humbly Craves yr. Honrs. mature Consideration in Reference to my Losses, so hereby I may receave some Satisfaction As in Duty bound Shall pray

****

North Carolina State Archives
Colonial Court Records
CCR - 192
Miscellaneous Papers, 1675-1775
File Named: Indians - 1697-1758
Treaties, Petitions, Agreements, and Court Cases

Mr Hatch

Colonial Court Records
1675 - 1775

I have taken from Capt. William dove of the Schooner Rect[?] tenn pounds of powder for the use of the Marramuskite Indyans wch. pray charge in ye accots. as delivrd by my order for the publick Service and give the Captn Creditt for ye same, wch will obleidge

Ye Assured friend to Serve you

Chowan Prct [?]

Charles Eden
ye 18th 1719

Mr. Anthony Hatch powdre
Received at little River

****

North Carolina State Archives
Colonial Court Records
CCR - 192
Miscellaneous Papers, 1675-1775
File Named: Indians - 1697-1758
Treaties, Petitions, Agreements, and Court Cases

Pamlico in North Carolina ffeby 29th: 1703/4

To ye Honble ye Govr: and Council wee whose names are undr written Doe Hum present to yr Honrs

That wee have great reason to believe ye neighboring towns of ye Tuscororah Indians are of late dissatisfied wth ye Inhabitants of this place and Several actions and discorses of ye Bare River Indians and more than Ordinary familiarity of late yt is between them and ye Tuscorodos: Induses us to believe yt they are Indeavoring to persuade them yt ye English here designs a war against them ye 13th[?] occasions us to [?] yt if yor. Honrs does not speedily take Sum Care in ye mattr; wee may receive Sum preiudice from them the wch wee Suppose might bee prevented[?] and yt Sum of ye Cheifs of ye Indians would come in to yor. Honrs. if you would spedily please to hr. a good Interpreter here wth orders what to doe and

Colonial Court Records
1675 - 1775

Such of us as yr Honrs. Shall appoynt are ready to gve wth Such Interpreter wee pray yr. Honrs. will take Sum Speedy Care in ye [?] for our preservation as to yor. wisdom Shall serve much and remain yr. hum. Svtts.

Lyonell Reading	Wm. Britt
Richard Smith	Hum: Legge
Nicholas Tylor	Wm. Powell
Tho. Dereham	Edward (E) Gatlin
Levi Truewhitt	Tho. Poi[?]

Mr. Reading Sayes yt the Indians of late are more Impudent in Killing their Calves than formerly and openly [Faded] of it Mr. [?] Sayes the like.

****

North Carolina State Archives
Colonial Court Records
CCR - 192
Miscellaneous Papers, 1675-1775
File Named: Indians - 1697-1758
Treaties, Petitions, Agreements, and Court Cases

North Carolina Ye [Faded]
To the Hon. Governr. & Council

The Humble Petition of John Hoyter & Rest of
ye Chowan Indians
Humble Maner Complaining

That Where upon ye Humble Petition of ye Sd Indians to this Honrble Board in the time when the Honrble Henderson Walker Esqr was President of ye Council On Order was past that ye Govnr or Depty Should lay out a tract of Land for ye Sd Indians of Six Miles Square And allso another Order in ye time of the Honrble Landgrave Robt Daniel Esqr pursuent to ye former Order.In pursuance of ye aforsd Orders ye Depty Govenr Viz Capt Luton Came & undertook ye Sd Survey by Various Courses did Lay out a tract of Land for ye sd Indians but wholy Contrary to ye Intent & Meaneing of ye sd Order for ye Petitioners are very Confident that ye Intent of ye Councill was that such Land should be layd out for them as would produce Corn for their Support & the petitioners Do prey & are

Colonial Court Records
1675 - 1775

Ready to Averr that none other parcell of ye Sd Land in ye Sd tract Layd out will produce Corn being all pines & Sands & Deserts So that they have not their Land according to ye Intent & Meaneing of the Honble Board Neither for quality nor quantity it being not near six miles Square. Wherefore your Humble Petitioners Do Humbly Pray your Honrs to take our Disatisfied Condition into your now Consideration [Torn] your Petitioners may have Releife in ye Premisses [Faded] [Torn] for Bread And Yr Petitionrs shall Ever Pray

      His
   John I Hoyter
      Mark
   in Behalfe of Himself &
   Rest of ye Nation

****

North Carolina State Archives
Colonial Court Records
CCR - 192
Miscellaneous Papers, 1675-1775
File Named: Indians - 1697-1758
Treaties, Petitions, Agreements, and Court Cases

Sr
I desire you will present my [?] to his Honour Governor Archdell, and tell him I begg his pardon that I doe not waite uppon him, for I have [?] of great importants, that I cannot possible Come as yet the indyans plays the Roge with mee they have allmost Kild all my hoggs and I am [?] to get a share with them; I could nott find my heart to [?] Sum of them out of there [?] I have six men and horses out a hunting up Marrotoc and [?] bears find a Cabin in the woods but I Eather find hogs bones or hoggs flesh or Cows, if this be Suffered, there will bee none living, I wish, Sum [?] might bee [?] this Assembly to prevent it [?] have [?] of mine from Governor Sothell for my plantation at ye log house, and Survay by Mr. [?] I desire you will get mee a paton, from Governor Archdell for ye log house land if in hand god willing to waite uppon ye Governor with in the ten days and Soe I Rest your Sarvant
Janu: 25 1696   Willm [?]

I have [?] Capt. Walker, to proseed ageanst [?] and Thomas

Colonial Court Records
1675 - 1775

palmer not John pray Speaks
>Yours
>W [?]

These
ffor Mr. William Glover
at the Assembly

****

North Carolina State Archives
Colonial Court Records
CCR - 192
Miscellaneous Papers, 1675-1775
File Named: Indians - 1697-1758
Treaties, Petitions, Agreements, and Court Cases

>Mr: Kingmans Deposition
>In & abt: ye Month of Septembr: 1707

I Being yn: att Panticough & Archibald Holmes comeing yn: on board my Sloop to ta: Sevll: Others told me yt they Expected ye Indians Every day to Come & Cut their throats & yt they had no [?]son to head ym: or Else they would goe & Secure all ye Panticough Indians, & yt he ye sd: Holmes Made Severall efecting words on Majr: Gale wch: he ye Sd: Depont: does not now remembr: and ffurther Saith nott
>Robt Kingman

Capt. or Jurat Quarto
2[?] Febry Ano Dm: 1707/8
Cora Me

W [?]

****

North Carolina State Archives
Colonial Court Records
CCR - 192
Miscellaneous Papers, 1675-1775
File Named: Indians - 1697-1758

Colonial Court Records
1675 - 1775

Treaties, Petitions, Agreements, and Court Cases

Att A Councill hold att the House of Captn. John Hecklefield in Little River Aprill ye 12th 1704.
                            sent the Lords Deputyes

Ordered that the Surveyr Generall or Deputy Shall (with what Expedition is Possible) Upon Complaint of the Yawpim Indians Lay out for the sd Indians (where they now live) four Miles Square of Land or the Quantity Not injuring any of the Old Settlements which was made before the Order of Councill bearing Date in October 1697 And Mr. John Hawkins Mr. Thomas Tayler Mr. Robert Morgan & Mr. John Relfe or any three of them are hereby required to attend the Surveyr. or Deputy in laying out the Same

To John Anderson Deputy Surveyr

To be diverted to Captn. Tho:
Relfe to execute with Speed
& Make returne

****

North Carolina State Archives
Colonial Court Records
CCR - 192
Miscellaneous Papers, 1675-1775
File Named: Indians - 1697-1758
Treaties, Petitions, Agreements, and Court Cases

North Carolina Ss Charles Eden Esqr. Governor

These may Certify that Mr. William Churton has been in the County Service by my order as Interpreter to the Indians Twelve days Given under my hand at Chowan April the 13th 1721

                            Charles Eden
To Mr. Thomas West Treasurer
For Chowan Precinct: to pay

april 18 day 1721

Colonial Court Records
1675 - 1775

Received of Tho. West three pound Clame by order of
ye Governr.

Wm. his Churton
    Mark

****

North Carolina State Archives
Colonial Court Records
CCR - 192
Miscellaneous Papers, 1675-1775
File Named: Indians - 1697-1758
Treaties, Petitions, Agreements, and Court Cases

No. Carolina Ss.
To the provost Marshall of Albemarle County or his Deputy

Whereas Mr. James Fleming of Chowan has made Information That one William Ward did run away wth. a prest Gun & that one Christopher Dudley Did hinder his March agt. ye Enemy Indians, These are therefore to will & require you to Sumons the Sd. James Flemings personally to be at the next Genl. Court to be held for this province at Major John Hecklefields house at Little River the last Tuesday in March next & then & there to make good his Information And for ye so doing - this shall be yr. Warrant Dated ye 24th of February 1714/15

                Danl. Richardson & Dom Rege

Executed by me
Daniel Halsey[?]
Dept marshall

****

North Carolina State Archives
Colonial Court Records
CCR 192
Miscellaneous Papers, 1675-1775
File Named: Indians - 1697-1758

Colonial Court Records
1675 - 1775

Treaties, Petitions, Agreements, and Court Cases

To the Honrble Coll. Thomas Palock Prest.
Octobr the: 17: 1706

Honerbl Ssr
I thought it [Blotted out] my self butt not being well at prese[Blotted out] [?] I thought going from home might Increase itt theire fore I send my Son to give ye Accounte a boute the Indians they weare gon to Meahearin Towne no men at the Cabins uppon Lewis Williams Land I tould them to get together all the Indians and I would tell them my business, then I warned them of Lewis Williams his Land and to be gon with theire towne and Cabins outher wise they must Expeckt to be forced of if they did not be gon by the twenty day of this Instant making them Senseable the meaning plane of this warning making them Senseable the Evill and danger they would bring uppon them Selves if they did not hasten a way by the time limited And After a long consultation a mongst them selves, Their Answer it would Ruin them to Remove now, now all Indians is a going a great way of a hunting, Now is the time a yeare to gett Skins be sides they must Shell theire corne be for they can Remove it and bark will note Strip, now they cannot bueld up theire cabins a gaine neather have they Anny Land to goe too for the great towne is full they say but this winter they will provide themselves with land and Remove all they have by the Spring clear of Lewis Williams Land they desire to have liberty till the Spring but if they cannot have that liberty the Englis may work this winter uppon the land only they are verry doutfull they will Receave great damidges by Reson theire corne and Cabins lieth all open they desire that we might make no lise of them for they heare Som doth make a great manny lise of them, they did not give a misbehaving word to Anny body but weare verry ci[?]ell and Kinde, more Resons then I doe heare Expressin Excuse for their not Removing this winter
                                Tho Garrett
Your humble Servant to command

****

North Carolina State Archives
Colonial Court Records
CCR - 192
Miscellaneous Papers, 1675-1775

Colonial Court Records
1675 - 1775

File Named: Indians - 1697-1758
Treaties, Petitions, Agreements, and Court Cases

N Carolina May 14th 1701
Whereas Mr. Thomas Amy hath made Information to me yt he wth. some other men being in an Indian Canoe wth. ffive Indians who pretended to Carry them to ye English butt goeing ashore they took up a Gun and a bow and arrow and presented it at ye said Mr. Amy butt he haveing one of ye Indians in ye Canoe who could not readily Leap out he Secured him and pretended to Kill him wth. his Swoard upon wch. they ran away.
Wh[Torn] [?] his Maties. named I doe Impower the said Mr. Thos. Amy, Capt. Thos. Luton, Mr. Nicho. Tylor & Capt. Nicho. [?] and Mr. Wm. Barrow or any three of them to goe to ye Matchepungo or Bear River Indians and there to demand the aforesaid Indians to be delivered up to them who made [?] assault as also the Armes wch. they Conveyed away: and to use such other meanes in ye managemt. of ye Same affaire: as to you or any three of you shall think fit and if they shall deliver up ye Same Indians to bring them before ye Counsell heldon ye first Monday in June next and I doe in his Maties name to witt & require you to press Men, horses, boate, and other Canoes [?] as shall be by you thought meet for ye doeing hereof And I doe require and Command all his Maties. Subjects be obedient to you in ye fullfilling hereof And you are to Returne an acct. of your proceedings herein And for [?] you Shall doe in ye fullfilling hereof this Shall be your Wart.: Given under my hand ye 14th May Anno 1701

Henderson Walker

****

North Carolina State Archives
Colonial Court Records
CCR - 192
Miscellaneous Papers, 1675-1775
File Named: Indians - 1697-1758
Treaties, Petitions, Agreements, and Court Cases

Pampticough. June. ye 23d 1701

Honble. Srs.

Colonial Court Records
1675 - 1775

Thursday last I was wth. ye Bay River Indians, & acquainted them wth ye contents of ye Sworn Warrt. given them by Cpt dawe: Their Kings Southwell, & evring wth. their great men mett & sent for me to Southwells Cabin before I mentioned any thing of my message to them: They produced a paper containing 5 Articles concluded from them to ye English, & Sighned by Mr. Akehurst, Mr. Calloway, Cpt. Blount, & Mr. Slade. I told thm. ye Governor demanded 4 Indian men & a boy who had offered severall Indignities to some English Gentlemen on ye sand banks as for cocking a Gun & setting it to Mr Ameys breast, they utterly denied, their Story to me run of thus. 4 Indian men & one boy mett wth. some English in a canoe who belonged to a Vessell yt was cast away & stuck a ground as they terme it, ye English asked way to Roanoake ye Indians profered their services to bring thm. to ye English there. ye Gentlemen gave them 3 Clay potts full of Rum, fisher one of ye Indians saies he told ye English if they made ye Indians drunk they would be rude, & ye Indians gave ye English Venison & 20 black Drums, one of ye Indians got drunk hearing thm. talk of Ashly River made thm. afraid of being taken thither, they fled, & let fall 3 guns of ye English into ye water in this Escape, one of thm. was a great gun, all wch. [?] they have left with one Anthony, the English took forcibly from them 4 rawe Deer skins, one Otter, one hairy match Coat & 4 baskets of corn, they were Extraordinary [?] [Torn] to me although most of thm. drunk,they say they have done no harm to ye English, & hope they may not suffer ye English Displeasure for a thing they have not acted or intended. They would make me no positive answer as to delivering up ye Indians but alw[Torn]
[Bottom line torn]

[Editors Note: Next lines written horizontally in the margin.]

Told me they hoped they might not receave any breach of their articles from ye English. I have no more at present but remain
Yr Honble.
most humble. most obedient
& most Devoted Svt.

John Lawson

****

Colonial Court Records
1675 - 1775

North Carolina State Archives
Colonial Court Records
CCR - 192
Miscellaneous Papers, 1675-1775
File Named: Indians - 1697-1758
Treaties, Petitions, Agreements, and Court Cases

North Carolina Ss.

By ye Honble. President of ye Councill -- Whereas a Warrant was Directed by ye Honble. Henderson Walker Esqr president of ye Council &c, unto Capt Rich. Daw Mr Wm Barrow Mr Nich. Tilor enjoining them to Call to account the Bear River Indians Some of which having afsd very great [--?--] [Torn] to Thomas Amy Esqr & others with him Contrary to those Articles made with this Governt & said Warrtt hath not been returned

These are Therefore in his Maitis name to require & Comand you to [--?--] the aforsd Mr Nich Tilor Capt Rich Daw Mr Wm. Barrow to make their apearance before this board the third Day of ye Honble Court to be holden for this province to Answer theire Contempt in failing to make return of theire proceedings And to have before us att the Same time & place ye King of ye Bear River Indians & his great men in pursuance of theire treaty with this Govermt Given under our hands ye 3d Day of Jan 1701

To mr James Nevill   Hendsn. Walker
Depty Marshall att
pamplico to Execute &
[Faded] returne

These Served by mee
James Nevill
Deputy Marshll.

****

North Carolina State Archives
Colonial Court Records
CCR - 192
Miscellaneous Papers, 1675-1775
File Named: Indians - 1697-1758
Treaties, Petitions, Agreements, and Court Cases

Colonial Court Records
1675 - 1775

[Editor's Note: Lower left side of this document torn away]

Pampticoe the 25th of sbr: 1699

Articles of Agreement Made & Concluded on bye & between Daniel: Akehurst Caleb Callaway Thomas Blount & Henry Slade of or parte in behalfe of the Governt. of North Carolina & Sothell King of the Bear River Indians with his Great men on behalfe of the Sd Nation of bear **[Two words blotted out]** : Parts as followeth

1: The Sd Indians shall at all times if they are accused by any English men or Indians of Murdering any of the Kings Subjects they shall Send the Said Indians Soe accused in to the English Government or to Sum officer or to Answer the Sd Accusation

2: If any Shipp, or vessell Shall be Cast away on any Shore, & any of the men Shall be found that have Escaped the Seae they Shall relieve them with Provisions & Conduct them to Sum English Plantation for which they Shall have a Match coat to ware for each man So **[Torn]** **[?]**uche & what Goods they find on the Sea Should **[Torn]** shall deliver to the English Governments & they **[Torn]** **[?]** them reasonable Salvage for ye Same **[Torn]** groes they can take up that are runn a**[Torn]** Shall bring into the English as allsoe the **[Torn]** or vessell in which they are & Gov**[Torn]** Shall have a Match Coat for each **[Torn]**aken **[Torn]**tians Shall at all times assist the **[Torn]** against the English or any Indians **[Torn]** them

5: The Sd. King or Sum of his Great men Shall yearly & every year make their appearance at the Genirall Corte to be holden in July & then & their pay to pair of Skins as a Tribute to the English Government

                King Sothell
                signum
                Mathews
                signum
                Edmund [?]elly
                signum
                Capt: Gibbs
                signum
                Lewis [?]
                signum

Colonial Court Records
1675 - 1775

Geo: Ffisher
Signum

****

North Carolina State Archives
Colonial Court Records
CCR - 192
Miscellaneous Papers, 1675-1775
File Named: Indians - 1697-1758
Treaties, Petitions, Agreements, and Court Cases

To the Honourable Robert Daniel Esqr Deputy Governor and the rest of the Honourbl membrs in Counsel

The humble petition of the Inhabitants of Matchapungo
May it please yr honrs

Wee whose names are hereunto Subscribed do humbly adresse yr honors not only in behalfe of ourselves the Subscribers but all of the Inhabitants of this place most humbly praying that Some Speedy and effective Method may bee taken for restraining the Insolency and Continued abuses of the Matchapungo Indians by killing and destroying our hoggs and beating our other neighbors for endeavoring to prevent the same as Likewise the threatening to take our lives away for discovery of these their Villanies to prevent wh. King Charles in his own person (Whether out of [?] to see how wee would resent it or out of Real Kind[Torn] wee know not) came down in the night to give us [Torn]siner wh. and to this Instant they continue unpardonably [Torn] both in their speeches and actions, In all things rather [Torn] desire to a War wth us than a peace, And have accordingly [Torn] themselves nigh a Willdernesse whereupon the last Intim[Torn] they can easily repair wth out being pursued, Wherefor these [Torn] being taken for truths, As wee are ready to prove Do therefore hope and Confidently believe that yr honours will find it part of yr Christian duty to see us defended from these barbarous heathen, And that wee may not live in such dayly Jeapordy of our lives, wee Likewise return our most humble and unfeigned thanks to the Honourable Governor for his Kind and affectionate Lettr by [?] Encouragemt wee are Embolded to give yr Honours this further Information Not doubting but to obtain reliefe by such waye as yr

Colonial Court Records
1675 - 1775

honours shall think fitt to prescribe and yr petitioners as in duty bound will ever pray

Nicholas Daw
John Britt
Simon Ffosens[?]
Richard Jasper
Roger Monntaug
James Welch

Charles Smith
Richard Batchlear
Henry Slaid
Robert Holmes
William Win
Henry Eborn

****

North Carolina State Archives
Colonial Court Records
CCR - 192
Miscellaneous Papers, 1675-1775
File Named: Indians - 1697-1758
Treaties, Petitions, Agreements, and Court Cases

October ye 20, 1703

Samuel Slockum did Declare before me upon oath that there was Indan named [?] did ask him whether the English did intend to make war or no and he said no and the Indan saide that we do understand that you do intend for to make war with us by severall of our Indan where upon he Saide the Indans are now fully Resolved for to make triall of it for to see wich is the [?] and Samuel Sloakum Saith that several others Indans has told him that thare is 2 pertigular towns doe intend for to make war and that one and all are agreed for it except 3 Indans men of the Saide 2 towns wich are very much against it but as ffor any of the other towns as yet are not agreed as yett ffor to make war with the English, and further this Deponent Saith not

and So if you think fitt   Lyonel Reading
Sir Carry this with you
and give his honest account
of it

****

Colonial Court Records
1675 - 1775

North Carolina State Archives
Colonial Court Records
CCR - 192
Miscellaneous Papers, 1675-1775
File Named: Indians - 1697-1758
Treaties, Petitions, Agreements, and Court Cases

[Editor's Note: This is an undated document.]

Mr. Badham
    I have Sent you my Account of the Indian's Tryall upon a Special Court called and if the Cheife Justice does not think fitt to allow me more I Shall be contented - Case as follows, vizt. as Attorney Genl 2:10:0: ffor my Boat & one hand to fetch the prisoner from the presdts. 0:10:0

                              Yor. very Humble Servant
                              Dan: Richardson

If you could Spare me a dozen pounds of good Sugar I will either pay you for it before I goe or order Mr. Oglesby; as likewise a Kegg of about 3 or 4: Galls. or a Jugg which Shall be answered for the returne by me or him - pray yor. imediate answere

****

North Carolina State Archives
Colonial Court Records
CCR - 192
Miscellaneous Papers, 1675-1775
File Named: Indians - 1697-1758
Treaties, Petitions, Agreements, and Court Cases

[Editor's Note: Already Transcribed by Archives Personnel.]

March ye 28th 1702
President & Councill
North Carolina Ss

Colonial Court Records
1675 - 1775

The petition of Benjamin Blanshard John Campbell, Thomas Spivey ffrancis Rountree, Robert Rountree, Robert Lacitar, George Laciter and Nicholas Stallings in all humility
Complaineth

Whereas every of your Honrs petitioners hath a lawfull right in and to considerable tracts of land lying and being within this Province and bounding upon Bennet's Creyke and a Creyke now known by the name of Caret's Creyke as by your Honours petitionrs patents under the Seale of this Province and other grants and conveyances more at large doth and may appeare. And forasmuch as the Chowan Indians having their hunting quarters upon some of your petitioners lands aforesaid therfore doe pretend the said lands to be theirs not withstanding the patents and grants aforesaid in making and threatening your Honrs petrs by destroying their Stocks burneing their houses and other hostilities under pretence they are under your Honrs protection and no Englishman ought to Seate within four miles of their towne. the which your Honrs petitionrs well knowing that by an order of the Honourable Councill no Seatment ought to be made within the space of four miles aforesaid any wise to the prejudice of the said Indians neither that your Honrs petitionrs taken up any Land witingly within that distance yet to continue peace and tranquility with the said Indians your Honrs petitionrs hath offered to purchass their right (if any) to the Land held as aforesaid by your Honrs Petrs which they refuse and denyeth any seatment to be made theron for prevention wherof and that your Honrs petitionrs may have a peaceable enjoyment in their and every of their aforsd lands humbly implores that the said Indians Land may be laid out to them according to the aforesd order of Councill and if any of your Honrs petrs hapen to hold any land within the aforesd limited bounds it shall be by your petitionrs diserted and left out to the said Indians use that they as well as your Honrs petitionrs in their capacity may be found true and faithfull subjects. And that your Honrs petitionrs may enjoy their said lands in peace and safty and as in all duty bound shall aver pray, etc.

George Laciter	ffrancis Rountre	Benjamin Blanshard
Nicholas Stallings	Robert Rountre	John Campbell
Robert Laciter	His	
	Thomas x Spivey	
	Mark	

****

Colonial Court Records
1675 - 1775

North Carolina State Archives
Colonial Court Records
CCR - 192
Miscellaneous Papers, 1675-1775
File Named: Indians - 1697-1758
Treaties, Petitions, Agreements,and Court Cases

Att a Councill held att the House of Captn John Hecklefield in Little River Aprill ye 12th 1704

Prsent the Lords Deputyes

Ordered that the Surveyr Generall or Deputy Shall (with what Expedition is possible) Upon Complaint of the Yawpim Indians Lay out for the sd Indians (where they now live) four miles Square of Land or the Quantity Not injuring any of the old settlements which was made before the Order of Councill bearing Date in October 1697 And Mr. John Hawkins Mr. Thomas Tayler Mr. Robert Morgan & Mr. John Relfe or any three of them are hereby required to attend the Surveyr or Deputy in laying out the Same

To John Anderson Surveyr Etc.

To be directed to Captn Tho: Relfe to execute with Speed & make returne

[Editor's Note: This document has already been transcribed by Archives personnel.]

****

North Carolina State Archives
Colonial Court Records
CCR - 192
Miscellaneous Papers, 1675-1775
File Named: Indians - 1697-1758
Treaties, Petitions, Agreements, and Court Cases

North Carolina

Colonial Court Records
1675 - 1775

To the Honble John Montgomery Esqr. Chief Justice of the said province and his Assistants

The humble petition and Complaint of Samuel Scollay

Sheweth

That a Negroe Man slave called Scipio belonging to your petr. on the first day of October in the year of Our Lord One thousand seven hundred and forty one at Bertie County in the province afsd ranaway and defected and absented himself from the services and Employment of your Petr. his Master, and continued runaway and absent from your petitioner from the said first day of October one thousand seven hundred and forty one untill the first day of October One thousand seven hundred and forty two:

That Benjamin Hill of Bertie County in the province afd Gentleman during the whole time afd harboured assisted and entertained the said Negroe slave Scipio knowing the said Negroe man slave to be the property of your petr. and to have ranaway and willfully defected and absented himself from the Service and Employment of your petr. his said Master; Whereby the said Benjamin by force of the Act of Assembly of the said province in that Case made and provided hath not only incurr'd the penalty of forty shillings Proclamation money but also five shillings of Like money for every **[Torn]** of **[Torn]** afd the said Negroe man slave was absent from your petr. as afd Amounting in the Whole to One hundred and eighty four pounds ten shillings Proclamation Money.

Your petr. therefore prays that the said Benjamin Hill may be compelled by the Order, Decree or Judgement of this Court to pay to your petr. the one hundred & eighty four pounds ten shillings proclamation Money according to the form force and effect of the Act of Assembly in that Case made and provided And that your petr. may be otherwise relieved in the premises as to your Honours shall seem meet, And your petr. shall ever pray, &c.

Jos: Henderson for petr.

****

Colonial Court Records
1675 - 1775

North Carolina State Archives
Colonial Court Records
CCR - 192
Miscellaneous Papers, 1677-1775

Thomas Spencer Martha Johnson [Johnson marked through]

North Carolina
The information of ye Revd, Mr Jno Blacknall of Edenton in Chowan precinct clerk taken taken before Christopher Gale Esqr Cheif Justice of ye sd province ye 2d day of March 1725

Who saith on his oath yt upon ye 3d, 2d, day of March Thomas Spencer a white man of Curratuck precinct did in Edenton in Chowan precinct aforesd, joyne himself in Marriage according to ye form prescribed by ye Church of England to a Mulatto Woman named Martha (Johnson) Carel [Editor's Note: The surname of Johnson has been marked through and changed to Carel] of Curratuck precinct Contrary to ye direction of an Act of Assembly in yt Case made and provided, whereby he ye sd. Thomas Spencer has incurred a penalty of fifty pounds ye one half to ye informer, which this Informer therefore demands, ye other half to be applied according to ye directions of ye Sd Act

Jurat Coram me   Jno: Blacknall
Gale C.J.

****

North Carolina State Archives
Colonial Court Records
CCR - 192
Miscellaneous Papers, 1677-1775

North Carolina

Complaint being made that two Negroes & one Indian man belonging to James Coale have in the absence of their Master & Mistress robed the house and caryed away Several Goods and a trunk with wearing Cloaths: Thes are theirfore In the Name of the Paletine & Absolute Lords Proprietory Names do will & requier all persons to apprehend the said

Colonial Court Records
1675 - 1775

Negroes & Indian and them to conveie to their Master and all Constables and other officers are hereby required to make dilligent Serch in their respective precinct and to procure by Way of Hue & Cry the said Negroes to take & In Safe Custody to keep till they Can Safly Conveie them to their said Master   Given under my hand this 26th of 5th mo. 1698

Daniel: Akehurst

To be conveied from house to house from the North East Side of Pascotank river and soe to Curatuck.

General Assembly Sessions
1709 - 1776

Chapter Two
General Assembly Sessions records
1709 - 1776

Letter from E. Jennings, 20 September 1708, in the Preston Davie Papers #3406, Southern Historical Collection, Wilson Library, University of North Carolina at Chapel Hill
The University of North Carolina

My Lord   Virginia Septembr the 20th 1708

Haveing on the 24th of June last given my self the Honour of writing to your Lordship by her Majestys Ship the Garland and at the same time sent a duplicate by a Merchant Ship of that ffleet, I humbly beg Leave to be referred to that letter and the papers therewith sent without giveing your Lordship the Trouble of repeating anything. I then laid before your Lordship.

  I herewith send your Lordship the Journals of Council from the 15th of October 1706 to the 30th of April last an abstract of which I sent your Lordship in my last. There have been four meetings of the Council since cheifly intended for giveing the necessary orders for hastning the Merchants Ships in their joining Capt. Stewart in June and Commodore Huntington now, but the severe and extraordinary fevers and other sicknesses with which all parts of the Country have been afflicted for almost two months past & under whic severall of the members of the Council at this time labour hath hindred the reading the last proceedings of the Council so as to prepare them for your Lordship's view.

General Assembly Sessions
1709 - 1776

After the departure of her Majestys Ship the Garland, Commodore Huntington ordered out one of her Majestys Ships under his command to cruise, but that Ship did not proceed on the Service for severall days after haveing been obliged to go round to York River to take in bread and provisions dureing which time we had daily advices of the appearance of Privateers on our Coast, and after the man of War was out cruiseing One Capt. Tarleton of Liverpole was chased from his anchors at the mouth of York River by a Privateer Sloop, Whereupon at the Council held the 29th of July, upon Consideration of our danger It was the unanimous opinion of the Council that for the secureing this Coast and Trade against the Privateers it was necessary to have a fourth Rate man of war and a Brigantine or Sloop of about 8 or 10 Guns and Proportionably maned, the latter to give Chase to the Privateer Sloop in the Shoal water, where, by the Report of all the Captains of the men of war that had been discoursed on that Subject. It appeared very early for such Sloops to pass without comeing within Gun shott of a large Ship. I have by this Conveyance laid this matter before his Royal Highness the Lord high Admiral, And I humbly beg your Lordships favourable Recommendation thereof, for it is demonstrable from the boldness of those Privateers in comeing within our Capes even in sight of her Majestys Ships of war, that they place their cheif Confidence in the lightness of their Vessells and the impossibility of a large Ships following them among the Shoals. I must on this beg Leave further to observe to your Lordship that the Sloops which have been occasionally hyred here for the assistance of the men of war in that Service have never answered the end proposed, for besides the almost impossibility of procureing a good Sloop fitt for such a design, the difficultys the Captains of her Majties. Ships have pretended of divideing their men and of sending out the Sloop, without their Ships going in Company have made all services intended by them fruitless, so that the hyreing of them has been only a Charge to the Queens Revenue without any real advantage, and this consideration obliged the Council to advise the discharging of the sloop impressed last Summer, after she had been employed and paid out of the Queens Revenue for six weeks and yet in all that time not above five days out a Cruising.

Inform'd Your Lords in my last that we were under some apprehensions from the Tuscarora Indians, who had not complyed in delivering up some of their Nation suspected of a murther committed in this Colony last year, And in order to make them more yielding in that particular, it hath been thought fitt to prohibit all trade and commerce with them. This hath had some affect on them already, for they have made

General Assembly Sessions
1709 - 1776

Overture for an Accomodation, and I'm inform'd their coming in to compleat it, hath been only obstructed by the raging of a violent distemper among them for several weeks past.

I thought it necessary to advise with the Council concerning calling an Assembly, the cheif occasion for which at this time is the raising an additional ffund for finishing the Governors house, the whole Sum appropriated by Act of Assembly for that use being already expended and yet the rooff not raised nor any inside work done. I should have been very glad to have had an Assembly for this purpose, but the majority of the Council thought it too great a charge to the Country to have an Assembly now, and another on the arrival of the Govnr. (he being daily expected &) by whom they thought it was very probable her Majesty would send such directions as might make the calling an Assembly of absolute necessity, nor were they of opinion that either the danger of the Country from Privateers, nor the apprehension we were under from the Tuscarora Indians were sufficient grounds for calling an Assembly at this time, the presenting of the first being a work too great for this Country to undertake, and the danger of the latter not so apparent, since there was hopes of an Accomodation with those Indians.

A nation of Indians called the Saponies who were formerly Tributarys to this Governmt, and removed Westward about 20 or 25 years ago, have lately returned and prayed the protection of this Government, and Land to be assyn'd them for a Settlement, which by advice of the Council, I have granted them in consideration of their being one of those Nations included in the articles of peace made with the Indians in 1677. Their number is not considerable being only about 30 Bowman, but the character they have of being stout fellows and with all very friendly to our inhabitants, makes me hope their Settlement well be a kind of Barrier against the Tuscaroras or any other Indians that might be suspected to annoy us on that side since they'l be able to advise us of their motions soon enough to present both their and our dangers.

I have lately reserved her Majestys commands for paying unto Collo. Hunter £1418,,S. out of the Quitrents as a Compensation for the loss of his Equipage, & £500 Per annum out of the same Fund from the first of July 1707 till his arrival in this Government, and pursuant to her Majtys. commands I have passed a Warrant for the money Ordered for his assessage, and also for one years allowance to the first of July last, both which Sums will be remitted him by this Conveyance, But there's so all the less in the bank, that I am afraid the accruing allowance (which is ordered to be paid quarterly) cannot be paid till the next year if he stays out so

General Assembly Sessions
1709 - 1776

long. I hop'd to have sent your Lords copys of the accounts of her Majestys revenues of Quitrents and two shillings per hogshead, but the unfortunate absence of the Council has hindered their being audited, so that I must beg Your Lords patience till after our General Court when I hope to have the opportunity of sending by some of the Latter Ships.

    I am informed from North Carolina that there are very great Commotions in that Governmt. occasioned chiefly by the Quakers, who after they had prevailed with the Proprietors to send out the Deputy Governor, and give [?] the Council (who were most of their persuasion) a power to chuse their own President, first made an Election, and because they did not find that Gentleman for their own turn, voted him out again. They have had the cunning to set all that Country in a flame, and all but themselves in arms agt. one another. It would be tedious to to trouble yr Lords with an account of the proceedings of both partys wch look like the freaks of madmen than the actions of men of reason, there has been one man already unfortunately killed in the fray, and tho tis said they are coming to some accomodation yet by the best information I have it is not like to end so. I thought it my duty to acquaint tour Lords of this, as it happens so nigh this her Majestys Colony, tho I hope it will have no ill consequences on us. I am with the greatest respect

        My Lord
        Your Lordships
        Most Oblidged & Most Obedient
        Servt.

        E. Jenings

****

Memorial of the General Assembly of South Carolina, 9 April 1734 in the Preston Davie Papers #3406, Southern Historical Collection, Wilson Library, University of North Carolina at Chapel Hill
The University of North Carolina

        Memorial of the General Assembly of South Carolina
                       April 9, 1734

To the Kings Most Excellent Majesty.

General Assembly Sessions
1709 - 1776

The humble Memorial and Representation of the State & Condition of Your Majesty's Province of South Carolina from the General Assembly of the said Province

Your Majesty's most Dutifull Subjects of this Province having often felt with Hearts full of Gratitude the many signal Instances of your most sacred Majestys peculiar favour & protection, to these distant Parts of Your Dominions, and especially those late Proofs of Your Majesty's most gracious and benign Care, so wisely calculated for the Preservation of this Your Majesty's Frontier Province on the Continent of America by your Royal Charter to the Trustees for establishing the Colony of Georgia in America, and your great goodness so timely applied in promoting the Settlement of the Swiss at Purysburgh. Encouraged by such Views of Your Majesty's wise and paternal Care, extended to Your remotest Subjects, and excited by the Duty which we owe to Your most sacred Majesty to be always watchfull for the support and Security of Your Majesty's Interest, especially at this very Critical Conjuncture, when the Flame of War breaking out in Europe may very speedly be lighted here in this Your Majesty's Frontier Province, which in Situation is known to be of the utmost Importance to the General Trade, and Traffic of America, We therefore Your Majesty's most faithfull Governor, Council & Commons conven'd in your Majesty's Province of South Carolina crave Leave with great Humility to represent to Your Majesty the present State and Condition of this Your Province, and how greatly it stands in need of Your Majesty's gracious and timely Succour in Case of a War to Assist our Defence against the French and Spaniards, or any other Enemies to Your Majesty's Dominions, as well as against the many Nations of Savages which so nearly threaten the Safety of Your Majesty's Subjects.

The Province of South Carolina and the new Colony of Georgia are the Southern Frontiers of all Your Majesty's Dominions on the Continent of America, to the South and South West of which is situate the strong Castle of Augustine, garrisoned by 400 Spaniards who have several Nations of Indians living under their Subjection, besides several other small Settlements and Garrisons near the Appellachys, some of which are not eighty Miles distant from the Colony of Georgia   To the South West and West of Us the French have already erected a considerable Town near Fort Thoulouse on the Moville River and several other Forts and Garrisons, some not above 300 Miles distant from our Settlements; And at New Orleans on the Missisippi River, since her late Majesty Queen Ann's War, they have exceedingly increased their Strength and Traffick, and have now

General Assembly Sessions
1709 - 1776

many Forts and Garrisons on both sides of that large River for several hundred Miles up the same. And since His most Christian Majesty has taken out of the Missisippi Company the Government of that Country into his own Hands, The French Natives of Canada come daily down in Shoals to settle all along that River, where many regular Forces have of late been sent over by the King to Strength the Garrisons in those Places; And according to our best and latest Advices they have 500 Men in Pay constantly employed as Wood Rangers to keep the Neighboring Indians in Subjection, and to prevent the distant ones from disturbing their Settlements, Which management of the French has so well succeeded, that we are well assured they have wholly now in their Possession, and under their Influence the several numerous Nations of Indians that are situate near the Missisippi River, one of which is called the Choctaws by Estimation consist of about 5,000 fighting Men, and who were always deemed a very Warlike Nation, lies on this Side of the River not above 400 Miles distant from our Out Settlement, among whom as well as several other Nations of Indians, many French Europeans have been sent to settle, whom the Priests and Missionaries among them encourage them to take Indian Wives, and use divers other alluring Methods to Attach the Indians the better to the French Alliance; by which Means the French are become throughly acquainted with the Indian way of Warring and living in the Woods, and have now a great Number of white Men among them, able to perform a long March with an Army of Indians upon any Expedition.

  We further beg Leave to inform Your Majesty, that if the Measures of France should provoke Your Majesty to a State of Hostility against it in Europe, we have great Reason to expect an Invation will be made here upon Your Majesty's Subjects by the French, and the Indians from Missisippi Settlements. They have already paved the way for a design of that Nature, by erecting a Fort called the Alabama Fort alias Fort Lewis, in the Middle of the upper Creek Indians, upon a Navigable River leading to Moville, which they have kept well Garrisoned, and mounted with fourteen Pieces of Canon, and have lately been prevented from erecting a second nearer to Us in that Quarter, The Creeks are a Nation very bold, daring and active, consisting of about 1,300 fighting Men, and not above 150 Miles distant from the Choctaws whom though we heretofore have traded with, claimed and held in our Alliance; Yet the French on Account of that Fort, and a superior Ability to make them liberal Presents, have been for some time striving to gain them over to their Interest and have succeeded with some of the Towns of the Creeks which if they can be secured in Your Majesty's Interest are the only Nation here

General Assembly Sessions
1709 - 1776

which Your Majesty's Subjects can depend upon as their Barrier against any Attempts, either of the French or their confederate Indians.

We most humbly pray Leave further to inform Your Majesty, that the French at Moville perceiving that they could not gain the Indians to their Interest, without buying their Deer Skins (which is the only Commodity the Indians have to Purchase Necessarys with) and the French not being able to dispose of those Skins, by Reason of their having no Vent for them in Old France, they have found Means to encourage Vessels from hence New York, and other Places (which are not prohibited by the Acts of Trade) To truck those skins with for Indian Trading Goods, especially the British Woollen Manufacture, which the French dispose of to the Creeks and Choctaws and other their Indians, By which Means the Indians are much more alienated fro our Interest, and on every Occasion object to us that the French can supply them with Strouds and Blanketts as well as the English, which would have the contrary Effect if they were wholly furnished with those Commodities by your Majesty's Subjects trading among them. If a Stop were therefore put to that pernicious Trade with the French, the Creek Indians chief Dependance would be on this Government, and that of Georgia, to supply them with those Goods, by which Means great part of the Choctaws living next the Creeks, would see the Advantage the Creek Indians enjoyed by having British Woollen Manufactures wholly from Your Majesty's Subjects, and thereby be invited in a Short time to enter into a Treaty of Commerce with us, which they have lately made some offers for, and which if effected, will soon lessen the Interest of the French with these Indians, and by Degrees attach them to that of your Majesty.

The only Expedient we can propose to recover and confirm that Nation to Your Majesty's Interest, is by speedily making them Presents, to with draw them from the French Alliance and by building some Forts among them, Your Majesty may be put in such a Situation, that on the first Notice of Hostilities with the French Your Majesty may be able to reduce the Albama Fort, and we may then Stand against the French and their Indians, which if not timely prepared for before a War breaks out, we have too much Reason to fear we may be soon overrun by the united Force of the French, the Creeks, and Choctaws, with many other Nations of their Indian Allies; for should the Creeks become wholly Enemies, who are well acquainted with all our Settlements, We probably should also soon be desert'd by the Cherokees, and a few other small tribes of Indians, who for the Sake of our Booty would readily join to make us a Prey to the French and Savages. Eversince the last Indian War, the Offences given us then by

General Assembly Sessions
1709 - 1776

the Creeks, have made that Nation very jealous of Your Majesty's Subjects of this Province; we have therefore concerted Measures with the Honourable James Oglethorpe Esqr., who being at the head of a new Colony will (we hope) be successfull for your Majesty's Interest among that People. He has already by Presents attach'd the Lower Creeks to the Services of Your Majesty & has [?] undertaken to endeavour the fixing a Garrison among the upper Creeks the expence of which is already in part provided for in this Sessions of the General Assembly of this Province, We hope therefore to prevent the French from encroaching further on Yr. Majesty's Territories, until your Majesty is graciously pleased further to Strengthen and secure the same.

    We find the Cherokee Nation has lately become very insolent to Your Majesty's Subjects Trading among them notwithstanding the many Favours which the Chiefs of that Nation received from Your Majesty in Great Britain, beside a considerable Expence which Your Majesty's Subjects of this Province have been at in making them Presents, which inclines us to believe that the French by their Indians have been tampering with them; We therefore beg Leave to inform Your Majesty that the building and mounting some Forts also among the Cherokees, and making them Presents, will be highly necessary to keep them steady in their Duty to Your Majesty, lest the French may prevail in Seducing that Nation, which they may the more readily be inclined to from the Prospect of getting considerable Plunder in Slaves, Cattle and Commodities, which they very well know they have among us: Several other Forts will be indispensably necessary to be a Cover to Your Majesty's Subjects settled backwards in this Province, as also to those of the Colony of Georgia, both which in Length are very extensive; For though the Trustees for establishing the Colony of Georgia by a particular Scheme of good Managemt. painfully conducted by the Gentleman ingaged here in that charitable Enterprize, have put that small part of the Colony, which he has been yet able to establish, in a fencible Condition against the Spaniards of Florida, which lye to the Southward, Yet the back Exposition of these Colonys, the vast Number of French and Indians which border the Westward must in Case of War cry greatly aloud for your Majesty's gracious and timely Succor. The Expences of our Safety on such an Occasion we must in all Humility acquaint your Majesty either for Money or [?], can never be effected by your Majesty's Subjects of this Province, who in Conjunction with Georgia do not in the whole amount to more than 3,500 Men that compose the Militia, and wholly consist of Planters, Traders and other Men in Business.

General Assembly Sessions
1709 - 1776

Besides the many Dangers which by Land we are exposed to from so many Enemies that lie on the Back of us, we further beg Leave to represent to your Majesty, the defenceless Condition of our Ports and Harbours, where any Enemies of your Majesty's Dominions may very easily by Sea invade us, there being no Fortifications capable of much Resistance; Those in Charles Town Harbour are now in a very ruinous Condition, occasioned by late violent Storms and Hurricanes, which already cost this Country a great deal of Money, and now require several Thousands of Pounds to repair the old and build new ones to mount the Ordnance which your Majesty was graciously pleased to send us, which with great Concern we must inform Your Majesty we have not yet been able to accomplish, being latterly obliged for the Defence and Support of this Your Majesty's Province and Government, to raise by a Tax on the Inhabitants a Supply of above 40,000 Paper Currency Pr. Annum, which is a considerable Deal more than a third part of all the Currency Money among Us, a Charge which Your Majesty's Subjects of this Province are but barely able to sustain.

Since Your Majesty's Royal Instructions to your Majesty's Governor here, an entire Stop has been put to the Duties which before accrued from European Goods imported, and if a War should happen or anything extraordinary to be further expensive here, we should be under the utmost Difficulties to provide additionally for the same, least an Increase of Taxes with an Apprehension of Danger should drive away many of our present Inhabitants, as well as discourage others from coming here to settle for the Defence and Improvement of Your Majesty's Province, there being several daily moving with their Families and Effects to North Carolina, where there are no such Fears and Burthens.

We must further beg Leave to inform Your Majesty, that amidst our other perilous Circumstances we are subject to many intestine Dangers from the great Number of Negroes that are now among us, who amount at lest to 22,000 Persons, and are three to one of all Your Majesty's white Subjects in this Province, Insurrections against us have been often attempted and would at any time prove very fatal if the French should instigate them, by artfully giving them an Expectation of Freedom. In such Situation We most humbly crave Leave to acquaint Your Majesty, that even the present ordinary Expences, necessary for the Care and support of this Your Majesty's Province and Government, cannot be provided for by your Majesty's Subjects of this Province, without Your Majesty's gracious Pleasure to continue those Laws for the establishing the Negroe and other Duties for seven Years, and for appropriating the same which now lie

General Assembly Sessions
1709 - 1776

before Your Majesty for Your Royal Assent and Approbation; And the further Expences that will be requisite for the erecting some Forts and establishing Garrisons in the several necessary Places, so as to form a Barrier for the Security of this Your Majesty's Province, we most humbly submit to your Majesty.

Your Majesty's Subjects of this Province with Fullness of Zeal, Duty and Affection to Your most gracious and sacred Majesty are so highly sensible of the great Importance of this Province to the French, that we must conceive it more than probable if a War should happen, they will use all Endeavours to bring this Country under their Subjection; They would thereby be able to supply their Sugar Islands with all sorts of Provisions & Lumber by an easy Navigation, which to our great Advantage is not now so practicable from the Present French Colony's. Besides the Facility of gaining them to their Interest, most of the Indian Trade on the Northern Continent, they might then easily unite the Canadees and Choctaws with the many other Nations of Indians, which are now in their Interest. And the several Ports and Harbours of Carolina and Georgia, which now enable Your Majesty to be absolute Master of the Passage through the Gulph of Florida, and to impede at your Pleasure the Transportation home of the Spanish Treasure, would then prove so many convenient Harbours for your Majesty's Enemies by their Privateers or Ships of War to annoy a great part of the British Trade to America, as well as that which is carried on through the Gulph from Jamaica, Besides the Loss which Great Britain must feel in so considerable a part of its Navigation, as well as the Exports of Masts, Pitch, Tar and Turpentine, which without any Dependance on the Northern Powers of Europe are from hence plentifully supplied for the use of the British Shipping.

This is the present State and Condition of Your Majesty's Province of South Carolina, utterly incapable of finding Funds sufficient for the Defence of this wide Frontier, and so destitute of White Men that even Money itself cannot raise a sufficient Body of them, We therefore with all Humility beg Leave to lay ourselves at the Feet of Your Majesty, humbly imploring Your Majesty's most gracious Care in the Extremities We should be reduced to, on the breaking out of a War; And that Your Majesty will be graciously Pleased to extend Your Protection to Us, as Your Majesty in Your great Wisdom shall think most proper.

South Carolina
In the Council Chamber the 9th of April 1734.

General Assembly Sessions
1709 - 1776

Robert Johnson   Tho. Broughton President
                        Paul Jenys   Speaker

****

North Carolina State Archives
General Assembly Sessions Records
1709 - Jan. 1760, Box #1
February-March, 1754
Joint Resolutions

Joint Resolutions - Mar 9 concerning payment to commanding officer of the forces to be raised for the expedition against French & Indians.
                    In the Genl. Assembly Mar 9, 1754
Resolved,
        That the Publick Treasurers pay by Warrant from the President or Commander in Chief to the Commanding Officer (or his order) of the forces to be raised in this Province for the Present Expedition against the french and Indians at Ohio the Money remaining in their hands for the use of the Several Forts respectively, and that the same be replaced, in the Treasury for the Use of the said Forts out of the 12,000 pounds to be stamped and Emitted in virtue of an Act passd this Session (Intitled an Act for Granting to his Majesty the sum of 40,000 pounds &C) and apply'd for Raising and Subscribing the said forces.
9th Mar 1754   Sam Swann Speaker
By Order W Herritage Clk
Gent of his Majesty Honble Council
The Above is a Resolve of this House & sent you for Concurrence
        By order Wm Herritage Clk
March 9th 1754 In the upper House
                Concurred with
                Ja Murray P.
                by Order John Devis

****

North Carolina State Archives
General Assembly Sessions Records
1709 - Jan. 1760, Box #1
Lower House Papers

General Assembly Sessions
1709 - 1776

Dobbs 1754

Gent. of His Majesty's Council
Mr. Speaker, & Gent. of the Assembly

  His Majesty having been graciously pleas'd to Honour & intrust me wth. the Government of this Province, I have taken the earlyest Opportunity of making wth. you in full Assembly, to consult you upon what may lend to the Peace & Happyness, Increase & Improvement of this Province and to consider of proper Laws to secure the Rights & Properties & improve the Trade of this Colony, and to unite the Affections of all the Members of the Society that all may concur in promoting your General Wealth and Happyness.

  As the first and greatest Principle & Foundation of all social Happyness is the Knowledge of true Religion & the Practice of Morality & Virtue to know love & adore the Divine Being as we ought, & to obey the Precepts he has reveal'd to us - so I think it my Duty in the first place to recommend to you the pro[?]ing ap[?]perfund to support a sufficient Number of learned pious Clergyman to reside in the Province, and to accomodate them with Houses Gleebs & Parish Clerks, to enable them to instruct the Inhabitants & the rising Generation in the principles of true Religion & Virtue, in such a prudent Manner without Tythes, as to prevent Contests & preserve a Harmony between the Clergy & Lastly, that their Interest may be the same, & they may have Leisure as well as Inclination to instruct their flock in Christian Principles

  Next in this Duty to his Majesty, who like a beneficient Father has given to this Colony a permanent property in their Lands, reserving to himself a very small Acknowledgmt. of Quit Rent, who has protected it in it's infant state from all foreign Ensults, & has maintained & supported it in all it's Civil & Religious Rights, Priviledges by a true Christian Liberty of Conscience, & in the happyest Constitution of the Globe; I must earnestly recommend it to you that in return for his Majesty's paternal Care, you make an effectual Law for the spec[Torn]asy Collection of the Quit Rents wch. his Majesty has been graciously pl[Torn] to apply for the Eare of this Colony the **[Faded]** due the Officers of this Establishment and towards their annual Support and are necessary to preserve your peace & to have Justice to yourselves, as well as in Gratitude to the best of princes, who is not only the Father of his people, but the Benefactor of Mankind, I am convinced you will readily agree to.

General Assembly Sessions
1709 - 1776

After these I must recommend to your Consideration the making effectual Laws to secure Peace & Properties, & to obtain your Rights, & have Justice distributed in the speedyest & easyest Manner without dilatory Law Proceeding, & also Laws to promote Trade & Industry in Order to support your Credit at home & abroad, by making effectual Laws to recover just debts without Chicanery or tedious Delays, & all small debts in a summary way, wch. will promote Our economy & Industry, & prevent Indolence & Sloth. Since a Paper Currency has been found beneficial hitherto from the want of Bullion or Coin, I must recommend to you the keeping up your Paper Credit, by making your paper Bills a permanent fund of Credit upon Land Security by a Loans Office, and to provide sufficient fund to pay off & cancel the Bills of Credit already issued in a short time, a plan of which shall be communicated to you - This with a general Inspection Law, & employing Inspectors in all your Seaports to view and support the Credit of your Exports, & a proper economy wth. Industry mut necessarily occasion a Ballance in your favour, & consequently a Return in Gold or Silver, & will demonstrate that Honesty in Trade as well in all other Dealings is the best Policy.

The extending our Trade into the Continent, & our Colonies into the fine Countrys beyond the Mountains being of the utmost Consequence to this & all our Colonies, I must earnestly recommend it to you to make a Law to lay our Indian Traders under proper Regulations, & to promote an Intimacy of friendship and living in Harmony wth. our Indian Neighbors & Allies, that we may be enabled to civilize & make them industrious, & to incorporate wth. them, by carrying on an equitable Trade wth. them, & treating them wth. Christian Benevolence This at least we owe to them upon Account of our possessing their happy Climate & Country & we shall not only profit by their trade, but make them our steady friends, & by extending our Allyances to distant Nations we may enlarge our trade over the whole northern Continent, & form an impregnable Barrier against our ever active Enemies the French, who in time of profound Peace have not only headed their Indian Allies, & have prevail'd wth. them to make Depredations massacre in cold Blood and scalp several of the Inhabitants of this & our other Colonies, but have enter'd wth. an armed force, & erected forts in the Countrys belonging to his Majesty, as well as of our Indian Allies, & therefore I am commanded by his Majesty to recommend it to you in the strongest Manner to provide a supply to assist the Colony of Virginia, whose Country is invaded & his Majesty's Troops slaughtered for endeavouring to repel these Invaders - the fire wch. has caught your Neighbors house has lately spread into your own, your Religion Liberty &

General Assembly Sessions
1709 - 1776

property are all at stake, if they [?] repell'd & drove back to their inhospitable Colonies. But as this Subject is of the utmost Importance, & it will be tedious to explain the French plan calculated for the Ruin of Britain & these Colonies at this time, as soon as you fall upon Busyness I shall lay it before you in a more ample Manner, that you may see the Necessity of a speedy & effectual Supply.

      Mr. Speaker & Gent. of the Assembly

  I am instructed & have it in Command from his Majesty to look out and fix upon a convenient & healthy Situation for the Seat of Government & Courts of Justice, which may best answer the whole Province, & lay it before his Majesty for his Approbation. When that is fix'd your own prudence & Wisdom will suggest to you, whether you shou'd not have a fund provided to erect public Buildings for the Residence of the Governor, & for public offices & Courts of Justice, since the Credit & Increase of the trade of the Province depends in great Measure upon the Healthyness & Increase of the Capital, & having all the public Offices together.

  I am also commanded by his Majesty earnestly to recommend to you the raising a suitable fund without Limitation of time to support the Dignity of the present & all future Governors & to answer the Contingencies and Emergencies of Government, the Payments of the offices & Clerks of ye Council & Assembly, for the repairing of Fortifications, Storehouses & Magazines when erected, which Establishment will be always necessary for your Security & Defense; his Majesty having been graciously pleas'd to give you a 1000 firelocks & Accoutrements for the use of this Province, and I have a well grounded Expectation that proper Artillery wth. Military Stores will be granted to the several forts when erected, and an independent Company provided that a powder Duty be again granted to supply the Magazines in the Province.

  It is with great Concern that I observe that from the late Divisions in the province the proper Du[Torn] laid on for the Support of the Establishment & for making the paper Currency have not been properly levied from the disputing the legality of the Assembly in passing & continuing those Duties, by which Means the Charges of Government have not been paid, & the public Debt increas'd, as this Bone of Contention is happyly laid aside by his Majesty's having minutely enter'd into an examination of ye Constitution & Laws of the province, by repealing several Laws it will be necessary for you to have all the present Laws revised, and where Laws have been repeal'd upon Account of some

General Assembly Sessions
1709 - 1776

improper Clauses, to re-enact them wth. unexceptionable Clauses, and to have the whole Laws ascertained, wch. may be best done by appointing Committees to sit upon them during the recess betwixt this & the next Session, to have them ready to be offer'd at next Assembly.

Gent. of his Majesty's Council
Mr. Speaker, & Gent. of the Assembly

Since his Majesty has been graciously pleas'd to intrust me wth. the Care & Improvement of this Province, as it is my Duty, so it shall be my constant Care to promote true Religion & Virtue and the Wealth Peace and Happyness of the Colony, & to increase & improvise its trade - As a Union of Affections & acting together for the general good of the Province is not only a prudent & right Measure, but absolutely necessary to be pursued to improve the Colony in wealth & trade, it is my determined Resolution to encourage & countenance only those who shall heartily concur in so good of purposes, which must improve the Market, support the Credit, establish Justice, & give Strength & Weight to the Colony, & induce Merchants, Artizans, & other Gentlemen of Learning, Merit, & Probity to purchase & reside in the Province.

****

Copy of the King's Instructions, in Miscellaneous Papers, OP-517/ Unit 2, Southern Historical Collection, Wilson Library, University of North Carolina at Chapel Hill
University Of North Carolina

[Editor's Note: There is no specific date on this document.]

Copy Kings Instruction to the Govr. No. 109 Respecting Indian Lands.

Whereas the Peace and Security of Our Colonies and Plantations upon the Continent of North America does greatly depend upon the Amity and Alliance of the several Nations or Tribes of Indians bordering upon the said Colonies, and upon a just and faithful Observance of those Treaties and Compacts which have been heretofore solemnly entered into with the said Indians by Our Royal Predecessors, Kings and Queens of this Realm;

And Whereas notwithstanding the repeated Instructions which have been from Time to Time given by Our Royal Grandfather to the Governors of Our several Colonies upon his Head, the said Indians have made and do still continue to make great Complaints that Settlements have

General Assembly Sessions
1709 - 1776

been made and Possession taken of Lands the Property of which they have by Treaties Reserved to themselves, by Persons claiming the said Lands under pretence of Deeds of Sale, and Conveyance illegally, fraudulently and surreptitiously obtained of the said Indians; And Whereas it has likewise been represented unto Us that some of Our Governors or other Chief Officers of Our said Colonies regardless of the Duty they Owe to Us and of the Welfare and Security of Our Colonies, have Countenanced such unjust Claims and Pretensions by passing Grants of the Lands so pretended to have been purchased of the Indians;

    We Therefore taking this Matter into Our Royal Consideration; as also the fatal Effects which would attend a Discontent amongst the Indians in the present situation of Affairs, and being determined upon all Occasions to support and protect the said Indians in their just Rights and Possessions, and to keep Inviolable the Treaties and Compacts which have been Entered into with them, Do hereby strictly enjoin and Command, that neither Yourself nor any Lieutenant Governor, President of the Council or Commander in Chief of Our said Province of North Carolina do, upon any pretence whatever upon pain of Our highest Displeasure, and of being forthwith removed from Your or his Office, pass any Grant or Grants to any Person whatever of any Lands within or adjacent to the Territories possessed or ocupied by the said Indians or the Property or Possessions of which has at any Time been reserved to or claimed by them. And it is our further Will and Pleasure that You do Publish a Proclamation in Our Name strictly enjoining and requiring all Persons whatever who may either wilfully or inadvertently have seated themselves upon any Lands so reserved to, or claimed by the said Indians, without any Lawful Authority for so doing forthwith to remove therefrom;

    And in Case You shall find upon strict Enquiry to be made for that Purpose, that any Person or Persons do claim to hold or possess any Lands within Our said Province upon pretences of purchases made of the said Indians, without a proper License first had and obtained either from Us or any of Our Royal Predecessors, or any Person Acting under Our, or their Authority; You are forthwith to cause a Prosecution to be Carried on against such Person or Persons, who shall have made such fraudulent Purchases, to the End that the Land may be recovered by due Course of Law. And Whereas the wholesome Laws, which have at different Times been passed in several of our said Colonies and the Instructions which have been given by Our Royal Predecessors for restraining Persons from purchasing Lands of the Indians without a License for that purpose, and for regulating the Proceedings upon such Purchases have not been duly

General Assembly Sessions
1709 - 1776

observed; This therefore our express Will and Pleasure that when any Application shall be made to You for License to purchase Lands of the Indians You do forbear to Grant such License until You shall have first transmitted to Us by Our Commissioners for Trade and Plantations the particulars of such Application as well in respect to the Situation as the extent of the Lands so proposed to be purchased and shall have received Our further Direction therein forthwith cause this Our Instruction to You to be made Public not only within all parts of Your said Province inhabited by Our Subjects but also amongst the several Tribes of Indians living within the same to the End that Our Royal Will and Pleasure in the Premises may be made known, and that the Indians may be apprized of Our determined Resolution to support them in their just Rights, and [Faded] Our Engagements with them.

****

Earl of Halifax Letter (#2963), Tracy W. McGregor Library, The Albert H. Small Special Collections Library, University of Virginia Library

Grosvr. Square July ye 6th 1754
Sir

Tho' the Letters you will receive from the Board at which I preside will fully convey our thoughts to you on every point, on which it was our duty either to give our opinion of your past, or direct your future conduct; and tho' I have but short notice of his Majesty's Ship being to sail to soon as to morrow; yet I am unwilling to let her depart without acknowledging the receipt of the letters you have favored me with, and giving you, as a friend, such thoughts as occur to me on the present posture of Things, and the great national Business, which is committed to your care.

You seem to express some Surprise that you have not heard from me for some time past, but the reason that has occasion'd my Silence is I think pretty obvious. I was much concerned to hear of the French Designs on the River Ohio, but it was not from me you was to receive your positive Directions for the disappointment of them; It was matter of still greater anxiety To His Excellency Robert Dinwiddie Esquire to me to hear the

General Assembly Sessions
1709 - 1776

progress they had made in the Execution of them, and tho' I was well apprised of his Majesty's orders which were sent you by the Secretary of State, yet it was not necessary for me to give any interpretation of or Comment upon those orders: They were full and explicit, and spoke sufficiently for themselves.

You seem hitherto to have executed them with that diligence and spirit which the nature of the Service and the circumstances of the times require; and I will not doubt of your steady and unwearied perserverance in the same, till you have accomplisht the important Work with which you are charged: a field of Honour is open to you, such as has seldom presented itself to our American Governors, when they have complain'd of French Incroachments on his Majesty's Territories. Your Zeal for the Public Service has not been check'd, nor have your Remonstrances remain'd unanswer'd, so as to leave you in perplexity or doubt how you are to proceed, on the contrary your part has been plainly mark'd out to you, you have the orders of the Crown for what you are to do, and your hands have been strengthen'd for the Execution of them: If you succeed, you will gain such a degree of credit, arising from this unforeseen opportunity, as you never could have flatter'd yourself with the hopes of when you first enter'd upon your Government; if you fail, shame and disgrace will be the portion of those, who have been employ'd on the occasion in Support of the British Cause; and the future ruin of his Majesty's Provinces in North America will probably be the consequence of our miscarriage.

The Support given you from hence must prove beyond your expectation, because it is beyond your requisition: It was agreed that a supply of money should be sent you, when you had asked none; and when you intimated the necessity, the Sum was instantly enlarged, tho' you sent no estimate of what you thought was immediately necessary, or what would probably, or might become so; And here I cannot help observing to you that in a matter of so high importance, on the issue of which the Security, I may say the very being of his Majesty's Empire in North America may depend, it was your duty to have formed and transmitted home a certain and infallible plan for the defeat of the French Projects, whether the expence attendant on the execution of such plan was likely to be defray'd by the Province of Virginia and the neighboring Governments, or whether it was to fall on the Mother Country: The first Object of your Attention should have been to have planned the means of preventing the mischief, leaving to future consideration the proportions of expence to be born by Great Brittain and her Colonies. I wish it had been done, as it

General Assembly Sessions
1709 - 1776

would have saved the Loss of much time, and as it would have been an easier task to have prevented the Evil, than it may be to remove it.

The absurd and false Economy, the ill-timed deficiency of Spirit, and lethargic insensibility of the Colonies (for probably to all three causes the present Backwardness may be ascribed) is not enough to be wonder'd at. Even Self-Interest, which operates in most corners of the World, and in other cases may have had it's effects in America, is a passion dead on the present Occasion. When Encroachments have formerly been made, and unnoticed by Government, What Patriot Lamentations have been made at home and abroad by all such as were more immediately concerned in the Welfare of the Colonies[?] They only desired to be at Liberty to act, and by their great Superiority of Numbers, and other advantages (many of which they certainly have over their Rivals) France would soon be afraid to show herself in America; now that at the time of the most pressing Danger His Majesty is pleased not only to permit but call upon them to defend themselves, and unasked to deal out his Succours for their encouragement, either from a niggard hope that the Mother Country will do all, or other causes equally unjustifiable, they for the most part appear as unconcerned at the Event as if their properties lay in Asia or Africa. Nothing has as yet been done but by Virginia and North Carolina, and the Supply granted in either Place has been given in a manner derogatory of the Prerogative of the Crown, and inconsistent With it's Governor"s Instructions. If what they have voted proves insufficient for the removing French Encroachmts., a secret Comfort I suppose is still proposed, in as much as by taking advantage of the necessity of the times, and their own danger, they themselves have been able to make an encroachment upon their constitution, and the Just Rights of the King, who would save them. If Virginia would only have executed her own laws, all possibility of danger would have been removed. I think her Militia consists of 19000 Men, and was last year reported to be in good order: It often happens that the Militia does not consist of good Soldiers, but that of Virginia I presume does not consist of good or bad, and only subsists by it's name; If so, I see good reason why it could not march; no other good one can I conceive: For if the whole of which it is said to consist, or an half, or a Quartr., or the thirteenth Part had marched in time to the Ohio, the French would not have built two forts there, we should not have lost one, nor would the present Scene of hazard bloodshed and expence have open'd. I must confess I am curious to know from you What the good People of Virginia originally intended their Militia to be, when they passed the Law for it, and what ideas they now affix to it; And whether as they are not to operate against an Enemy, they

General Assembly Sessions
1709 - 1776

are kept for the purposes of a few particular Friends Indeed, Sir, from the little Information I have as yet had of this matter, I am equally ashamed and grieved at the Inefficacy of our Colony Laws, and impotency of our Colony Bands; for if the Militia Regulations in the other Provinces are the same, or equally observed with those in Virginia, I think a Man would not be hazard too much if he declared that 500 French might safely march from East to West thro' the heart of His Majesty's American Dominions. But to come more directly to the present State of Things-Our Fort taken, and the French in Possession of it, and Two more, with 100 Men and Cannon to support their unjust Pretentions; our Forces not yet assembled, and, when assembled, not likely to amount to more than 1000 Men, and most of them newly raised. In your Letters you seem to think you shall dispossess the French, and I think you will, for if our little Army should not succeed in the first attempt, yet if it can keep the Field (for I do not suppose the French can winter there) I shall please myself with hopes of your success. I will likewise still flatter myself with expectations that the neighbouring Colonies will exert themselves, and that your Force will daily increase. What has been done from hence ought and must instill a Spirit into them, unless the unfortunate Inhabitants of them are dead to every manly sensation.

    The money that is sent, and the Credit that is given you, I most earnestly recommend to you to manage with the utmost prudence and circumspection, to make use of neither, but where you judge it necessary for the publick Service, and not to consider what is given from hence as given for the Provincial Purposes, or the security of one Colony only, but as a Pledge His Majesty is Pleas'd to give his Subjects in North America of his Attention to and Protection of their Interests; and I most heartily hope that this paternal Mark of Royal Regard will be attended with the consequences it ought, and that when the Colonies fin how much His Majesty thinks of them, they will think it high time to think for themselves.

    Before I finish my Letter I must exhort your most Serious Attention to the several Indian Tribes. No Pains, no Presents must be spared that may effectually secure them in our Interests. Presents to the Cherokees, amongst whom I hear the French are endeavouring to build a Fort, and establish themselves, (which will be attended with most fatal consequences to his Majesty's Dominions) are absolutely necessary. I am informed that £700 in Presents will secure them, and obtain their leave for building a Fort in the upper Cherokee Country, that ought to be begun upon immediately. I hope therefore you will lose not a day in conferring with Mr. Glen upon carrying into execution a Work of such importance. I

General Assembly Sessions
1709 - 1776

desire to hear from you as often as you have opportunity of writing, and that you would be very full and explicit on every Point worthy my notice. I am, Sir, Yr. most obedt. humble Servant. [?] Halifax

P.S. As I foresee great difficulties in ye recovery of ye English Fort, or the taking the French Forts on the Ohio without large pieces of battering Cannon, I hope you have been able to supply yourself wth. some such either from Williamsburgh or some of the neighbouring Colonies. These cannot fail Leaving their effect, as the French have, I take for granted, none such to oppose agst. them. What Cannon they have I conclude are small pieces, & as I know ye difficulty yt. must be attend ye bringing even that from Canada, I think it very probable they have been taken from ye encroached Fort at Niagara, which may be thereby reduced to a defenceless State.

****

North Carolina State Archives
Governor's Papers, 1754

North Carolina   }   29 Augt 1754
Rowan & Anson County's }

At A Treaty held on Thursday the Twenty Ninth day of August one Thousand Seven Hundred and Fifty Four at the house of Mr. Matheus Tool, Between Alexander Osburn & James Cater Esqrs. Commissioners, and the Cataba Indians

Present James Carter   }
          &   }   Esqrs. Commissioners &c
     Alexdr. Osburn   }

King Hagler And Sundry of his head men and Warriors
    The Commission which was Sent by his Honr. the
        President to the above Commissioners, being Read in the presence of King Hagler and sundry of his head men and Warriors, after which it was Interpreted by Mr. Mattheus Tool, Together with the Letter which was also sent by his Honr. to Capt. McClenachan Andw. Pickens Esqr. and Others, as Concerning said Indians

General Assembly Sessions
1709 - 1776

After Each Sentence was Distinctly Interpreted by Mr. Tool, who was Sworn for that purpose the King Made the following Speech

Brothers and Wariors I am Exceeding glad to meet You here this day, and to have the Oppertunity of haveing a talk one with an Other in a Brotherly and Loveing manner, and to Brighten, and Strengthen, that Chain of Friendship which has so long remained between us and the people of these three Provinces, and I am Very Sorry to hear those Complaints that are Laid to our peoples Charge, But now will Open our Ears to here those Grievances & Complaints that shall be made by You against our Young men and Others, and we do Heartily Thank our Good Brother the President of North Carolina for his good Talk in his Letter to us, and also for his appointing You to meet here, to have this Discourse.

Then William Morrison Appeared, to Support the Complaints that was by him Made to the Officers at a late Court martial held in Rowan County, Concerning the Indian Insults to him at his own house, Some time before, when they Came to him at his mill and Attempted to throw a pail Water into his Meal Trough, and when he would prevent them they made many Attempts to Striek him with their guns over his head - To which Some of the Indians said what they Intended to do with the water was only to put a hand full or Two of the Meal into it to make a kind of a Drink which is their way and Custom.

The King also Said that it was well that one of them had killed him, for said he had they killed You or anybody Else we would Surely have killed him for they would not let him Live above the ground, but would put him under the ground, as Lately we have Done to one of our Young Fellows who got Drunk and in his Liquor met with a little girl in his way below the Waxhaw Settlement and kill'd her we were Imediately aprized of it [by] one of our own people, and we Soon Discovered who it was that Commited the fact whereupon we Directly Caused an Other young man the fellows own Cousin to kill him, which he readily did in the presence of some of our Brothers the white people in Order to Shew our Willingness to punish Such offenders.

Then Came James Armstrong William Young and William McNight, who Said Sundry things to the Indians Charge (to wit) Concerning the takeing Bread meat meal and Cloaths and also for Attempting to Take away a

General Assembly Sessions
1709 - 1776

Child, and Attempting to Stab men and women if Opposed by them from Committing those Crimes, To which the King & Some of the the Head men Answered

Brothers as You are Wariors Your Selves, You well know that we often times goe to War against our Enemies and Many Times we are Either makeing our Escape from our Enemies or in pursuit of them, which prevents us from hunting for meat to Eat when we are in Danger, least our Enemy Should Discover us; And as this is our Case many times we are forced to goe to Your houses when Hungry, and no Sooner we do Appear but your Dogs bark and as Soon as You Discover Our Comeing You Imediately hide Your Bread Meal and Meat or any Other thing that is fit to Eat about Your houses, and we being Sensible that this is the Case, it is True we Serch, And if we find any Eatables in the house we Take Some, and Especially from those who behave so Cherlish and ungratefull to us, as they are very well assured of our great need many times for the Reasons we now give, If we ask a little Victuals You Refuse us & then we [?] Take a Loaf of bread a little meal or meat to Eat, and then You Complain and say those are Transgressions, it is True there are many in those Settlements that are Very kind and curtious to us when or as often as we come they give us Bread and milk meat or Butter very freely if they have any ready and never do refuse whether we do ask or no, and if it should happen that they have nothing we goe away Contented with them, for we well know that if they had any thing ready we would have it freely & be not Refused by them & One of the Captains Named James Bullin Owned that not Long agoe he and his men were in pursuit of the Enemy and then on their Track he Came to James Armstrong's house, the above Complainant, who gave him a small Cake of Bread, and being Very hungry he Asked more for himself and his men, and being Told by Sd. Armstrong that there was no more ready in the house One of the Indians Lifted up a bag that lay in the house Under which they Discovered Some Bread which they had Suspected was hid from them, and takeing Some of it the Woman Struck one of them Over the head, which is the Cause of our Takeing Those things without leave that we would not do to those who are kind to us in Our Necessity when we Apply to them.

King   You I Remember Brothers Accuse our People with Attempting To take away A Child from one of Your people, but I hope You will not harbour this Thought of us so as to Imagine it was done in Earnest, for I am Informed it was Only done by way of a joke by one of our wild Young

General Assembly Sessions
1709 - 1776

men in Order to Surprize the people that were the parents of the Child, to have a Laugh at the Joke. But as to their Takeing other things Such as knives Cloaths or Such Things we own it is not right to do but there are some of our Young fellows will do those tricks Altho' by us they were often times Cautioned from Such ill Doings Altho' to no purpose for we Cannot be present at all times to Look after them, and when they goe to war or hunting Among the Inhabitants we generally Warn them from being Any ways Offensive to any white person upon any Consideration whatever.

King   Brothers here is One thing You Your Selves are to Blame Very much in, That in You Rot Your grain in Tubs out of which You take and make Strong Spirits You Sell it to our Young men And give it them, many times; they got Very Drunk with it this is the Very Cause that they Often times Commit those Crimes that is offensive to You and we and all thro' the Effect of that Drink it is all Very bad for our people, for it Rots their guts and Causes our men to get Very Sick and Many of our people has Lately Died by the Effect of that Strong Drink, and I heartily Wish You would do Something to prevent Your people from Dareing to Sell or give them Any of that Strong Drink upon Any Consideration Whatever for that will be a great means of our being free from being accused of those Crimes that is Commited by our Young men and will prevent many of the Abuses that is done by them thro' the Effects of that Strong Drink.

Commissrs.
King Hagler and Brethren here is one thing more that is Laid to Your peoples Charge by many of the white people, that is Your Comeing into our woods and Among our plantations and steale our horses mares and Young Creatures from us and Take them away and Sell them to others under a pretence of their being Your property, if Such Things as those were Done by any of our people to one An Other, our Laws and Customs are to put them to Death, or any Offender when Discovered or Catch'd in Any Such heinous fact, or for smaller facts they are punished According to the Nature of the Crime; but when Your people do Any of those things we have no Remedy but are obliged to Apply our Selves to You, that the Offenders may be punished According to the Nature of the Crime And According to Your Manner and Customs, and if those Offences are by You permited to be done it will be a great means to Breake that Strong Chain of Friendship that has been so Long made Between us, it will also be a meanes to cause [diss]entione Among You and us and make us act and

General Assembly Sessions
1709 - 1776

behave towards one An Other as tho' we were Entire Enemies to One An Other, if this should be our Case the Great King Your Father and ours would be much Displeased with You [Torn] us, as he Looks upon us as his own Children and so [Torn]the the President who he sent here in his Stead as A guardian over us and You, but on the Other hand whilst we behave well to Each Other it will Cause them to Rejoice and they will be ready and willing to protect us from the Impositions of Insults of Any Other Natione or that would attempt to take our properties from us or You.

Commissrs.
You Remember in the Letter the President wrote to You by Capt. McClenachan and the Other Gentlemen he told You that he had understood that Mr. Glen the Governor of South Carolina Incouraged You to Drive all the white people from the Land within Thirty miles of Your Nation, if he has Told You so You Cannot Expect that this man Loves You or the white people, Because he well knows that the great king Your Father & ours gave those Lands to his Children and also he Gave it into the Care of the President of North Carolina to Divide According to his Discretion Among his people and not to the Governor of South Carolina and it is his desire and pleasure to do Justice Between You and us, for he Looks upon You and us as his own people and would rejoice to here of our Unity and Friendship to Each Other, for whilst we behave thus to Each Other and Stand by Each Other we need not fear any Opp[Torn] that should attempt or come to Dismay us.

King   Brothers and Wariors You Talk Very well and as to Your talk about our people takeing Your Horses and Mares, it is Very True there are a great many of our Creatures that Run Amongst the white peoples a[Torn] there are also Many Stole from us by these people for it is not Long agoe Since we [Torn] a white man with some of our Horses and [Torn] him to Justice, but was not punished a[Torn] Represented to us while agoe.

Commissrs.
Who was that Justice You Carried him before

Indians
Before Mr. McGirt in South Carolina below the Waxhaw Settlement

Commissrs.

General Assembly Sessions
1709 - 1776

This Offence was not in our power to punish for we have no Authority in An Other Government so that we are Excuseable in this Case -

King   As to our Liveing on those Lands we Expect to live on those Lands we now possess Dureing our Time here for when the Great man Above made us he also made this Island he also made our forefathers and of this Coulor[?] and Here (Shewing his hands & Breast[?]) he also fixed our forefathers and us here to Inherit this Land and Ever Since we Lived after our manner and fashion we in those Days had no Instruments to Support our living but Bowes which we [Torn]bated with stonesn knives we had none, and as it was the Custom in those days Cut our hair, which we Did by Burning it of our heads and Bodies with Coals of Fire, our Axes we made of Stone We bled our Selves with fish Teeth Our Cloathing were Skins and Furr, instead of which we Enjoy those Cloaths which we got from the white people and Ever Since they first Came Among us we have Enjoyed All those things that we were then Destitute of for which we thank the White people, and to this Day we have Lived in A Brotherly Love & Peace with them and More Especially with these Three Governments and it is our Earnest Desire that Love and Friendship which has So Long remain'd Should Ever Continue.

King   Our Brother the Governor of Virginia Sent for us not Long Agoe, we gladly answered his Call, and he Entertained us and shook hands with us Very kindly, and had he Indulged us we would have Gone with the white people to War against their Enemies the French, but Guns and Amunition being not Sufficient to Supply the white people who were then going out, we were forced to Return Back to our Nation again untill further Instructions from him. We understand that Our Brothers and the french has had a battle and that Several of our friends were Kill'd I am heartily Sorry for it.

We Never had the pleasure of Seeing our Good Brother the President of North Carolina as yet, but this Let our Brother know that we want to be brothers and Friends with him & all his people, and with the great king Over the Water, and all his Children, and to Confirm the same I shall as Soon as I get home I will Call all our Nation Together and Charge the Young men and Wariors Not to Misbehave on any Consideration Whatever to the white people and as we do Expect an Everlasting Friendship between You and [Torn] we Expect your kinds to us for Ever, as you may [**Torn**] Friendship and kinds often to you.

General Assembly Sessions
1709 - 1776

And Tell Brother the President of North Carolina that if this war Continues between the white people and the french that I and my people are ready and Willing to Obey his Orders in giveing All possible Assistance in my power to him when Called by him or the Governor of Virginia and As A pledge of the same Take our Brother this letter as a token of Everlasting Friendship and return him Thanks for our good Talk this Day with Each Other

Then they Shook Hands all round   King Hagler
A True Coppy as to me Delivered by Mr.
Matthew Toole Interpreter at the Above Treaty

                 Jno. Dunn

****

North Carolina State Archives
General Assembly Sessions Records
GASR-OS, Box #1
October 1748 - December 1757

Folder Name: September-October, 1755 - Bills
Subfile Title: October 9: Bill to prevent the exportation of provisions and livestock from this province to the French or neutral posts.
    Whereas Supplying the Subjects of the French King with Provisions from this Province in the Present time of Danger may contribute towards the facilitating of their Designs of making Encroachments & Depredations on his Majesty's Territories in the Northern Provinces For Prevention whereof - - Be it Enacted by the Governor Council & Assembly and it is hereby Enacted by the Authority of the same that from and after the first day of November next; no person or persons whatsoever shall export out of this Province into any Port belonging to or in the Possession of the French King or any of his Subjects or into any Neutral Port, any Indian Corn, Pease, flower bread Rice beef Pork Live Stock or other Provisions whatsoever or sell, vend or dispose of any such in any such Port, or to any Master Commander or other Person Concerned in Navigating any Ship belonging to the said French King or any of his Subjects
    And every Master of any Ship or other Vessel which after the Aforesaid first day of November next shall be Laden in any Port within

General Assembly Sessions
1709 - 1776

this Province shall before his Ship or Vessell shall be cleared out by the Collector of the Customs in the said Port enter into Bond with two or more good and Sufficient Securities, to the Governor or Commander in Chief for the time being in the Penalty of five hundred pounds Proclamation money with Condition that he will not vend, sell or dispose of any such Provisions then on board his Ship or Vessel contrary to the Directions of this Act And Moreover shall take the following Oath, to wit, "I A.B. do Swear that I will not directly or indirectly vend, sell or dispose of, or knowingly Suffer or permit any person or persons on board my Vessel to vend sell or dispose of any Indian Corn, Pease Wheat flower, bread beef Pork live Stock or other Provisions on board my said Vessel to any of the Subjects of the French King contrary to the directions of the Act of Assembly intituled an Act to prevent the Exportation of Provisions and live Stock to the French or Neutral Ports so help me God."

And every such Collector is hereby Impowered Authorised and required to take such Bond and Security and Administer such Oath, And shall and may receive of every such Master or Commander for the same five shillings & five pence Proclamation money

And no Collector shall clear out any Ship or Vessel or deliver up the Register until the Master or Commander thereof, shall have given such Bond & Security and taken such Oath as aforesaid. And every Collector failing or neglecting to take such Bond or Administer such Oath shall forfeit and pay the sum of Five hundred pounds Proclamation money to be recovered in the name of the Governor or Commander in Chief for the time being and the Informer with Costs by Action of Debt Bill Plaint or Information one half to the use of this Province towards defraying the Contingent charges thereof and the Other half to the use of the Informer. And if any Suit shall be Prosecuted on the said Bond the Penalty thereof when recovered shall be applied & delivered in like manner

And be it further Enacted by the Authority aforesaid that this shall continue and be in force for and during the space of Two Years after the aforesaid day of November next and from thence to the end of the next session of Assembly and no longer

And for the better discovery of Violations of this Act Be it Enacted by the Authority aforesaid that every Master or Commander of any Ship or Vessell Laden in this Province which after the Aforesaid first day of November next shall be cleared out by any Collector as aforesaid shall within Twelve Months after being so Cleared out Produce to, and lodge with the Collector from whom he had such Clearance Certified under the hand & Seal of a Collector of the Customs in some one of his Majestys

General Assembly Sessions
1709 - 1776

Plantations of his having delivered his Cargoe in some Port of such Plantation and thereupon return the Collector shall deliver up such bond to be Cancelled And if such Master or Commander shall fail or neglect to produce such Certificate and lodge the same with the Collector within the time aforesaid, such failure or Neglect shall be deemed a Forfeiture of his Bond. Provided nevertheless that if no suit shall be commenced on such bond within Two Years from the date thereof, the same shall be held & deemed to be Null and Void any thing herein contained to the Contrary Notwithstanding

A Bill to prevent the Exportation of Provisions & live Stock from this Province to the French or Neutral Ports

9th October 1755
In the Assembly read the first time & Passed
By Order of Wm Herritage Clke
Mr Wyatt Mr Wynne

In the Upper House Octbr 9, 1755 read the first time & passed by Order
Richd: Spaight Clk

9 Octobr 1755
In the Assembly Read the Second time and Amended
By Order Wm Harritage Clke
Mr. Bell Mr. Harvey

10th Octbr 1755
In the Upper House read the second time and Amended
By Order 11 of October 1755 Richd: Spaight Clke.

In the Assembly read the third time & passed
By Order Wm Harritage Clke
Mr. Brown Mr. Pain

In the Upper House Octr 11, 1755 read the third time & passed
Orderd to be enforced

****

North Carolina State Archives

General Assembly Sessions
1709 - 1776

General Assembly Sessions Records
GASR-OS, Box # 1
October 1748 - December 1757

Folder Name: September - October, 1755, Bills
Subfile Title: October 1: Bill for granting a further aid to his majesty to repell the French and Indians in their alliance from their encroachments on his majestie's territories in America

    A Bill for granting a further aid to his majesty to repell the French and Indians in their Alliance from their Encroachments on His Majestie's Territories in America and other Purposes

    Whereas the Subjects of the French King in pursuance of their wicked and destructive Designs to render themselves Masters of the American Continent have erected forts on his Majestie's Lands And in Conjunction with the Indians in their Interest committed divers Murthers on his Subjects and still continue to perpetrate such horrid Cruelties and unparalleled Barbarities the Prosecution of which if not speedily prevented may not improbably terminate in the Completion of their iniquitous Schemes and the Destruction of the British Colonies; This Assembly moved with the Consideration of the Sufferings of their Fellow Subjects and earnestly desirous to show their Duty and Loyalty to their Sovereign and uninvariable Attachment to his Interest Have granted to his Majesty for aid of ten thousand pounds to enable His Excellency the Governor to protect the Frontier of this Province and to assist the other Colonies in Defense of his Majestie's Territories and to repel the French from their Encroachments And Whereas there is not in the Treasury any Money unappropriated out of which the aforesaid Sum can be paid Be it enacted by the Governor Council and Assembly and by the Authority of the same That the sum of Seven thousand two hundred pounds appropriated for building and finishing Churches and purchasing Glebes under a Suspending Clause in an Act intituled An Act for granting to His Majesty forty thousand pounds in publick Bills of Credit at the Rate of Proclamation Money to be applied towards defraying the Expence of raising and subsisting the forces for his Majestie's Service in this Province to be sent to the Assistance of His Majestie's Colony of Virginia and for other Purposes therein mentioned and also the Sum of two thousand pounds appropriated for and towards finishing the publick Buildings under the same suspending Clause in the before recited Act amounting in the

General Assembly Sessions
1709 - 1776

whole to the sum of nine thousand and two hundred pounds Be Received by the publick Treasurers from the Commissrs. appointed for [?] the Sum of 40,000 pounds which they? hereby required and empowered to pay to the sd Treasurers on Demand to wit four thousand and six hundred pounds to the Treasurer of each District within this Province and by them paid to such person or persons as the Governor or Commander in Chief for the time being shall appoint and receive the same for which the said Treasurers shall receive no more than one [?] And the persons appointed by the Governor or Commander in Chief to Receive [?] same shall account therefore to the Assembly when required

And that the said Sum of nine thousand two hundred Pounds may be replaced in the hands of the Treasurers And also to raise the Sum of Eight hundred pounds to be applied with the said nine thousand two hundred pounds and this Act is directed Be it further enacted by the Authority aforesaid That a Poll Tax of two shillings per Taxable be levyed on each taxable Person within this Province for and during the space of five years from the passing of this Act and no longer which Tax be collected paid and accounted for at the same time and in the same Manner and under the like Penalties as the Tax imposed by an Act of Assembly intituled An Act for granting an Aid to his Majesty for the Defense of the Frontier of this Province and other Purposes And as the same shall be paid shall be applied to the Payment of the said Eight hundred pounds to such person as the Governor or Commander in Chief For the Time being shall direct And to replacing the said Sum of nine thousand two hundred pounds

And Be it further Enacted by the Authority aforesaid That the said Ten thousand pounds hereby granted to His Majesty or so much thereof as shall be necessary for the Purposes of this Act shall be applied in Manner following that is to say one thousand pounds to defray the expense of erecting one or more Forts at such Place or Places on the Frontier of this Province as the Governor or Commander in Chief for the time being shall appoint and for the better Accomodation of the Company formed for Defence of the same And the sum of Nine thousand pounds for the Expence of raising paying Cloathing and accomodating three Companies consisting of fifty Men each exclusive of Commissioned officers which Companies shall march or be transported to such of the Northern Colonies as his Excellency the Governor or Commander in Chief for the time being shall think most conducive to his Majestie's Interest and be employed [?] the troops in his Service

And be it further enacted by the Authority aforesaid That the Officers and Soldiers of the aforesaid three Companies to be raised in

General Assembly Sessions
1709 - 1776

Virtue of this Act on or from the Time of their being Commissioned and inlisted have and receive the same and be under the same Disipline and Regulation with the other Officers as the Soldiers appointed and raised for the same Service

And Be it further enacted by the Authority aforesaid That all such Monies as shall be raised by Virtue of the Tax herein before directed more than shall amount to the said Sum of ten thousand pounds and so much of the said ten thousand pounds as shall remain after the Disbursements for the several Services herein before mentioned according to the true Intent and Meaning of this Act shall by the Governor Council & Assembly be applied towards paying the contingent Charges of Government

And That the Troops in Virtue of this Act intended to be raised may be well paid and cloathed Be it enacted by the Authority aforesaid That the Governor or Commander in Chief for the time being shall and may direct the Manner of remitting the necessary part of the sum granted for that purpose by appointing such persons as he shall think proper to purchase Commodities in his Province and to ship them to any other of the British Colonies in which it may be thought they may to the greatest Advantage be disposed of and to direct the person or persons to whom the same shall be consigned to pay over the Money arising from the sale of such Commodities to the Paymaster of the said Troops to be appointed by the said Governor or Commander in Chief of this Province

And whereas in the present Time of Danger the inlisting of Voluntiers may be attended with great Difficulty and Delay To the End therefore that the aforesaid three Companies may be compleated in the most expeditious Manner Be it enacted by the Authority aforesaid That on or before the first Day of January next after the passing of this Act Every Captain of a Company of each respective Regiment and Captain of any Independant Company within this Province shall give in a List of the Names of all the single Men on his Muster roll to the Colonel or chief Commanding Officer of the Regiment residing in his County under the Penalty of Ten pounds to be recovered by a Warrant from the Colonel or Chief Commanding Officer the Use of his Majesty to be accounted for and aid to the Governor or Commander in Chief for the time being and applied to the Purposes intended by the Tax imposed by this Act And Every Colonel or Chief Commanding Officer of each Regiment respectively shall after the Receipt of such List in the presence of the other field Officers and Captains of the Regiment or the Majority of them on or before the first day of february next after passing this Act cause so many Men to be draughted out of the Number as the Govr. by his Warrant under his hand & Seal shall

General Assembly Sessions
1709 - 1776

direct regard being had to the Number [?] each particular Regiment so that there be an Equal proportion of Each And every field Officer & Captain who shall Refuse fail or Neglect to make such Draught Pursuant to such Warrant shall forfeit and pay the Sum of Twenty pounds Proclamation Money to be received in any Court of Record in this Province by Action of Debt (Editor: Part of page missing) of single men whose Names shall be so given in as aforesaid And the Persons who shall be so draughted shall thenceforth be deemed and are hereby declared to be inlisted Soldiers and shall be intitled to the same Pay and be under the same Regulation and Disipline as other inlisted Soldiers And in Case of Desertion or Neglect of Duty subject to the same Punishment Provided always that if the Officers to be employed by the Governor or Commander in Chief for the time being to raise the aforesaid three Companies shall inlist Voluntiers so as to compleat their Companies without taking all the Men who shall be so draughted It shall and may be lawful for them to discharge so many of the said draughted Men as can be spared without rendering their Companys incompleat

Provided also that if any person so draughted as aforesaid can and will procure one other able Man to inlist as a Voluntier in his Majesties Service in his stead at any time before this Company shall march or be transported from this Province The Person so procuring such Voluntier to inlist shall be discharged any thing herein to the contrary notwithstanding

And Be it further enacted by the Authority aforesaid That the Companies to be raised in Virtue of this Act may be continued and kept Pay until the [?] Day of November which will be in the year of our Lord one thousand seven hundred and fifty six if necessary for his Majesties Service and no longer

A Bill for Granting Further Aid to His Majesty to Repell the French & Indians in their Alliance from their Incroachments on his Majestys Frontiers in America & other purposes

1 Octr 1755
In the Assembly read the first time & pass
By order of the Assembly
Mr Starkey Wm Harritage Clke

1 Octr 1755
In the Upper House Read the First Time & Pass
By order Richd. Spaight Clke

General Assembly Sessions
1709 - 1776

2d Octr 1755
In the Assembly Read the Second Time and Amended & Passd.
Mr. Relfe, Mr. Spier

Octr 4, 1755
In the Upper House read the second time and passed with Amendmts.
By Order Richd. Spaight Clke.

4th Octr 1755
In the Assembly Read the Third time & Amended
By order Wm Herritage Clke

Octbr. 6th 1755
In the Upper House read the third time & passed
Mr. Ashe, Mr. Vail
Ordered to be Engrossed

****

North Carolina State Archives
General Assembly Sessions Records
1709 - January, 1760, Box #1
Lower House Papers

14 Jan 1755

Gentlemen of His Majesty's Council,
Mr. Speaker and Gentlemen of the Assembly

  The steady Zeal you have shewn for his Majesty's Person & Royal Family and Support of His Government, and securing the Payment of his Quit Rents, and the unanimity with which you have proceeded in doing every thing necessary according to your present ability for the Peace security & Defence of this and ye adjoining Colonies, and in securing your Religious Rights & properties from French Incroachments and papal Tyranny requires my returning You sincere Thanks, which I shall faithfully represent to his Majesty.
  Your Application and the Dispatch you have made in preparing or passing many necessary Laws, for these Improvements of the Trade, easy

General Assembly Sessions
1709 - 1776

Distribution of Justice, and for the Maintenance of an Orthodox Clergy, well deserves the Thanks of your Constituents, & of all who wish well to this Province.

I am particularly obliged to you for the favourable Sentiments which you have expressed of my endeavours to serve his Majesty's, and to promote the peace security and Improvement of this Colony according to the Trust His Majesty has reposed in me.

Mr. Speaker and Gent. of the Assembly

I returned you in particularly my hearty Thanks for ye Supplys you have granted for the Defence of this Colony and for the Assistance of Virginia and Contingencies of Government, with which you have entrusted me, which I shall endeavour to apply with the greatest of economy for his Majesty's Service and Security of this Province

Gentlemen of His Majesty's Council
Mr. Speaker and Gentlemen of the Assembly

As your close Attendance and your Private Affairs will require your separating at this time and returning to your several Counties, I most earnestly recommend to you the promoting Peace & Harmony in your several Counties, and that you will exert yourselves in your several Districts in putting in Execution the several Laws formerly and now made for promoting true Religion and Virtue, the due Execution of Justice, and promoting the Trade & Improvement of this Province, and to take care that the Supplies you have so chearfully granted be duly and carefully levyed & paid in, to answer the Purposes for which they are granted, without which Your Lives Religion Libertys and Properties can't be secured, nor the Government be enabled to defend you, as all Laws are a dead Letter if not duly inforced and put in Execution.

****

North Carolina State Archives
Governors Papers, 1756

Fom Job Carr Abot. the Hatteras Indians Lands

General Assembly Sessions
1709 - 1776

In Obedience to the Governors Command I have Made a digilent Inquiery into the Complaint of Thomas Elks Indian and I find the greatest parte of his Complaint to be Eronias for I find it Set forth in the Complaint of Sundery persons that came and indeavour to dispossess him and the Rest of the Indians Which is a Small Numbour for there is butt **[Faded]** Man beside him Selfe and one Small boy of the Male I**[Faded]** and I have Strictly Examined the Sd. Thomas Elks What pers**[Faded]** they were that [**Faded**] the Indians and he answered Me None but Thomas Robb Junor and demanded of the Said Robb Junor his Reason of his Incroachment uppone the Indian Land and he the Sd. Robb denied that he had don it or intended to do it for he desered No More than his one and accordingly produced a plot and pattin for a pece of Land Containing 320 acres Which Was Surveyed to his grandfather Mr Henry Dayvis in yr 17[?]6 beginning at the Indian Town and Rainging to the Northward and for the better Cleareing up the Matter I Caused Mr Hezeciah Farrow and Capt Jacob Farrow to appeare before Me one the Spot and Strictly Examined them one theire Corperal Oath one the holy Evangelest of all Mity god Concerning the boundary of the the Indin Land Which the deponants declareth that they know bound to the aforesd. Indian Land Nor Quantity Except the Possession Line betweene the aforesd. Thoms. Robb Junor and the Indians Which they Redily Shewed for the said Indians Never had any Grant or Patting for it as Ever they Were acquainted With or had any Knowledg of further the deponants Sath Not & So that I humbly Conceive a[?] they **[Faded]** No Right to Complaine Seaing they have no grant or patting for any Lands neither is Thoms. Elks Intiteled to the Royelty for he is but a Son in Law to the Late King Elks desesed and part of the Maromosceat Line of Indians for the tru Line of the Hatteras Indians are mostly dead So I Shall Commit it to Your Excellencys worthy opinion and I assert this above under My hand and Seale

Dated one Hatteras this 10th of august
Anno dominy 1756   Job Carr

****

North Carolina State Archives
General Assembly Sessions Records
GASR-OS Box # 1
October 1748 -December 1757

General Assembly Sessions
1709 - 1776

Folder Name: November-December, 1757, Bills
Subfile Title: December 10: Bill for preserving peace and keeping correspondence with the Indians, etc. (with Governor's message)

Whereas it has been represented to this Assembly that divers Persons under pretence of dealing with the Cherokee & Catawba Indians have committed many Frauds and irregularities to the great disturbance of those People which if permitted may be the Cause of their [?]

Wherefore the better to preserve Peace & Harmony with the said Indians and to prevent the like Irregularities for the future Be it Enacted by the Governor Counsel and Assembly and by the Authority of the same That from and after the first Day of May next no Person whatsoever shall presume to deal or Traffick with either the Catawba's or Cherokee's or other Western Indians within the limits of this Province without having first obtained a Licence or Permission for such purpose from the Honble. Edmund Atkins Esqr. his Majestys Agent for and Superintendant of Indian Affairs in Virginia North & south Carolina and Georgia and given Bond with two Sufficient Sureties in the Sum of Two Hundred Pounds Proclamation money payable to the said Edmund Atkins or his Successor in Office with Condition that he or those he shall employ shall demean theirselves honestly and innoffensively to the Indians with whom he shall have Licence to deal and duly observe such Instructions and orders in writing as shall for the purposes aforesaid and for the better regulation of Trade be given to him from time to time by the said Edmund Atkins or his Successor in office

And be it further Enacted by the Authority aforesaid That if any Reason whatsoever shall after the said **[Last line torn away from document]** within the Limits of this Province without having obtained a Licence or Permission agreeable to the direction of this Act it shall and may be Lawful for the said Edmund Atkins or his Successor in Office to cause the Person so offending to be Arrested and to seize his Goods and to cause the Goods so seized after Ten Days notice by Advertisement to be sold at Public Auction and the Money arising by such Sale to lay out for presents to be distributed among the said Indians in such manner as the sd. Edmund Atkins or his Successor in Office shall then In most likely fix and confirm the said Indians in Friendship and Amity with his Majestys **[Torn]** And to cause the Person so Arrested to enter into bond to the said Edmund Atkins or his Successor in Office in the Sum of Two hundred Pounds Proclamation Money with Condition That he shall not thereafter deal with

General Assembly Sessions
1709 - 1776

any of the said Indians contrary to the form and effect of this Act And in Case the person so offending shall fail or refuse to give Bond and Security as aforesaid, The sd. Edmund Atkins or his Successor in Office shall and may Cause such offender to be sent to the Public Goal of the District wherein such offence was Committed till he shall before the Supreme Court or the Chief Justice or one other of the Justices of the sd. Supreme Court Justices enter into Recognizance with two sufficient sureties in the Sum of Five Hundred Pounds Proclamation Money for his good Behaviour **[Bottom of page torn away from document]**

Authority aforesaid That if a **[Torn]** Edmund Atkins or any other Person or Persons shall be sued for or by Reason of any Act or **[Torn]** by him or them done agreeable to the direction of this Act he or they may plead the General Issue and give this Act in Evidence. And the Plaintiff if he be **[?]** on the Trial shall pay double Costs. And Be it further Enacted That this Act shall continue and be in force two years from the first day of May Next, and no longer

In the Upper House 12th Decr 1757. Read the third Time - Ordered to be Engrossed
            By Order Jno Smith Clk

Exd
J Murray
J Ashe

****

North Carolina State Archives
General Assembly Sessions Records
1709 - Jan. 1760, Box #1
September-October, 1756

    Mr. Speaker and Gentlemen of the Assembly 19 oct 1756
    Mr. Dinwiddie the Lieut. Governor of Virginia Having Acquainted me, That He was sending Commissioners To Treat with the Cherokees and Catawbas, and to Confirm the alliances with them, and that it would be of service to His Majesty and the Colonies That Commissioners shou'd be sent From this Province to Joyn them, and to Make and Confirm Our Alliance with them, I accordingly sent a

General Assembly Sessions
1709 - 1776

Commission to Captain Hugh Waddell to Joyn with the Virginia Commissioners and treat with them which He Accordingly Did, and was out upon the Treaty with the Cherokees and Catawbas above a Month, for which He has had no Allowance And therefore Recommend it to you, to Allow him what is Proper for His Trouble and Attendance
Arthur Dobbs

****

North Carolina State Archives
General Assembly Sessions Records
1709 - Jan. 1760, Box #1
May, 1757
Joint Resolutions

Joint Resolutions
May 23--Appointing County Commisaries to provide necessaries for Indian allies

Gent: of His Majesty's Hon'ble Council
    This House have Resolved that Mr Robert Harris be Appointed Commisary for Granville County to Provide Necessarys for the Indians in Alliance with us on their March in the Service of the Public from their Several Nations to and from Virginia or any part of this province, and Mr. James Watson for Orange County Mr. George Smith for Rowan County, and Mr. Martin Piper for Anson County for the purposes aforesaid and that they be allowed Eight pence p. Diem for Each Indian they shall find with Necessarys as above said to which Desire Your Honors Concurrence
23 May 1757   Sam Swann   Speaker
By Order Wm Harritage Cke
Sent by Mr. Whitmill
    In the upper House of Assembly
    Concurr'd with

By Order	Matt. Rowan P.C.
Jn Smith Clk	Attention to:
	Arthur Dobbs

****

General Assembly Sessions
1709 - 1776

North Carolina State Archives
General Assembly Sessions Records
GASR-OS Box # 1
October 1748 - December 1757

Folder Name: November-December, 1757, Bills
Subfile Title: December 10: Bill for preserving peace and keeping correspondence with the Indians, etc. (with Governor's message)

Whereas it has been represented to this Assembly that divers Persons under pretence of dealing with the Cherokee & Catawba Indians have committed many Frauds and irregularities to the great disturbance of those People which if permitted may be the Cause of their [?]

Wherefore the better to preserve Peace & Harmony with the said Indians and to prevent the like Irregularities for the future Be it Enacted by the Governor Counsel and Assembly and by the Authority of the same That from and after the first Day of May next no Person whatsoever shall presume to deal or Traffick with either the Catawba's or Cherokee's or other Western Indians within the limits of this Province without having first obtained a Licence or Permission for such purpose from the Honble. Edmund Atkins Esqr. his Majestys Agent for and Superintendant of Indian Affairs in Virginia North & south Carolina and Georgia and given Bond with two Sufficient Sureties in the Sum of Two Hundred Pounds Proclamation money payable to the said Edmund Atkins or his Successor in Office with Condition that he or those he shall employ shall demean theirselves honestly and innoffensively to the Indians with whom he shall have Licence to deal and duly observe such Instructions and orders in writing as shall for the purposes aforesaid and for the better regulation of Trade be given to him from time to time by the said Edmund Atkins or his Successor in office

  And be it further Enacted by the Authority aforesaid That if any Reason whatsoever shall after the said **[Last line torn away from document]** within the Limits of this Province without having obtained a Licence or Permission agreeable to the direction of this Act it shall and may be Lawful for the said Edmund Atkins or his Successor in Office to cause the Person so offending to be Arrested and to seize his Goods and to cause the Goods so seized after Ten Days notice by Advertisement to be sold at Public Auction and the Money arising by such Sale to lay out for presents to be distributed among the said Indians in such manner as the sd.

General Assembly Sessions
1709 - 1776

Edmund Atkins or his Successor in Office shall then In most likely fix and confirm the said Indians in Friendship and Amity with his Majestys **[Torn]** And to cause the Person so Arrested to enter into bond to the said Edmund Atkins or his Successor in Office in the Sum of Two hundred Pounds Proclamation Money with Condition That he shall not thereafter deal with any of the said Indians contrary to the form and effect of this Act And in Case the person so offending shall fail or refuse to give Bond and Security as aforesaid, The sd. Edmund Atkins or his Successor in Office shall and may Cause such offender to be sent to the Public Goal of the District wherein such offence was Committed till he shall before the Supreme Court or the Chief Justice or one other of the Justices of the sd. Supreme Court Justices enter into Recognizance with two sufficient sureties in the Sum of Five Hundred Pounds Proclamation Money for his good Behaviour **[Bottom of page torn away from document]**

Authority aforesaid That if a **[Torn]** Edmund Atkins or any other Person or Persons shall be sued for or by Reason of any Act or **[Torn]** by him or them done agreeable to the direction of this Act he or they may plead the General Issue and give this Act in Evidence. And the Plaintiff if he be **[?]** on the Trial shall pay double Costs. And Be it further Enacted That this Act shall continue and be in force two years from the first day of May Next, and no longer

In the Upper House 12th Decr 1757. Read the third Time - Ordered to be Engrossed
                By Order Jno Smith Clk

Exd
J Murray
J Ashe

                6 Decr. 1757

Having received a Letter from the Lords Commissioners for Trade and Plantations recommending Edmond Atkins Esquire to me, appointed by his Majesty Agent and Superintendant for Indian Affairs in the Provinces of Virginia North and South Carolina and Georgia I herewith send you a Copy of said Letter along with a Letter from Mr. Atkins representing what he thinks very proper to be passed into a Law to have a Law passed of the same Nature through all the provinces that all may act in Concert, I think

General Assembly Sessions
1709 - 1776

what is proposed with some Alterations will be of great Service to his Majesty and the Colonies and therefore recommend it to you for your Consideration in Order to have your Thoughts in Case it should be too late to pass a Law this Session to shew our Willingness to act in Concert with the rest of the Colonies

Arthur Dobbs

To Samuel Swann Esquire
Speaker of the House of
Assembly

Folder Name:May, 1757 bills
Subfile Title:May 20: Bill for Granting a further aid to his majesty for the assistance of South Carolina and the defense of the frontiers of this province.

A Bill for Granting a further Aid to his Majesty for the Assisting of South Carolina and the Defence of the Frontiers of this Province and other Purposes.
    Whereas our Neighboring Province of South Carolina is Threatened with a Formidable Invasion from the French and Indians their Interest and Alliance, And our own Frontier much Exposed in the time of War, And this Assembly being Desirous to Shew their Duty and Loyalty to his Majesty and to Contribute such further Aid as the necessary Circumstances of their Constituants will Admit to Enable his Excellency the Governor to Furnish our Quota toward the Support of the Common Cause.
    Be it Enacted by the Governour Council and Assembly by the Authority of the same that the sum of Five Thousand three hundred & Six Pounds be Granted to his Majesty. And that Two Companies shall be Raised and Subsisted, Each of which said Companies shall Consist of One hundred Men Exclusive of one Captain, Five Lieutenants & one Ensign and one Surgeon & one Adjutant to both Companies Which Companies with all Possible Dispatch shall March to South Carolina to be there Employed with the Troops in his Majestys Service in the Defence of the Inhabitants of that Province from the Hostile Attempts of the French & Indian Allies.

****

General Assembly Sessions
1709 - 1776

North Carolina State Archives
General Assembly Sessions Records
1709-January, 1760, Box #1
Committee of Claims

The Publick of North Carolina to Martian Phifer

To 47 Cherreke Ingons on thear way to Virginia to war against the French

To 1 Large Beef	£2.15.0
To Bred & Corn for thear horses	£1.5.0
To Flouer carred away 204 lbs at[?]	£52.8.6

May the 30 1757 Rec'd the Bove artickels for the use of the Ingons

By me - John Watts

The Publick of North Carolina To Martain Pifer

1758 July the 21 by King hagler & his Compeny on his way to Virginia to war To provisions £ "8"0

1757 Feby the 14 Capt. John & Eight more Cattaba Ingons on thear Return from Virginia for Necessary Provisions £"5"6

the 19 to 17 Cattabo Ingons on thear way to Virginia For Provisions
£" 9"

the 19 Capt. Bullen & Eight of his men for Provision £"5"6

1757 Feby 29 King hagler & his Compeny on thear way to Virginia To Expenses for Provisions £"13 "0

March the 3 Capt. George & Seven more on thear way to Virginia To Expenses for Provisions £"4"0

March th 20 Mr. Richard Smith & 30 od Cherrekes on thear way to Virginia To Expenses £"0"4

General Assembly Sessions
1709 - 1776

May the 29 King hagler on his Return from Virginia with his Compenet to Expenses £"1"5

June the 3 Frenche hura & his Compeney on thear Return from Virginia Expenses £"10"2

Sept. 14 one Creek Ingon & his Interpertor with a Express to the Governor of Charlestown To Expenses £"4"8

Octr. the 4 to 4 Cattabo Ingons on thear Return from Virginia To Expenses £"4"8

Anson County, North Carolina Octr. 13, 1757
This Day Came Martin phifar Before the [?] a majestrate of A. County and made oath that the above Account is just and true as it Stands Stated and that he hath Receaved no part Nor parcil Securety or Satisfactions for the Same - Sworn Before
     Nathl. Alexander
     Alexr. Cathey

****

North Carolina State Archives
General Assembly Sessions Records
Over Sized Records, Box #1
October, 1748-December, 1757
Bills

Folder Name: November-December, 1757, Bills
Subfile Title: December 10: Bill for preserving peace and keeping correspondence with the Indians, etc. (with Governor's message).

Whereas it has been represented to this Assembly that divers Persons under pretence of dealing with the Cherokee & Catawba Indians have committed many Frauds and irregularities to the great disturbance of those People which if permitted may be the Cause of their [?] Wherefore the better to preserve Peace & Harmony with the said Indians and to prevent the like Irregularities for the future Be it Enacted by the Governor Counsel and Assembly and by the Authority of the same That from and after the first

General Assembly Sessions
1709 - 1776

Day of May next no Person whatsoever shall presume to deal or Traffick with either the Catawba's or Cherokee's or other Western Indians within the limits of this Province without having first obtained a Licence or Permission for such purpose from the Honble. Edmund Atkins Esqr. his Majestys Agent for and Superintendant of Indian Affairs in Virginia North & South Carolina and Georgia and given Bond with two Sufficient Sureties in the Sum of Two Hundred Pounds Proclamation money payable to the said Edmund Atkins or his Successor in Office with Condition that he or those he shall employ shall demean theirselves honestly and innoffensively to the Indians with whom he shall have Licence to deal and duly observe such Instructions and orders in writing as shall for the purposes aforesaid and for the better regulation of Trade be given to him from time to time by the said Edmund Atkins or his Successor in office.

And be it further Enacted by the Authority aforesaid That if any Reason whatsoever shall after the said [**Last line torn away from document**] within the Limits of this Province without having obtained a Licence or Permission agreeable to the direction of this Act it shall and may be Lawful for the said Edmund Atkins or his Successor in Office to cause the Person so offending to be Arrested and to seize his Goods and to cause the Goods so seized after Ten Days notice by Advertisement to be sold at Public Auction and the Money arising by such Sale to lay out for presents to be distributed among the said Indians in such manner as the sd. Edmund Atkins or his Successor in Office shall then In most likely fix and confirm the said Indians in Friendship and Amity with his Majestys [**Torn**] And to cause the Person so Arrested to enter into bond to the said Edmund Atkins or his Successor in Office in the Sum of Two hundred Pounds Proclamation Money with Condition That he shall not thereafter deal with any of the said Indians contrary to the form and effect of this Act And in Case the person so offending shall fail or refuse to give Bond and Security as aforesaid, The sd. Edmund Atkins or his Successor in Office shall and may Cause such offender to be sent to the Public Goal of the District wherein such offence was Committed till he shall before the Supreme Court or the Chief Justice or one other of the Justices of the sd. Supreme Court Justices enter into Recognizance with two sufficient sureties in the Sum of Five Hundred Pounds Proclamation Money for his good Behaviour [**Bottom of page torn away from document**] Authority aforesaid That if a [**Torn**] Edmund Atkins or any other Person or Persons shall be sued for or by Reason of any Act or [**Torn**] by him or them done agreeable to the direction of this Act he or they may plead the General Issue and give this Act in Evidence. And the Plaintiff if he be [**?**] on the Trial shall pay double

General Assembly Sessions
1709 - 1776

Costs. And Be it further Enacted That this Act shall continue and be in force two years from the first day of May Next, and no longer.

In the Upper House 12th Decr 1757. Read the third Time - Ordered to be Engrossed
                     By Order Jno Smith Clk

Exd
J Murray
J Ashe

****

North Carolina State Archives
General Assembly Sessions Records
Over Sized Records, Box #1
October, 1748-December, 1757

Folder Name: November-December, 1757, Bills
Subfile Title: December 10: Bill for preserving peace and keeping correspondence with the Indians, etc. (with Governor's message)

Whereas it has been represented to this Assembly that divers Persons under pretence of dealing with the Cherokee & Catawba Indians have committed many Frauds and irregularities to the great disturbance of those People which if permitted may be the Cause of their [?]

Wherefore the better to preserve Peace & Harmony with the said Indians and to prevent the like Irregularities for the future Be it Enacted by the Governor Counsel and Assembly and by the Authority ofthe same That from and after the first Day of May next no Person whatsoever shall presume to deal or Traffick with either the Catawba's or Cherokee's or other Western Indians within the limits of this Province without having first obtained a Licence or Permission for such purpose from the Honble. Edmund Atkins Esqr. his Majestys Agent for and Superintendant of Indian Affairs in Virginia North & south Carolina and Georgia and given Bond with two Sufficient Sureties in the Sum of Two Hundred Pounds Proclamation money payable to the said Edmund Atkins or his Successor in Office with Condition that he or those he shall employ shall demean theirselves honestly and innofensively to the Indians with whom he shall

General Assembly Sessions
1709 - 1776

have Licence to deal and duly observe such Instructions and orders in writing as shall for the purposes aforesaid and for the better regulation of Trade be given to him from time to time by the said Edmund Atkins or his Successor in office

And be it further Enacted by the Authority aforesaid That if any Reason whatsoever shall after the said **[Last line torn away from document]** within the Limits of this Province without having obtained a Licence or Permission agreeable to the direction of this Act it shall and may be Lawful for the said Edmund Atkins or his Successor in Office to cause the Person so offending to be Arrested and to seize his Goods and to cause the Goods so seized after Ten Days notice by Advertisement to be sold at Public Auction and the Money arising by such Sale to lay out for presents to be distributed among the said Indians in such manner as the sd. Edmund Atkins or his Successor in Office shall then In most likely fix and confirm the said Indians in Friendship and Amity with his Majestys **[Torn]** And to cause the Person so Arrested to enter into bond to the said Edmund Atkins or his Successor in Office in the Sum of Two hundred Pounds Proclamation Money with Condition That he shall not thereafter deal with any of the said Indians contrary to the form and effect of this Act And in Case the person so offending shall fail or refuse to give Bond and Security as aforesaid, The sd. Edmund Atkins or his Successor in Office shall and may Cause such offender to be sent to the Public Goal of the District wherein such offence was Committed till he shall before the Supreme Court or the Chief Justice or one other of the Justices of the sd. Supreme Court Justices enter into Recognizance with two sufficient sureties in the Sum of Five Hundred Pounds Proclamation Money for his good Behaviour **[Bottom of page torn away from document]** authority aforesaid That if a **[Torn]** Edmund Atkins or any other Person or Persons shall be sued for or by Reason of any Act or **[Torn]** by him or them done agreeable to the direction of this Act he or they may plead the General Issue and give this Act in Evidence. And the Plaintiff if he be [?] on the Trial shall pay double Costs. And Be it further Enacted That this Act shall continue and be in force two years from the first day of May Next, and no longer

In the Upper House 12th Decr 1757. Read the third Time - Ordered to be Engrossed

      By Order Jno Smith Clk

Exd
J Murray
J Ashe

General Assembly Sessions
1709 - 1776

****

North Carolina State Archives
General Assembly Sessions Records
1709-January, 1760, Box #1
Joint Committees

30 NOVR. 1757
     Mr. Speaker and Gentlemen of the Assembly
  Mr. Brown having brought me down from the Catawba Nation some papers containing a strong Talk from King Hagler and the Sachems desiring that we wuo'd finish the fort we have begun and make a Law to prevent Spiritous Liquors being sold to their Young Men, I have sent the papers to you and desire you may take them into your Consideration, and raise a sufficient Supply to finish the fort, but as there have been several Contradictory sent to the North and South Provinces wou'd not have the Money issued until Mr. Atkins who has a Commission from his Majesty to transact all Indian Affairs in the Southern Provinces shall arrive in South Carolina, and then proceed to the Catawba Towns and know from the Indians whether it is agreeable to them that we should finish the fort, and if they shou'd appear to dislike it, then the Sum raised may be appropriated to other Publick Services in the Province
Arthur Dobbs
30 Novr. 1757

10 Dec 1757
  I think it very necessary at this Time of Danger that a post shou'd be appointed to carry on a Correspondence with the Northern Provinces to Suffolk and with South Carolina at Wilmington
  I don't find that you have taken Notice of what I recommend from his Majesty to tou to give a proper allowance to a Storekeeper for the Military Stores which he has been graciously pleased to give for the Defence of this Province of at least 4000 pounds Value for which I am to oblige the Storekeeper to give great Security and to correspond twice a Year with the Board of Ordnance to give them a State of the Stores and it wou'd give me great Uneasiness to be obliged to acquaint his Majesty that you refused to Comply with his Recommendation after receiving so gracious a Bounty to secureth Safety of this Province.
  These several things I must recommend to your Consideration before I can think of closing this Session.

General Assembly Sessions
1709 - 1776

Arthur Dobbs

To Samuel Swann Esqr.
Speaker of the House of
Assembly
    10 Decr. 1757

---

14 Decr. 1757
Gentlemen
    I thank you for the Supply you have granted to his Majesty for the support of 3 companies to defend the forts and Western Frontier of this Province, but wou'd have wish'd for the good of the Province that you had kept up the 2 Companies stipulated as our Quota to assist our neighboring Colonies if necessary, as they were raised by his Majesty's Recommendation for the Safety of all the Colonies - I wish your parsimony at this critical Time may not be the occasion of a much greater Expense and Trouble to you if these Companies shou'd be wanted for then I must assemble you soon to meet again, and it will be a much greater Expense to raise and cloth so many more men, and if it shou'd not be agreed to if found necessary for his Majesty's Service, I am under Apprehensions that our Dividend of his Majesty's Bounty to this Province of 15,000 pounds which I expect, wil be employed for his Majesty's Service out of the Province
    I shall only recommend to you the Support of the Laws and the preservation of the peace of the Province in your Several Counties upon your Return home, and particularly to supress the Spirit of protecting and harbouring of Deserters contrary to Law so dangerous to the future Safety of this Province.
[Editor: Letter from Governor Dobbs]

****

North Carolina State Archives
General assembly Sessions Records
1709 - Jan. 1760, Box #1
November-December, 1758

    Dec. 18: Bill for repealing an act therein mentioned

General Assembly Sessions
1709 - 1776

Whereas One Act of Assembly intitled "An Act for preserving peace and continuing a good Correspondence with the Indians in Aliance with his Majesty's subjects has not produced the Good effects hoped for. But on the contrary is likely to alienate the affections of the said Indians from the Inhabitants of this Province

Be it therefore enacted by the Governor Council and Assembly and by the Authority of the same, That the said recited act and every Clause and Article thereof shall be from henceforth repealed and Made Null & Void

****

North Carolina State Archives
Granville County
Miscellaneous Records, 1722, 1747-1920
C.R.044.928.8

The Examination of Thomas Hugens Senior of Granville County Taken before Me Robert Hicks Esqr. one of his Majesties Justices of the Peace for said County this 21st Day of febuary 1759 The Said Thomas Hugens being charged before me by Edward More of said County that the said Thomas Hugens Did lately felloniously steal in His own Hous a pack belonging to a cherokee Indian Containing the following artikels to wit 1 small Bottal belonging to Richard Smith 2 yds Red Shroud 2 yds Ditto blew 1 french Blanket & wild[?] 1 Chekerd Shirt 3 yds White Linning 4 yds Riben 2 blew 2 Ditto Red 1 pipe hatchet 1 1/4 yds white plains & wild[?] 1 Brich clout of the said Cherokee Indian To the value of five pounds & procklamation Money He the Said Thomas Hugens Did Uppon his Examination by me the said 21st Day of febuary Declare as followeth to wit that the Indians under the Conduct of Richard Smith unpacked ther Horses & Spred There Goods In His yard and further Saith He never knew Smith or the Indian or Mist aney thing until the next Day Smith came Back to make Enquiry aughter the pack that was Lost But he could give Him no Intiligence there of he the Said Hugen Being Drunk & not all the time the Indian was at His Hous and further this Examinant Saith Not
Test} Robert Hicks

The Examination of James Mitchell of Granvil County Taken before Mee Robert Hicks Esqr: Uppon oath the Said James Mitchell Declareth he saw

General Assembly Sessions
1709 - 1776

aughter the son of Thomas Hugens being about Eighteen years old as he believes take the Indians pack and tows it behind the Dore of the Hous as he Sd. Mitchell was standing in the yard on which the Dore was shut about four Minutes then the Dore being opened & a Girl the Daughter of Thomas Hugens being about Eleven years old came out of the hous with a bundel under her arm Covered with an old gown or petticote which She Carried of Sum Distance to a branch the Said Aughter Hugens called out to Her obet it is now two late to wash it being then about Sunset Richard Smith aughter the Indians pack was Missing came back to Hugenses from there to David Mitchell the Indian being with Him who owned the pack David Mitchell Informd Him that his Brother James Mitchell had seen the passage as above Related on which **[Faded]** sent for James Mitchell **[Faded]** up to Hugenses with him next morning which he Did but Hugens Denied He or aney of his family Had Seen aney thing of the pack missing Aughter Hugens being then not at Home but Come home while They were there but was very unwilling to come to the hous, His Mother Called out to him you Good for nothing son of a bitch you was seen to have the Indians pack Mr. Mitchell Says he saw the Indians pack opened which he took to be the Same that Aughter Hugens towed behind the Dore and that he saw the following Goods In it: to Wit Remnant Red Shrouds 1 Ditto blue 1 Permanent white Linning 1 french blanket 1 pipe Hatchet and the Checkerd Shirt and further This Examinant Saith Not
Test Robert Hicks   febuary 21st 1759

The Examination of Edward More taken before me Robert Hicks Esqr: This 21st: Day of febuary 1759 Taken uppon oath the Examinant Saith he was present with Richard Smith when the Indian Mist His Pack Smith had a small bottel missing on which Sum star was made but the bottel was soon found in hugens chest they Smith Mr: More & the Indians Set off up the Rod about four miles Said the Indian to Smith he had Left H pack & must go back for it Richard Smith Said he was afraid the Indian would never git his pack again Mr: More Asked what Valew it Might be he said about four or five pounds worth of Goods in Riding about 2 Miles further Mr: Smith mist His wollet on which he went Back in Serch of the Wollet & Indians pack when Mr: More understood what had passed at the hous concerning the pack he asked the girl who carried the bundel to the branch what she went there for she Said she only went to wash her face Mr: More saith he believes Aughter Hugens is about Eighteen year old & further this Examinant Saith Not

General Assembly Sessions
1709 - 1776

Test Robert Hicks

By virtue of a warrant from Mee Thos: Hugens Senior & his wife & Thos: hugens Junior & Aughter Hugens Son of Thos Hugen Senior all were brought before Mee & Aughter Broke Custody & was ordered to be hue & cried by me

---

The Examination of Thomas Hugen Junior taken before mee on oath this 21 Day of febuary 1759 Saith he was not at home & Could give no manner of aney Acct: of the matter & that he never Saw the goods but Saith his sister went to the Branch to wash a shirt for aughter hugen & to go up Grasey creek and further this Examinant Saith not

Test Robert Hicks

****

North Carolina State Archives
General Assembly Sessions Records
1709 - Jan. 1760, Box #1
November, 1759, - January, 1760
Bills

Mr. Speaker and Gentlemen of the Assembly

       Having recd. by an express from Colo. Waddell a letter sent to him by Governor Lyttleton and a letter acquainting me that the Militia refuses to march against the Cherokees under pretence that it is out of this province, and by law they are not obliged to march out of this province, I therefore send you the several Letters an papers sent to me and as there is no time to [?] hope you will immediately pass some resolutions [torn] and pass a short Bill to explain and enforce the Militia and oblige the Militia to act when ordered for the publick good and Defense of the province and to procure Satisfaction for the Depredations of hostile Indians
26 Novr. 1759   Arthur Dobbs

****

General Assembly Sessions
1709 - 1776

North Carolina State Archives
General Assembly Sessions Records
April-May, 1760, Box #2
Bills

"And for the Greater encouragement of such persons as shall enlist voluntarily to serve in the said Companies And other Inhabitants of this province who shall undertake any Expedition in Alliance against the said Cherokees and other Indians in Alliance with the French. Be it further enacted by the Authority aforesaid; That each of the said Indians who shall be taken captive during the Present War by any Person as aforesaid, shall and is hereby declared to be a slave and the absolute right and Property of him who shall be the Captor of Such Indian "
[Editors note: Five pounds was paid from Public Treasury for every Indian killed.]

****

North Carolina State Archives
General Assembly Sessions Records
April-May, 1760, Box #2
Committee of Claims

Your Committee recommend to the House that a proper Allowance be made for the taking of an Indian Scalp Produced by Mr. John Frohock: taken by Henry Harmon who went with a partie under the Command of Captn. Tage[?] Allowed by the House

Cornelius Harnett Esqr was Allowed his Claim of One Pound nine shillings & Eight Pence for holding an Inquest on the Body of one Menasses a Portagees he having paid the Jurors and other Charges &c.

****

North Carolina State Archives
General Assembly Sessions Records
May 26-27, 1760, Box #2
Resolutions

General Assembly Sessions
1709 - 1776

Thomas Kersey & Robert Campbell shot & wounded while taking scalps under Capt. Hugh Waddell - sums allowed for disabilities.

****

North Carolina State Archives
General Assembly Sessions Records
1709 - January, 1760, Box #1
Committee of Claims

North Carolina Ss.
Reports of the Committee of Public Claims held at New Bern, on thursday the 1st day of May Anno Dom. 1760.

     Present
     John Swann
The Honourable John Dawson Esqrs. Members of the
    Maurice Moore Council

    John Starky
    John Ashe
    Edward Nail
    Richard Caswell
    Willm. Bartram Esqrs. Members of
    Willm. Williams Assembly
    John Barrow
    John Frohock
    James Cary
    Anthony Hutchins

  The Committee Being met at the House of Mr. Perrigan Cox proceeded to make Choice of a Chairman. Mr. John Starkey was Chose Accordingly & at the same time Andrew Knox was Appointed Clerk set up an Advertisement Requiring all persons that have any Public Claims to Attend at the House of Mr. Perrigan Cox to Morrow After-Noon and so every day during this Session, As business may Require.

Martin Phifer Commissary for Supplying the Indians with Provisions &C Was allowed his claim of Forty Six pounds Eighteen Shillings and two pence Proclamation Money, Including the claims formerly allowed him, it being the ballance of his Account Laid before your Committee, For

General Assembly Sessions
1709 - 1776

Provisions by him found, and money Advanced for Provisions for the Indians going to, and returning from the War. After Deducting the monies in his hands arising from the Sale of Tooles brought from the Catawba Nation.

Thomas Allison was Allowed his Claim of two pounds five Shillings Procla. Money for a Steer for the Catawba Indians in May 1759.

The following Claims Produced to Your Committee from the Frontiers for Services done on the Expedition against the Cherokee, Ranging Companies, Waggoning &C was Allowed as follows to wit,

Capt. John Kuykendal and Company	Ranging	1759 409.17.0
Charles Harris	Waggoning	1760 24.0.0
Moses Alexander	Ditto	1760 24.0.0
Samuel Pattin	Apprizing Waggons	1760 0.15.9
Capt. Martin Phifer & Co.	Expedition	1760 77.0.[?]
Ditto & Co.	Ranging	February 1760 8.5.4
Capt. John Kerr & Co.	Expedition	1760 196.3.0

Capt. Terrys Account dated April the 12th: 1760 Rejected, it appearing to your Committee that he & Company Mutinied & Deserted

Colonel Nathl. Alexander,	Ranging	1760 45.4.[?]

General Assembly Sessions
1709 - 1776

Capt. Morgan Bryan & Co.	Ranging	July 1757 11.7.0
Ditto & Co.	Ditto	April 1759 21.13.0
Ditto & Co.	Ditto	May 1759 33.7.6
Ditto & Co.	Ditto	March 1760 5.6.8
Capt. Conrod Michael & Co.	Ranging	May 1759 14.15.8
Ditto & Co.	Ditto	July 1759 16.3.4
Ditto & Co.	Ditto	Febry 1760 28.8.6
Capt. Jonathn. Hunt & Co.	Ditto	May 1759 11.16.4
Leiut. Alexr. Dobbin & Co.	Ditto	1759 182.16.0
Capt. Elijah Teague & Co.	Ditto	March 1760 13.16.8

Colonel Alexander Osburn was allowed Fifty two pounds Eighteen Shillings, being the Ballance of his Account Laid before Your Committee for Services Done &C on the Expedition against the Cherokees; After deducting the Public Monees in his hands 52.18.0

Capt. James McManus & Co. 1759 & 1760	Ranging	12.2.2
Capts. Rutherford & Ker 1759 and Companies	Ranging	Octobr 309.19.0
Capt. Conrod Michael & Co. 1760	Expedition	117.14.8

General Assembly Sessions
1709 - 1776

Capt. Laurance Thompson   Ranging 1760 and Company Disallowed until it comes properly proved it being Suggested to be wrong charged by information of Mr. William Cummins

Capt. Evan Ellis & Compy.	Ranging	Octobr 1759 6.17.2
Lieut. Matthew Floyd & Co.	Ditto	Octobr 1759 126.3.8
Lieut. John Miller & Compy.	Ranging	Octob: 1759 60.0.8
Capt. Willis Ellis & Co.	Ditto	760 25.18.8
Ditto & Do	Ditto	1760 25.5.0
Lieut. William Luckie & Co.	Ditto	1760 10.5.4
Ensign William Giles & Co.	Ditto	June 1759 7.18.4
Lieut. Andrew Smith & Co.	Ditto	April 1760 14.4.0
Lieut. John McWhorter & Co.	Ditto	Febry 1760 10.18.10
Lieut. John Thompson & Co.	Ditto	1759 9.8.0
Capt. Elijah Teague & Co.	Ditto	June 1759 13.7.0
Ensign Philip Howard & Co.	Ditto	June 1759 32.8.0

General Assembly Sessions
1709 - 1776

Conrod Michael Waggonin on the Expedition			1760 33.15.0
Capt. Aventon Phelps & Co.	Ranging	May &	June 1759 32.8.0
John Olliphant	Ditto		1760 32.5.0
Henry Whora	Ditto		1760 27.0.0
Thomas Foster	Ditto		1760 32.5.0
John Long	Ditto		1760 10.8.0
John Dunn	Ditto		1760 45.15.0
Thomas Parker	Ditto		1760 42.0.0
Hugh Montgomery Waggoning on the Expedition			1760 45.15.0
Michael Robinson	Ditto		760 7.10.0
John Ryall	Ditto		1760 26.5.0
Capt. Morgan Bryan & Compy.	Expedition		1760 55.19.0

Capt. Brown was also Allowed twelve pounds two Shillings and two pence for Provisions furnished his Company on the Expedition Against the Cherokees

General Assembly Sessions
1709 - 1776

Capt. William Little & Co.	Expedition	1760 59.19.0
Capt. Anthony Hutchins & Co.	Ranging	1760 91.0.0
Henry Downs junr.	Waggoning	1760 20.5.0
Lieut. Samuel French & Co.	Ranging	1760 33.0.0
Capt. William Terry & Co.	Ditto	1760 36.0.0

Your Committee Recommends it to the house that a proper Person be Appointed to receive the Monies Allowed for the Expedition Against the Cherokees, to the Ranging Companies, for Waggoning &C And that he pay the same to the Several Persons Intitled to Receive it

Docter Andrew Scott was Allowed five Pounds Seven Shillings & ten pence Procla. Money for his Claim for Sundry Medicines for Soldiers belonging to Capt. Waddell & Capt. Paine in the Year 1758 As by Acct: Filed

Thomas Bashford of Rowan County was Allowed two pounds four Shillings and eight pence for his Claim for Provisions found the Cherokee Indians in the Year 1757 & 1758 as by Acct. Filed

Willis Ellis of Rowan County was Allowed seven Pounds nine Shillings & Six Pence proclamation Money for Entertainment for the Catawba Indians in the Year 1759, As by Account Filed

Charles Cogdell was Allowed Nine Pounds Seventeen Shillings & two Pence for Sundry Disbursements on a Command to the Cherokee Nation, As by Account Filed

Your Committee Recomends it to the House that a proper Allowance be Made for the taking of ten Indian Scalps (Produced by Colo: Hugh Waddell and Mr. John Frohock) taken by a party of Volanteers who

General Assembly Sessions
1709 - 1776

went out at their own Expense and has not brought any Charge Against the Public for the Same Allowed by the House and to be Equally divided amongst the adventurers in proportion to the Number of Scalps taken by Each respective Company   100.0.0
Wm Halsey is Allowed for a Horse Impressed   12.0.0

Charles Blount is Allowed six Pounds Proc. money for taking up three deserters belonging to Capt. [?] Company allowed heretofore but not paid

****

North Carolina State Archives
Anson County Miscellaneous Records
1759-1960
C.R.005.928.3
LIEN TRANSCRIPT

FILE NAME: "Request to pay John Rutherford for services in scouting parties against Indians 1764"

Sir   Septr 20th 1764

Pay to John Rutherford Esq the sum of Sixty three pounds ten shillings proc. money due to me as Lieitt. and to the Men under my direction under the Command of Colol. Nathl. Alexander when imployed on Scouting parties against the Indians agreeable to Act of Assembly - My Claime having been allowed of by the Assembly for which Service I have Received from Colol. Waddell the Sum of sixty three pounds **[Last Sentence Torn]**

[Back Side of Document States]

Rec'd of Jos: Montfort Decr. 2d Sixty two pounds thirteen & four on the within Order. Pd.

                    Jno. Rutherford

****

General Assembly Sessions
1709 - 1776

North Carolina State Archives
General Assembly Sessions Records
December, 1770-January, 1771, Box #4
House Joint Resolutions

Mr. Speaker and Gentlemen of the House of Assembly

I am to request You will exempt Mr. Joseph Fulford, now upwards of Eighty Years of Age, from the payment of Public, Parochial and County Taxes. He has been a Resident in the Province since the Year 1705 (near Twenty Years before the Indians were last drove from Cape fear River) Served Seven Years in the War against the Indians between the Years 1709 & 1719, and is at this present Time incapable of Labor; all which Circumstance make Him an Object of Your Indulgence. He is now an Inhabitant of Carteret County.

William Tryon
Newbern the 19. december 1770.

****

Council held at Newbern, 6 December 1773, in the North Carolina Court of Claims Papers, #2145, Southern Historical Collection, Wilson Library, University of North Carolina at Chapel Hill
[This collection has been returned to the North Carolina State Archive.]

At a Council held at Newbern 6th of decr. 1773

His Excy. was pleased to lay before the Board a Ltr. from Maj. Gen. Haldim[?] and Encls'd an extract of a Ltr. from the Superindt. of Indian Affairs for the So.ern District together with an affidavit of Ann Tranthaw[?] relating to the Murder of two Cherokee Indians by Hez: Collins on the frontiers of Georgia Upon which his Excy. had issued a procl. offering a reward of 200 lb proc m. for apprehending the murderer which was [?]: approved

****

General Assembly Sessions
1709 - 1776

Council held at Newbern, 6 December 1773, in the North Carolina Court of Claims Papers, #2145, Southern Historical Collection, Wilson Library, University of North Carolina at Chapel Hill
[This collection has been returned to the North Carolina State Archives.]

At a Council held at Newbern 6th of decr. 1773

H.E. [His Excellency] was pleased likewise to com: to the Board a Ltr. from H: Gov. Bull of So. Carolina acq: him that the Chief of the Catawba Ind: had complained to him in Council of their being interrupted in hunting & meeting with other acts of unkindness from our people in This province & desiring that the rights reserved to the Indians by the Treaty made at Augusta in the Year 1763 might be made known to them

****

Council held at Newbern, 6 December 1773, in the North Carolina Court of Claims Papers, #2145, Southern Historical Collection, Wilson Library, University of North Carolina at Chapel Hill
[This collection has been returned to the North Carolina State Archives.]

At a Council held at Newbern the 6th of Feby. 1773
The Ct. resumed the Consideration of Messr Neal Blackledge & Joneses Petition, the adverse parties being present Ordered a Resurvey to be made of the Mattamuskeet Lands.

****

At a Council held at Newbern 24 of May 1773
Read a petition of Richd. Blackledge & others in relation to the Mattamuskeet lands - Ordered that the adverse parties have notice to attend at next Court.

****

At a Council at Newbern the 23d. of March 1774

General Assembly Sessions
1709 - 1776

Due proof was made of the proper Advertisemt: being given of an intended application to the Assembly for an Act to appropriate two acres of Land at the Indian town in Currituck County & parish for the Use of a Chapel & Church yard.

****

At a Council held at Newbern the 16th Day of July 1774
On the appr. of Messrs. Blackledge & others ord'd that whereas an Order of Resurvey having issued at the Instance of Gibbs & others of the Mattamuskeet Lands, which hath been returned to this Court: Ord'd. that the said Gibbs &c pay the Expence of the sd. Resurvey & appear at the next Court of Claims to take a patent for the Surplusage, & pay in the Quit Rents due upon the old patent.

At a Council held at Newbern 26 Feb 1775
Read pet. of Henry Gibbs for a Resurvey - Granted.

****

Council held at Newbern, 6 December 1773, in the North Carolina Court of Claims Papers, #2145, Southern Historical Collection, Wilson Library, University of North Carolina at Chapel Hill
[This collection has been returned to the North Carolina State Archives.]

At a Council held at Newbern the 26 March 1774 His Excellency desired the advice of the Council as to the measures proper to be taken with Certain persons from this province who have settled on the Cherokee Lands, and Who, it is represented by His Majts. Superintendant of Indian Affairs, have given Umbrage to those people, & may probably involve ye province in a War with them.
      The Board recommend to his Excellency to issue a proclamation strictly requiring the people who have settled beyond the Indian Line to remove themselves forthwith; Or they must expect no protection from this Government.

****

General Assembly Sessions
1709 - 1776

From Wm. Moore to General Rutherford, 18 November 1776, in the Griffeth Rutherford Papers #2188-z, Southern Historical Collection, Wilson Library, University of North Carolina at Chapel Hill

Capt. Wm. Moore's Letter
On the Service of the United States

Brigadier General Rutherford

Dear Sir,
    After my Compliments to you, This is to Inform you, that Agreeable to your Orders I enlisted my Company of Light horse men, and Entered them into Service the 19th of Octbr. From thence we Prepar'd ourselves and March'd this 29th. Same Instant as far as Cathey's fort, Where we Join'd Capt. Harden and March'd Over the Mountain to Swannanoa, the Next day Between Swannanoa & French Broad River, we Came Upon fresh Signs of five or Six Indians, Upon Which we March'd Very Briskly to the ford of Homney Creek, where we Expected to Join the Tryon Troops, But they not meeting According to Appointment, we, were Necessitated to Encamp and Tarry for them, Our men being Extremely Anxious to Pursue the aforesaid Indians. After the moon Arose we Sent out a Detachment of 13 men Commanded by Capt. Harden & Lieut. Woods, they Continued their Pursuit About 8 miles and could Make no Discovery, Untill day light Appear'd, then they Discovered upon the fort, that one Indian had gone along the Road, they Pursued Very Briskely About five miles further And Came up with Sd. Indian, Kill'd and Scalp'd him, the Remainder of them, we Apprehend'd Had gone A Hunting off the Road, Upon which they Return'd Back to Camp, where we waited to Join the Tryons, they coming up Towards the Middle of the day we Concluded to Stay (to refresh our horses which were fatigued with the Over Nights march) till the Next morning But to our Great Disadvantage we lost Several of our Horses, which Detain'd us the Ensuing Day, then we Pursued our march as far as Richland Creek, where we Encamped in A Cove [**Smudged**] the Safety of our Horses, but in spite of all our Care, the Indians Stole three from us that Night, by which we Perceiv'd that the Enemy was Alarm'd of our Coming, we followed their Tracks the Next day as far as Scots Place, which Appear'd as if they were Pushing into the Nation Before us Very fast, & Numerous, from Scots Place we took A

General Assembly Sessions
1709 - 1776

Blind Path which led us Down to the Tuckysiege River through a Very Mountainous bad way, we Continued our march Very Briskely in Expectation of Geting to the Town of too Cowee before Night, But it Lying at A Greater Distance than we Expexted; we were Obliged to tie up our Horses, & Lay by till Next morning, when we found A ford and Cross'd the River, & then A Very large Mountain, where we Came upon A Very Plain Path, Very much Us'd by indians Driving in from the Middle Settlements to the Aforesaid Town, we Continued our march Along Sd. Path About two miles when we Came in Sight of the town, which lay Very Scattered, then we Came to a Consultation to us which was the best method to Attack them. But one Small Army Consisting of but 97 men, we found we were not Able to Surround it, So we Concluded and Rush'd into the Center of the town, in Order to Surprize it, But the Enemy Being Alarm'd of our Coming, were all fled Save two, who Trying to make their Escape Sprung into the River, and we Pursued to the Bank, & as they were Rising the Bank in the Other Side, we fir'd upon them and Shot one of them Down, & the Other Getting out Of Reach of our Shot, & making to the Mountain, Some of our men Cross'd the River on foot & Pursued, & Some went to the ford & Cross'd on horse, & headed him, Kill'd & Scalp'd him With the Other, then we Return'd into the town, and found that they had Mov'd all their Valuable Effects, Save Corn, Pompions, Beans, peas, & Other Triffling things, Of which We found Abundance in Every house, the town Consisted of 25 houses, Some of them New Erections, and one Curious Town house fram'd & Ready for Covering. We took what Corn we stood in Need of, and what Triffling **[Faded]** was to be got, and then Set fire To the Town, then we Concluded to follow the Tracks of the Indians, which Cross'd the River, & led us A Direct North Course, we Continued our march About A Mile, and then we Perceived A Great Pillar of Smoak Rise out of the mountain, which found Arose from the Woods being Set on fire, with A View as we Suppos'd to Blind their Tracks that we Could not Pursue them, Upon which Capt. Mcfadden & myself took a small Party of men in Order to make further Discoverys, and left the main Body Behind Upon A Piece of Advantageous Ground Untill our Return, we march'd Over A Large Mountain & Came upon A Very Beautifull River which we had no knowledge of, we Cross'd the river & Immediately Came to Indian Camps which they had Newly left, we went over A Second Mountain into A large Cove upon **[Faded]** of Sd. river, where we found A Great deal of sign, Several Camping Places & the first Burning Very Briskely, Night Coming on we were Obliged to Return to our main Body A While Before day, when day Appear'd we made Ready and march'd our

General Assembly Sessions
1709 - 1776

men Untill the Place we had Been the Night Before, our Advance Guard Being forward Perceiv'd two Squaws, And A lad, who Came down the Creek as far as we had Been the Night Before, and when they Perceiv'd our Tracks they were Reatreating to the Camp from whence they Came, which was within 3 Quarters of a mile, the Signal was Given, then we Pursued And took them all three Prisoners, Unfortunately our men Shouted in the Chase And fired A Gun, which Alarm'd them at the Camp & they made their Escape into the Mountains, the Prisoners led us to the Camp where we found Abundance of Plunder, of Horses And Other Goods, to the Amount of Seven Hundred Pounds, we took Some horses Belonging to the Poor Inhabitants of the frontiers which we Brought in, & Delivered to the Owners. Our Provisions falling Short, we were Oblig'd to Steer homewards, that Night we lay upon A Prodigious Mountain where we had A Severe Shock of an Earthquake, Which Surpriz'd Our men Very much, then we Stear'd our Course About East & So. East two days thro' Prodigious mountains which were Almost Impassable, and Struck the road in Richland Creek Mountain, from thence we march'd to Pidgeon river, Where we Vandued off all Our Plunder, then there Arose A Dispute Between me & the whole Body of Officers & all Concerning Selling of the Prisoners for Slaves, I Allow'd that it was our Duty to Guard Them to Prison, or some Place of Safe Custody till we got the Approbation of the Congress Whether they Should be Sold Slaves or not, and the Greater Part Swore Bloodily that if they were not Sold for Slaves upon the Spot, they would kill and Scalp them Immediately Upon which I was Oblig'd to give away, then the 3 Prisoners was Sold for £222, The Whole Plunder we got, including the Prisoners Amounted About 1100, our men was Very Spirited & Eager for Action, and is Very Desirous that your Honour would Order them Upon A Second Expedition, But our Number was too Small to do as Much Execution as we would Desire, from Pidgeon river we march'd home and Every Man Arived in Health and Safety to their Respective Habitations, Capt. Mcfadden is Going to see your Honour at Congress, and if I have Been Guilty Of A Mistake in my Information, its Possible he may Acquaint you Better. Col. McDowell[?] Capt. Davidson and me has sent for one of the Squaws this Day to Come to my house, in Order to Examine her by an Interpreter, & we will Give you as Good an Account as we Can Gather from her, Concerning the State of the Indians, Dear Sir, I have one thing to remark, which is this, that where there is Seperate Companys United into one Body, withou A head Commander of the whole I Shall never Embark in Such an Expedition Hereafter, for where Every Officer is

General Assembly Sessions
1709 - 1776

a Commander there is no Command, No more at Present But Wishing you Sir, With all true friends to Liberty all Happiness.
               I am Sir
               Yours &c
Novembr. ye 18th 1776   William Moore

General Assembly Sessions
1777 - 1789

Chapter Three
General Assembly Sessions Records
1777 - 1789

From Richard Caswell to Waightstill Avery, 12 June 1777, in the Richard Caswell Papers #145, Southern Historical Collection, Wilson Library, University of North Carolina at Chapel Hill

1. Richard Caswell became Grand Master of Masons for the jurisdiction of North Carolina.
2. Contains a letter appointing Waightshill Avery, William Sharpe, Robert Lanier, and Joseph Winston Esquires, as Commissioners to work in conjunction with Commissioners from Virginia & South Carolina to fix a boundary between the Cherokee Indians and the White People.

20 April 1777
Letter from Governor Richard Caswell in New Bern, to Thomas Burke, in Philadelphia serving in Congress. "... from the Westward induces a Belief that we shall be involved in an Indian War, the states of Virginia & South Carolina have appointed Commissioners to Treat with the Indians ..."

12 June 1777
State of North Carolina   Commission of the Treaty
                               with Cherokees

General Assembly Sessions
1777 - 1789

To Waightsill Avery, William Sharpe, Robert Lanier, and Joseph Winston Esquires, Greeting.

    Out of the Assurance We have of your Integrity, Abilities, and Fidelity to the State, We do hereby appoint you the said Waightsill Avery, William Sharpe, Robert Lanier, and Joseph Winston, Commissioners on the Part and behalf of this State; to Act in Conjunction with the Commissioners appointed by the States of Virginia, and South Carolina, or either of them; in establishing a Peace, and fixing a Boundary Line, between the Cherokee Indians and the White People.

    You, or any two, or more of you, are therefore, to proceed to Long Island, on Holsten, on the twenty sixth day of this Instant, or at such Time, and Place, as may agreed upon by the Commissioners of the aforesaid States, for the Purpose aforesaid; And you, or any two, or More of you, are hereby invested with Competent Power, to Negociate the aforesaid Treaty; and in any Acts by you, as in Conjunction with Commissioners of either of them, done, shall be Obligatory on this State.

    Witness Richard Caswell Esquire Governor Captain General and Commander in Chief of the said State under his hand & Seal at Arms at New Bern the 12th day of June Anno Dom 1777. And in the first Year of our Independence.

By His Excellys. Command   R. Caswell
J. Glasgow Sec.

****

**North Carolina State Archives
General Assembly Sessions Records
November-December, 1777, Box #1
Joint Select Committee**

Report of the Committee app'd to take into Consideration
the Memorial of Edge Tomlinson
Rejected

Report of the Committee for inquiring into the conduct of Alexander Gaston and William Tisdale esquires, upon the Memorial of John Edge Tomlinson

M Benbury Chairman -- M Maclaine Clerk

General Assembly Sessions
1777 - 1789

All the members present except Mr Person

Your Committee having before them the Persons accused, and the witnesses on both sides, proceeded to inquire into the truth of the allegations set forth in the memorial, and find that they are admitted to be true. The Justices in their justification or excuse alledge that M Tomlinson had treated his servant with great inhumanity for leaving his service, and that they did not think him safe in his possessions, unless he would give security that he would be forth-coming for him at Court, and until then, use him well; and at the same time they introduced the Clerk of Court with the minutes thereof, wherein it appeared that after Mr Tomlinson had refused giving security in the mode required, Mr Gaston had ordered the Indian into the care of Mr Tisdale until Court, and that the Court (present Alexander Gaston, William Bryan, Nathan Bryan, John Bryan, William Tisdale, Emanuel Simmons, William Randall and Andrew Blanchard, esquires) had offered to return Mr Tomlinson his Servant he giving such security as Mr Gaston & Mr Tisdale had before required; and the trial was postponed to another term that Mr James Blount, who first purchased the Indian after his importation, might have time to produce some testimony to the Court

Your Committee find from uncontroverted testimony that his Excellency the Governor, John Cooke esquire attorney at law did upon being informed of Mr Tomlinson's complaint and the proceedings of the Justices, advise Mr Tisdale in whose possession the Indian then was, and before the County Court had taken cognizance of the matter, that the proceedings were illegal, and that Mr Gaston & Mr Tisdale had acted out of the line of their duty, and that it would be best for Mr Tisdale to return the Indian to Mr Tomlinson.

  Your Committee find that the act of assembly concerning servants and slaves, directs, in cases when any person demand freedom, that the magistrate before whom many claim of freedom shall be made shall
"cause the pretended owner of the person complaining together with such evidence, or evidences as shall be material, to appear before him, and after examination taken in writing, shall bind them over to the next County Court."
  Your Committee also find that Mr Gaston & Mr Tisdale, not only deprived Mr Tomlinson of his servant without any evidence whatever, but expressly contrary to the plain meaning of the act of assembly, and against

General Assembly Sessions
1777 - 1789

the advice of gentlemen whom they must know to be competent Judges, and could not be supposed to be biased it appearing that Mr Cooke had declined accepting a fee from Mr Blount or being at all concerned in the dispute.

Your Committee are of opinions that had no advice been given, it was the duty of Mr Gaston & Mr Tisdale to have asked it, at Court from those long acquaintance with our laws, and experience as magistrates qualified them to give such advice: Therefore

Resolved by this Committee that the said Alexander Gaston & William Tisdale, as magistrates of Craven County have wantonly and against better information violates their duty as Magistrates, with intent, as appears to your Committee, to injure and oppress the memorialist and that their conduct renders them unworthy of acting in the respectable office of Magistrates.

Resolved that an execution of power without right, from whatever cause it proceeds, is oppressive to the people, and merits the severest censure of the laws; and that such exertion, particularly at this time, is pernicious and inflammatory, and tend to Disunite the good people of this State, and to drive them into measures against the cause of liberty.

Resolved that the clause in the Act of Assembly, here in before-in part recited, directing, that trials in cases of claims to freedom, shall be determined, by the County Courts, without any formal process of law, is of a dangerous tendency, and directly contrary to the 14th Section of the declaration of Rights; and that the said clause, and all other acts and clauses of the like nature, are inconsistent with our present happy constitution; for thereby a free man may be deprived of the principal part of his property, without a trial by Jury

All which is submitted

1st December 1777   Thos: Benbury   C:
Committee

****

North Carolina State Archives
General Assembly Sessions Records
November-December, 1777, Box #1
Senate Joint Resolution

Message from the Senate relative Jno. Montgomery

General Assembly Sessions
1777 - 1789

Resolve of the Senate Deciding James Miller to keep an Indian Boy as his Property
Dec 6 1777

State of North Carolina
    In the Senate 2 December 1777
On Motion Resolved, That Mr James Miller of Tryon County be directed to detain in his Possession an Indian Boy, taken Prisoner from the Cherokee Nation, which he now has, untill the Commissioners who shall be hereafter appointed by the General Assembly to treat with the said Nation shall otherwise direct.

Saml. Ash S.S.
In the House of Commons
4 Decr. 1777 Read & Concurred with By Order John Hunt C.H.C.

****

North Carolina State Archives
General Assembly Sessions Records
January-February, 1779, Box #1
Senate Joint Resolution

State of North Carolina
    Whereas Mr. James Robertson Superintendant of Indian Affairs for this State hath resigned his paid Appointment and it appearing that it is at the earnest Request and Desire of the Indians that Mr. Ellis Harling should succeed said Robertson in the Appointment Resolved therefore that the said Ellis Harling be & he is hereby appointed Superintendant of Indian Affairs for this State that he be allowed the same pay as the said James Robertson was allowed & that His Excellency the Governor be requested to grant him a Commission for that purpose & that his Excellency return a talk to the Raven of Chota in answer to the talk given by him to our Superintendent on the 23, december last.
Allen Jones S.S.
    In the House of Commons 29 Janr. 1779
Concurred with
By Order John Hunt CHC Thos. Benbury S:C:

****

General Assembly Sessions
1777 - 1789

North Carolina State Archives
General Assembly Sessions Records
April-May, 1780, Box #1
House Joint Resolution

State of Georgia
In Council
Augusta March 16th 1780

      The Petition of Mr Adam Tate was presented to the Board setting forth, that he traded formerly to the Indian Nation to the Year One thousand Seven hundred and Seventy Three, at which time he returned to this State (then Province) from whence he went to the place of his Nativity North Carolina, where he resided to the Year One thousand Seven hundred and Seventy five when his concerns not being altogether settled in West Florida he went there and returned last August to this place, and from thence to North Carolina, to become a Citizen of that State, but was rejected on a supposition of his being a Certain David Tait who is Commissary or Deputy Superintendent in the Creek Nation on the part and behalf of his Britainnick Majesty

      And whereas it appears from the Certificate of a number of respectable Citizens of this State, as also from the Affidavit of Mr. Martin weatherford, that the said Adam Tate is not the supposed David Tate who is a Commissary or Superintendent as aforesaid, but that he has always been esteemed by them as a true friend to the United States. And this Board being willing to do justice to the said Adam Tate as far as in their power lies, in order that he may be entitled **[Last line in document torn].**

Resolved
      That his Honor the President be requested to give the said Adam Tate, a Certificate under his Hand and the Great Seal of the State, in order that he may return to North Carolina, and produce the same to the Governing Powers of that State, that they may do therein as to them may seem most meet, this Board being of Opinion that the said adam Tate is a true friend to the American Cause
Extract from the Minutes
Saml. Stirks[?] S.E.C.

General Assembly Sessions
1777 - 1789

By his Honor Stephen Heard Esqr. President of the Executive Council, and Commander in Chief of the said State

    Agreeable to the request contained in the aforesaid resolution of the Honorable the Executive Council of the said State I do hereby certify that the said Adam Tate is not the supposed David Tait a Commissary or Superintendent of Indian Affairs on the part and behalf of his Britainnick Majesty in the Creek Nation, but that the said Adam Tate has demeaned himself as a good and faithful Friend to the American Cause since the Commencement of the same, as has appeared to us. In Testimony whereof I have hereunto set my Hand, and Ordered the Great Seal of the said State to be affixed, this Seventeenth day of March in the Year of our Lord One thousand Seven hundred and Eighty, and in the fourth Year of American Independence
By his honors Command
Saml Stirks[?] S.E.C.

By his Honor's Command
Edward Jones Sec:y of the State of Georgia

State of Georgia   }
Richmond County   }

    Personally appeared before me the within named Martin Weatherford, who being duly sworn on the Holy Evangelist **[Rest of line torn.]** say, that some time in October last past, that he was on his way to West Florida upon some cor**[Faded]** respecting this State heard in the Creek Nation many people speaking of the within named Adam Tate who in conversation passed under the denomination of Rebel Tate at the **[Faded]** calling him a Traitor to his King, and declaring that if ever they could lay hold on him they would confine him and deprive him of his property and this deponent further more declares on his oath aforesaid as he hath heretofore sworn that for **[Faded]** the **[Torn]** named David Tait Commissary or Superintendent aforesaid at West Florida when he the said Deponent was last there
Martin Weatherford
Sworn before me the 17th March 1780
Edward Jones Secy.

****

General Assembly Sessions
1777 - 1789

North Carolina State Archives
General Assembly Sessions Records
April-May, 1782, Box #1
Joint Select Committee

To the Honourable the General Assembly of the State of North Carolina
    The Memorial of Richard Henderson, John Williams, Thomas Hart, Nathaniel Hart, James Hogg, William Johnston, The Heirs of John Lutrell deceased, David Hart and Leonard Henly Bullock humbly Sheweth

    That your Memorialist moved as well by the desire of increasing the strength and Population of America in general and of this State in particular (both of which appeared to them to be in danger of suffering great restriction and depression from the Plans adopted by the Crown of Great Britain, the then Sovereign thereof) as by the hope of making a provision for their posterity; did by fair open and bonafide treaty, Purchase for valuable consideration actually paid from the Cherokee nation of Indians, a certain parcel of their Lands which they had immemorially held, and occupied as their hunting Grounds, That their Land purchase contains among other Lands the following situated within the limits of this State, that is to say, all the Lands lying on the Waters of the Cumberland River, Powel's River & Clynch River on the South side of the Virginia Line, and also all the Lands lying between the Holston River and Clynch, from the Long Island in Holston, running down that River to where the course of Powel's Mountain strikes the same and thence along the course of said Mountain to a point from which a Northwest Course will hit or strike the head of the most southerly branch of Cumberland River, thence down the said River including all it's Waters on the South side of the Virginia Line, as will more fully appear by two separate Deeds granted to your Memorialists by the said Indians, dated the 17th day of March 1775.
    That although your Memorialists were so fortunate as to satisfy the Indians very fully, yet the circumstances of the war have rendered it hitherto ineligible to settle the said Lands, and your memorialists relying on the Equity of their Country, and the Provisions made by the General Assembly, that nothing in the Act for opening a Land Office in this State contained, should be construed to prevent or bar any persons being subjects of this State, and claiming property in any Lands therein by conveyance or Grant from any Nation of Indians, from the right of Trial by Jury, or a hearing before the General Assembly of this State at a future day, have

General Assembly Sessions
1777 - 1789

discontinued all their attempts for the improvement of their purchase, lest by encouraging emigrations during the war, they might be instrumental in weakening the defence against the common enemy.

But your Memorialists having learned that some measures are in agitation for divesting this State among others, of the Lands lying within their Limits to the westwards of the Mountains, for the benefit of the Confederacy of the United States; and also that the General Assembly are minded to appropriate certain Lands on the Western Waters as a reward for the faithful services of their Officers and Soldiers. Your Memorialists are desirous of strengthening the claims of the State to those Lands by ceding to them the title acquired from the Cherokee Nation thereto by the Deeds and Grants above mentioned trusting that the General Assembly will make them Grants for each parcels of the said Lands as they in their wisdom shall deem an ample Compensation for the risques, trouble and expence incurred by your Memorialists in obtaining the said Grants, and the services by them rendered to the State in obtaining the Cession from the Indians, and Strengthening the claims of the State to the Lands aforesaid and whereas it is just and right that the general Assembly be well informed of the nature and importance of the Cession proposed by your memorialists, and of the Nature and Validity of the Titles they have acquired, as well as the compensation to be made to your Memorialists; They hope that the Honourable the General Assembly will, during this Session take this matter with the Papers relative thereto under their serious consideration, or if they shall judge that the investigation of this affair will require more time and attention than the General Assembly can bestow thereon. Your Memorialists humbly pray that the same be referred to able and learned commissioners who may compleat the Enquiry in the recess of the Assembly, and report fully thereon to the next Session, and in the mean time that care be taken to provide that no act passed or appropriation made shall affect the title of your memorialists, or prevent their obtaining the just and reasonable compensation to which with all humility they think they may pretend. And your Memorialists persuade themselves that this prayer will appear the more reasonable as they have not yet had a trial by Jury, or a hearing before the General Assembly of the State, agreeably to the provision Quoted in this their memorial. And your Memorialists shall ever pray &c

Hillsborough, May 7th 1782　}James Hogg and Wm. Johnston For themselves & the other Memorialists
Memorial of James Hogg & William Johnston

General Assembly Sessions
1777 - 1789

Mr. Sharp, Mr. Person, Mr. Shelby, Mr. Phifer, Mr. Hawkins, Mr. Harden, Mr. Moore, Mr. Williams, Mr. Coor, Mr. Bledsoe.

Memorial of James Hogg & W. Johnston referred 9 May   (Entd.)

In Senate 9th May 1782
North Carolina
    Mr. Speaker and Gentlemen
Mr. Moore, Mr. Bledsoe, Mr. Coor, and Mr. John Williams will act with the Gentlemen by you appointed to consider of the Memorial of James Hogg & William Johnston
By Order
Rd. Caswell Sp.
John Haywood CS

****

North Carolina State Archives
General Assembly Sessions Records
April-May, 1782, Box #2

                      To the Honble the Genl. Assembly
The Memorial of the Subscribing Officers of Burke and Rutherford Counties doth represent.

      That the Frontiers of said Counties have been much distroyed by the Indians during a War that still continues; That several Hundred Men Women & Children have been drove from their Homes, their Plantations laid waste & many Houses burnt - About fifty of the Inhabitants (A List of whose Names are hereto added) have fallen Victims to the Rage of the Savages; being killed in their usual barbarous Manner.
      Your Memorialists complain that the above Facts **[Torn]** to have been neglected or passed over as unworthey the favourable Notice of the Legislature or Executive Power of this Government; and pray that some Committee may inquire into the Facts; and make Report of the [**Torn**] Mode of Carrying out the **[Torn]** to Secure the Frontiers; and the best means of obtaining a permanent Peace. And that in the Mean time a few of the Frontier Inhabitants most exposed may be exempted from mallitia drafts to serve out of the State.
                      C. McDowell

General Assembly Sessions
1777 - 1789

James Miller

A List of The Kiled and Wounded By the Indians in the County of Rutherford

William Grant
Elizabeth Grant
Two of the Humphreys
William Kindell
Widow Hannah & 2 Childr.
Saml. Wilson
Lewis Jenkins
Neley Mills
Mr. Moor
Mary Step Scalped
& Allin Hinson

Capt. George Dickey
Elias McFaden
James Bryant
John Gray Cor[?]
George Russell
Nathen Shipley
Thos. Dills
James Buttler
James Cheek & 3 Children
Curtions Williams
2 Children & one Negroe
of Richard Ledbetter

many others Kiled and Carried Away from Said Country Which I Can Not Recolect
Certifyed Pr.   James Miller
Capt. William Nevels
Capt. Jos McFadine   }
      &   } old Compy
Capt. John Watsons   }
All Done Since the Last Trety preposed By the Indians

Killed and Wounded **[Editor: Burke County]**

Samuel Davidson
James White
Abraham Collet
Robert Cain
Jas. Lowgan
John Gardner
James Justes
John Davidson
Anne Davidson
and a Child About 16 Mts. Old
Elisabeth Henson

General Assembly Sessions
1777 - 1789

William Spenser
Zepheniah Crook
John Hanry[?]
& 2 men on grassey Creek
John Lee
Suke
Mery McFalls
Alderson Spradling
& One Negroe Wench the Property of G Watson

Certifyed by me Joseph McDowell of Burke County
The people killed by the Indians since the Last perposels of treaty by the Indians

---

North Carolina
    In the House of Commons 14 May 1782
Mr Speaker & Gentlemen
    We send for your Concurrence a Resolve for the protection to the frontiers of this State, which we propose instead of referring the Petition from Rutherford & Burke Counties
By order J. Hunt Clk   Thos. Benbury SC

North Carolina
    In Senate 14 May 1782
Mr Speaker & Gentleman
    This House have appointed Mr Wade and Mr Isaacs who will Act in Conjunction with such Gentlemen as you may appoint as a Committee to take under Consideration the Memorial from the Inhabitants of Rutherford & Burke Counties
By Order Jno Haywood Ses   Rd. Caswell Sp.

North Carolina   In Senate 14 May 1782 Mr Speaker and Gentlemen
    The Resolve of your House for the Petition of the Frontiers of this State we return you Concurred with
By Order Jno Haywood   Rd. Caswell Sp.

The four frontier Companys
Capt. Wood, Capt. McDowell, Capt. Neele, Capt. [?]

General Assembly Sessions
1777 - 1789

****

North Carolina State Archives
General Assembly Sessions Records
April-May, 1783, Box #1
House Joint Resolutions

        Richd. Henderson &c
       All'd 200,000 Acres of Land

North Carolina
  In the House of Commons 8 May 1783
Resolved that Richard Henderson for himself and Company, for their expences trouble and Risque in settling the Lands by him purchased of the Cherokee Indians be allowed the full quantity of two hundred Thousand Acres of Land in Powells Valley, beginning in the dividing line between North Carolina and Virginia, where the same is nearest to the old Indian Town extending down Powels River on both sides thereof, four Miles Wide to the Mouth of the said River, then down Clinch River on both sides thereof Twelve Miles Wide so far as to include the Compliment of two hundred Thousand Acres.

By Order
Edward Starkey Sp.
J Hunt CHC
In Senate 9th May 1783
read and Concurred with
Rd. Caswell Sp.
By Order J Haywood CS

****

North Carolina State Archives
General Assembly Sessions Records
April-June, 1784, Box #2

   A Message from his Excellency the Governor

In the House of Commons 29 May 1784, read & referred to a joint committee the members chosen

General Assembly Sessions
1777 - 1789

Mr Hawkins, Mr Blount, Mr Davie, & Mr Hooper
By Order   J Hunt   CHC

In Senate 29th May 1784, read & referred to Mr Jones, Mr Macon, & Genl. Rutherford
By Order
J Haywood   ClK

To the Honourable the General Assembly
Gentlemen
    If it is the sense of the Honble. Legislature that the late intended Treaty with the Cherokee should be still conducted under the Directions of the Executive: I request that the Treasurers be directed to pay out of the Collection of the Taxes of the Year 1783 the Sum allotted by Act of Assembly to defray the Expences that will accrue in holding said Treaty, that Money not being retained out of the late Emission in Halifax Treasury: As Waggons are ready to proceed with the Indian Goods to the Place destined for this purpose, as soon as Money can be advanced to the Owners for their Travelling Expences.
                  Alex. Martin
May 28th 1784.

Report on the Govrs. Message
Rejected

The Committee to whom was referred the Message of his Excellency the Governor respecting the Holding a Treaty with the Cherokee Indians Report that it is the Sence of the Committee that the Treaty with the Cherokee Indians Should be Still Conducted under the Direction of the Executive and that the Governor be and hereby is Authorised to Issue Warrants Directed to Either of the Treasurers for one Thousand pounds to Defray the Expence of Such Treaty to be paid Out of the Tax for the Year 1783, That being the Sum allow'd by Act of Assembly passed in the Year aforesaid for Defraying the Expence of said Treaty.

In House of Commons 2 June 1784
Read and rejected
Tho Benbury   SC
By Order   J Hunt   CHC

General Assembly Sessions
1777 - 1789

Govr. to Transmit to Congress Copy of an Act

North Carolina

In the House of Commons 2 June 1784

    Resolved that the Governor be directed to transmit immediately to Congress a Copey duly authenticated of the Act passed this Session of Assembly entitled an Act Ceeding to the Congress of the United States in Congress Assembled certain Western Lands therein mentioned and authorizing the Delegates from this State to execute a deed or deeds for the same, and that he inform Congress of the measures begun by this State for carrying on a Treaty with the Indians what goods have been purchased by this State for that purpose and to what amount and where they are lodged; that he further inform them, that in case Congress should accept the Cession intended, the said goods may yet be applied to the purpose of carrying on the said Treaty under the Sole direction of Congress, they giving credit to this State for the amount of the Goods in the account of the United States with this State; the Congress also taking upon themselves every other expence that may attend the said Treaty.

By Order J Hunt CHC   Tho Benbury SC

In the Senate June 2nd 1784
The within Resolve was read and concurred with
By Order J Haywood Clk   R. Caswell Sp.

****

North Carolina State Archives
General Assembly Sessions Records
April-June, 1784, Box #2

    A Message from his Excellency the Governor

In the House of Commons 29 May 1784, read & referred to a joint Committee the members chosen
Mr Hawkins, Mr Blount, Mr Davie, & Mr Hooper

General Assembly Sessions
1777 - 1789

By Order J Hunt CHC

In Senate 29th May 1784, read & referred to Mr Jones, Mr Macon, & Genl. Rutherford
By Order
J Haywood ClK

To the Honourable the General Assembly
Gentlemen
      If it is the sense of the Honble. Legislature that the late intended Treaty with the Cherokee should be still conducted under the Directions of the Executive: I request that the Treasurers be directed to pay out of the Collection of the Taxes of the Year 1783 the Sum allotted by Act of Assembly to defray the Expences that will accrue in holding said Treaty, that Money not being retained out of the late Emission in Halifax Treasury: As Waggons are ready to proceed with the Indian Goods to the Place destined for this purpose, as soon as Money can be advanced to the Owners for their Travelling Expences.
                            Alex. Martin
May 28th 1784.

               Report on the Govrs. Message
                        Rejected

The Committee to whom was referred the Message of his Excellency the Governor respecting the Holding a Treaty with the Cherokee Indians Report that it is the Sence of the Committee that the Treaty with the Cherokee Indians Should be Still Conducted under the Direction of the Executive and that the Governor be and hereby is Authorised to Issue Warrants Directed to Either of the Treasurers for one Thousand pounds to Defray the Expence of Such Treaty to be paid Out of the Tax for the Year 1783, That being the Sum allow'd by Act of Assembly passed in the Year aforesaid for Defraying the Expence of said Treaty.
In House of Commons 2 June 1784
Read and rejected
                      Tho Benbury SC
By Order J Hunt CHC

General Assembly Sessions
1777 - 1789

Govr. to Transmit to Congress Copy of an Act

North Carolina

In the House of Commons 2 June 1784

Resolved that the Governor be directed to transmit immediately to Congress a Copey duly authenticated of the Act passed this Session of Assembly entitled an Act Ceeding to the Congress of the United States in Congress Assembled certain Western Lands therein mentioned and authorizing the Delegates from this State to execute a deed or deeds for the same, and that he inform Congress of the measures begun by this State for carrying on a Treaty with the Indians what goods have been purchased by this State for that purpose and to what amount and where they are lodged; that he further inform them, that in case Congress should accept the Cession intended, the said goods may yet be applied to the purpose of carrying on the said Treaty under the Sole direction of Congress, they giving credit to this State for the amount of the Goods in the account of the United States with this State; the Congress also taking upon themselves every other expence that may attend the said Treaty.

By Order J Hunt CHC   Tho Benbury SC

In the Senate June 2nd 1784
The within Resolve was read and concurred with
By Order J Haywood Clk   R. Caswell Sp.

****

North Carolina State Archives
General Assembly Sessions Records
November-December, 1785, Box #1

No. 28
a Letter from Genl. Sevier to Govr. Caswell
Dated 14th May 1785
His Excellency Richd. Caswell Esqr
Governor
Answered 17th June 1785
No. Carolina

General Assembly Sessions
1777 - 1789

State of Franklin
Washington County
14 May 1785

Sir,
    Governor Martin have lately sent up into our Country a manifesto, together with letters to private persons, In order to Stir up Sedetion and Inserection, thinking thereby To destroy that peace and Tranquility which Now so greatly Subsists Among the peaceful Citizens of this Country.
    First in the Manifesto he Charges Us with a revolt From No. Carolina, by declaring our Selves independant Of that State; Secondly, that designs of a more dangerous Nature and deeper die, seem to glare in the Western Revolt, the power Usurped over the Western Vacant Territory; the Union deriveing No Emolument from The same; Not Even the part intended No. Carolina By the session; And that part of her Revenue Is seized by the New Authority and appropriated To different purposes intended by your Legislature.
    His Excellency is pleased to Mention, that one Reason we have Assigned for the Revolt, as he Terms it, is that the goods were stoped from the Indians that was to Compensate them for the Western Lands, And that the Indians had Committed Murder In Consequence thereof. He is also pleased To say that he is well informed to the C, And that no Hostilities has been Committed on that Account; But on the other Hand, provocations are daily given the Indians, And one of those Cheifs Murdered With Impunity.
    In answer to the Charge Relative to which his Excellency is pleased to Call the Revolt; I must beg Leave to differ with him in Sentiments on that Occasion; For your Own Act declare to the World, that this Country was Ceded off to Congress; And one part of the Express Conditions was, that the same should be Erected Into one or More States; And we believe that Body was Candid, and that they full believed A new State would tend to the Mutual Advantage of all parties, that they was as well Acquainted with our Circumstances at that Time, As Governor Martin Can be Since; And That they did not think a new Government Here would be led away with the pageantry of a mock government without the Essentials; And leave Nothing among us but a shadow as Represented.
    But if governor Martin is Right in his Suggestion, we can only say that the Assembly of No. Carolina deceived us, And were Urging us On

General Assembly Sessions
1777 - 1789

into total Ruin, and Laying a plan to destroy That part of her Citizens, she so often Confessed, Saved the Parent State from Ruin.

But the people Hear, Neither at that time, nor The present, Haveing the most distant Idea of any such intended deception, and at the same Time well knowing, How pressingly Congress had Requested Cessions to be made of the Western Territory Ever since the 6th of September and 10th of October in the year Eighty; These several Circumstances Together with a Real Necessity, to prevent Anarchy, promote our own Happiness, and to provide Against the Common Enemy that always infest this part of the World, Induced and Compelled the people hear to Act as they have done, Innocently thinking at the same time, your Act Tolerated then to the Separation; Therefore we can by no Means think it can be Called a revolt or known by such a Name. As to the second Charge it is entirely groundless, We Have by No Act whatever, Laid hold of one foot of the Vacant Lands, Neither have we Appropriated any of the same to any of our Use or Uses - but intend everything of that Nature For a further deliberation, And to be Mutually settled According to the Right and claim of each party;

As to that part of Seizing the public Money, it is as Groundless as the former, For no Authority Among us whatever, has Laid hold or Appropriated one farthing of the same, to our Uses in Any shape whatever, but the same is Still in the hands of the Sheriffs and Collectors, and on the Other hand, we have passed such laws, as will both Compel and Justify them, in setting and paying Up, to the Respective Claimants of the same; All of which will Appear In Our Acts, which will be laid before you, And will fully evince to the Reverse of Governor Martins charge in the Manifesto;

Very True we Suggest that the Indians have Committed Murders in Consequence of the delay of the goods, Near forty people have been Murdered since the session Bill passed, some of which in our own Counties, and the Remainder on Caintuck path, and it is Evidently known to be the Cherokees, and there frequent talks proves they are Exasperated at getting nothing for their lands, and in all probability had the goods Been furnished, No Hostilities would have been Committed;

The murder Committed with impunity, Alludeing to Major Hubbards killing a half breed, which Governor Martin called a Cheife, (but never any such thing Among the Indians) we can't pretend to say what information his Excellency has had on this Subject more than the Others or where from; This we know, that all the proof was had Against Hubbard, and that ever can be had; Which is; The Indian first, Struck, and then

General Assembly Sessions
1777 - 1789

discharged his Gun at Hubbard, before the Indian was killed, by Hubbard - As Governor Martin Reprobates the Measure in so great a degree; I can't pretend to say what he might have done, but must believe, that had any other person Met with the same insult from one of those bloody Savages who have frequently Murdered the Wives and Children of the people of this Country for Many years past; I say Had they been possessed of that Manly & Soldierly Spirit, that becomes an american, they must have Acted Like Hubbard.

I have now observed to your Excellency the principal Complaints in the Manifesto, And such as I think is worth observation, and have Call'd forth Such proofs, as must fully evince to the Reverse of the Charge and Complaints set forth.

The Menaces Made Use of in the Manifesto, Will by No Means intimidate Us; We mean to pursue our Necessary Measures, and with the fullest Confidence believe, that your Legislature when Truly informed of our Cool proceedings, will find No Cause for Resenting any thing we Have done.

Most Certain it is, that Nothing has been Transacted here, out of my disregard to the parent State, But we still Entertain, the same high Opinion & Have same regard and affection for Her, that Ever we Had, And would be as Ready to Step Forth in her defence, as Ever we did, should need Require it.

Also our Acts and Ourselves Will Evince the World, that we have paid all due Respect to your State, first in Takeing Up her Constitution, & then her Laws, Together with Nameing Several New Counties, And Also An Academy after some of the first Men in your State, The Repeal of Cession Act, we Cant take Notice of, As We Had declared our Seperation, before the Repeal; Therefore we are bound to Support It, with that manly firmness that becomes free men.

Our Assembly Sits again in August, at which Time it is Expected Commissioners will be appointed To adjust and consider on such Matters of Moment as will be Consistent With the Honour and interest of each party.

The disagreeable and sickly time of the year Together with the greate distance from Newbern, As Also the short Notice; puts it out of the power of any person to Attend from this Quarter at this time.

Our Agent is at Congress, And daily Expect Information from that Quarter, Respecting our present Measures, and to advise thereon.

We are informed, that Congress have Communicated to your State Respecting the repeal of the Session Act; Be that as it may, I am

General Assembly Sessions
1777 - 1789

Authorized to say, nothing will be Lacking in Us, to forward every thing that will tend, to the Mutual Benefit of each party, And Conciliate all Matters whatever.

I have the Honour to be With Greate Regard and Much Respect, Your Excellencies Mo. Obedt. Humbl. Servt.

His Excellency }   John Sevier
Govr. Caswell }

In H.C. 21 Nov. 1785

****

North Carolina State Archives
General Assembly Sessions Records
November-December, 1785, Box #1

No. 8
Copy of a Letter to The Honble.
Ben Hawkins, Andrew Pickens & Joseph Martin Esqrs.
Comrs. for Treating with the Southern Indians
in Answer to theirs of 19 July 1785, Charleston
Kinston 23d July 1785

Hon'ble Benjamin Hawkins, Andrew Pickens, and Joseph Martin Esqrs. Comrs. for Treating with the Southern Indians - Charleston
No. Carolina Kinston 23d. July 1785

[Editor's Note: Words appearing below in brackets have been struck through by the author of the letter.]

Gentleman,

I had the Honor to receive your Letter of the 19th of June the 10th Instant, but was [which I had it not in my power] not able to Convene the Council until Yesterday, when the same was laid before that Board, the Members of which, [as well as myself] being anxious to fulfill the requisition of Congress [in answering such drafts as you may make on this State to enable you to carry into effect the expectations of Congress respecting the Treaties they have empowered you to make with the Cherokees & other Southern Indians] Have , notwithstanding the State is Labouring under many difficulties for want of Money Advised me to draw on the Treasury to the Amount of one third of the thirteen thousand dollars,

119

General Assembly Sessions
1777 - 1789

this I mean to do so as to get the Money into my private Secretary's hands ready to Answer Your Drafts by [the first of Octo.] the Second Monday in October next, And I think I can venture to engage that [Sum & shall be then ready] you shall meet with no disappointment at that Time, But Gentlemen you will be pleased to Observe that it will be with great Labour & expence in sending to different parts of the State that I expect to be able to Collect this Sum in proper Money, that Money I Know will not answer your purposes in No. Carolina & Georgia, And whether you would wish me to endeavour to effect an exchange for Hard Money in this State or to remit any of the produce of the State to Charleston to try to raise the Hard Money there or Purchase Bills upon Charleston, you will be pleased to Advise me as early as possible.

    I thank you for the information you have been pleased to give me respecting the offers & disposition of the Creeks & the disorderly White People who are amongst them, And shall be happy in receiving any further Communications from you which you shall think proper to make.

    Colo. William Blount is appointed Agent for this State to Attend the Treaties Which you are to hold under the Authority of Congress and I flatter myself he will set out so as to Arrive at Galphinton by the time you have appointed to [hold] open the Treaty there.

With Sentiments of esteem & respect
I am, Gentlemen Your Most Obedt. Servt. Rd. Caswell

****

North Carolina State Archives
General Assembly Sessions Records
November-December, 1785, Box #1

No. 22
Copy of a Letter to the Honble. Col. Wm. Blount & Col. Joseph Martin Comrs. appointed to Treat with the Cherokee Indians inclosing their Commission. Kinston 3d. Septr. 1785

No. Carolina, Kinston 3d. Septr. 1785

Gentlemen,
    You will receive herewith a Commission appointing you to Treat with the Cherokee Indians in Consequence of which you will be pleased to receive and distribute the Goods destined by the General Assembly to be

General Assembly Sessions
1777 - 1789

given to the said Indians, at or near Fort Rutledge in the State of South Carolina; at the same Time, that a Treaty is to be held, next month, by the Commissioners appointed by Congress for Treating with them.

In this Business I refer you to the Act of Assembly for your Government, and request that you will report to me your proceedings, in Time to be laid before the General Assembly on the first Monday in November next.

With Great respect and esteem
I am, Gentlemen
Your Most Obedient
and very humble Servt.
R. Caswell

Hon'ble Colo. William Blount
Col. Joseph Martin

****

North Carolina State Archives
General Assembly Sessions Records
November-December, 1785, Box #1

No. 23

Copy of a Letter to The Hon'ble Wm. Blount Esqr. Agent for the State of North Carolina to Attend the Treaties to be held by Commissioners appointed by Congress to treat with the Cherokee & other Southern Indians.

Kinston 3d. September 1785

Sir,

Herewith you will receive a Commission appointing you Agent for this State to Attend the Treaties to be held by Commissioners appointed by Congress with the Cherokees and other Southern Indians.

I am therefore to request you will repair to Golphinston in the State of Georgia in Time to be present at the Treaty to be held by the said Commissioners there, with the Cherokee Indians on the third Monday in September Instant, and from thence, after the business of the Treaty being

General Assembly Sessions
1777 - 1789

Compleated, you will proceed to the Treaty to be held on Keowee in the State of South Carolina, at each of which Treaties, as the representative or Agent of the State, you will be pleased to use your best endeavours to advance the Interests of the State, and prevent any encroachment, upon, the Territory or Liberties of the same.

As I have nothing particularly to recommend to your Attention, at present, I can only add that your Country has the utmost relyance on your Integrity and Abilities and that I have the strongest Confidence in your inclination to serve her in this Business in which I wish you the Greatest success.

You will be pleased to make me a report of your proceedings in Time to be laid before the General Assembly in November next.

With Great respect & esteem I have the honor to be, Sir, your most Obedt. & very humble Servt.

          R. Caswell
The Honble, William Blount Esqr.

****

North Carolina State Archives
General Assembly Sessions Records
November-December, 1785, Box #1

No. 24

Copy of a Letter to the Honble. Ben Hawkins & other Comrs. appointed by Congress to Treat with the Cherokee & other So.Ern. Indians   Kinston 4th Septr. 1785

No. Carolina, Kinston 4th Septr. 1785

Gentlemen,

I have the Honor to enclose you a Duplicate of a Letter addressed you the 23d. July since which I have not been favored with any of your Commands.

Colo. William Blount the Agent appointed to Attend the Treaties in behalf of this State, will deliver you this and is able to give you any information respecting the State of Affairs here, to them I beg leave to refer you.

General Assembly Sessions
1777 - 1789

    I hope to be able to answer your Draughts by the Time mentioned in my former but it will be with great difficulty & trouble that the money can be obtained.
    I wish you great Success in your negotiations with the Indians and am with great regard & esteem

        Gentlemen,
            Your Most Obedient and
            very humble Servant
                R. Caswell

Honble Benjamin Hawkins
Andrew Pickens &
Joseph Martin Esquires

****

North Carolina State Archives
General Assembly Sessions Records
November-December, 1785, Box #1

                        No. 30
Memorial of the Counties of Washington, Sullivan, & Greene in western part of North Carolina - by their Genl. Assembly to Congress, delivered the 16th May 1785, by Wm. Cooke their Special Agent.
                    recd. 12 July 1785
                          R.C.
        To the Honorable the Continental Congress
    The Memorial of the freemen by their Representatives in General Assembly met, who were included within the limits ascertained by an Act of the General Assembly of the State of North Carolina Ceding certain Vacant Lands to Congress.
                      Humbly Sheweth
That having in many instances discovered the friendly disposition of Congress not only to guard the liberties of the States now in the Union but also to Incourage the erection of New States on the western side of the Appalachian Mountains, And finding the disposition of North Carolina to comply with the Requisitions made by Congress requesting liberal Cessions of vacant western Territory which Requisitions being complied with by North Carolina, She immediately stoped the goods she had

General Assembly Sessions
1777 - 1789

promised to give the Indians for the said land, which exasperated them that they began to commit hostilities on our frontiers, in this situation we were induced to a declaration of Independence not doubting but we should be Excused by Congress when she came to hear the reasons that called for such a declaration, and when she was assured that it was Necessity rather than choice, as North Carolina seemed quite reguardless of our on interest, and the Indians daily murdering our friends and relatives without distinction of age or sex, and we are sorry to inform Congress, that notwithstanding the Act of Cession must have bound North Carolina at least in Honour to have continued the Act in force for the space of twelve months from the passing of the same, unless Congress should have refused to accept the Cedure, yet North Carolina has repealed the Cession Act, and claims a sovereignty over a County whose prayers she has rejected and whose interest she has forsaken. Impressed with every sentiment of duty and respect we earnestly request Congress to accept the offered Cession and to receive us into their federal Union that we may enjoy all the rights referred to us in the Cession Act and which freemen are entitled to.

And we humbly pray that you will be pleased to call upon our Agent for such further information as you in your wisdom shall think proper, in whose Integrity we confide, and earnestly pray that you will adopt such suitable measures as may promote the peace and prosperity of those who wish ever to be found a Zealous and useful part of the people that form so dignified a Union, and your Memorialists shall ever pray.

Signed Landon Carter S.S.
Wm. Cage S.C.

By Order
Thomas Talbot C.S.
Thomas Chapman C.C.

****

Manuscript Reading Room
Special Collections Department
Duke University Library
Durham, North Carolina 27706
Richard Caswell Papers, 1777-1790

The State of North Carolina, by the
Grace of God, Free and Independant

General Assembly Sessions
1777 - 1789

To the Honorable Colonel William Blount and Colonel Joseph Martin Greeting

    Out of the Assurance we have of your Fidelity, Integrity and Abilities, We do hereby Nominally Constitute and Appoint you the Said William Blount and Joseph Martin Commissioners for holding a Treaty with the Cherokee Indians. You observing such Instructions as you shall from Time to Time receive from our Governor or Commander in Chief for the Time being, and conforming yourselves to our Laws relative to Indian affairs

    Witness our Trusty and well beloved Richard Caswell Esquire our Governor Captain General and Commander in Chief under his hand our Great Seal at Kinston the third day of September Anno Dom 1785 and in the Tenth year of our Independence

****

Letter from Thomas Green, 10 September 1785, in the Preston Davie Papers #3406, Southern Historical Collection, Wilson Library, University of North Carolina at Chapel Hill.

Box # 3
Folder # 210

Hon. Sir
    Since I have had the Hon. of seeing you, have Agreeable to the late law of Georgia made a Demand in (behalf of the State) of the county of Bourbon, Respecting Which no decisive answer hath been Yet Given by the Spaniards, Who continue Still to hold possession of the Garrison, In Consequence of the arrival of Capt. Devonport who came down the River after me I left him at the Natchez and Went to the Nation in order to deliver to the Indians some talks Agreeable to your Honrs. Request, Being Informed that a Certain Mr. McSaint a Spanish Commandment, was then in the Choctaw Nation Endeavoring to draw them Over to their party &c, However Sir, their Answer to my talks and also my Opinion of the disposition of those tribes I Will Acquaint you in the latter part of my letter &C, -

General Assembly Sessions
1777 - 1789

Dayly preparations are making at the Natchez in Preparing the fort, a large Quantity of Military Stores, brought up from Orleans and also A number of Troops, which, Gives me Great Reasons to think they have no Inclination to Give it up in an amicable manner

As Capt. Davenport and myself Arrived at Natchez in two parties I came there a few days before him Was Verry Coldly Received and my men Ordered away in three Days and myself they Would have Confined and Sent to Orleans had I not have Evaded it by withdrawing to the Nation, as for Capt. Davenport and his men they Confined them to their boats about three weeks and were not Suffered to Set their foot on land, (himself & Capt. Smith only Excepted) After which they were brought up to The Fort and there kept Confined for some considerable Time After Which they were Suffered to go into the Neighborhood only confined to tarry at a Certain house appointed for that purpose Untill Further Order, in Which Situation they Remain at Present &c -

Agreeable to my Instructions I presented the Commission of the peace to the Gentleman Appointed, therein, who all Accepted the same Except Taciter Gilliard, Sutton Banks, and Mr. John Ellis, who Utterly Refused the same at the same time Denying that the State of Georgia had any Right Or Claim to the Natchez, and Endeavored to Seduce A number of the Inhabitants from paying any Aligence to sd. Authority by Representing both its Officers, and Constitution in as Deriding manner as possible, Aledging, that Congress, had the only Right of the Disposal of sd. lands, and of course Would be laid out in a New State -

Hond. Sir I beg leave to Inform you that from the high Opinion I have of your Merit, and your Ardent desire to make our Western Country happy I may take the liberty without Giving Offense, to Recommend to your Honr. the building and fortifying, of Two Strong Garrisons on the River Mississippi Viz. one at the Chickasaw Bluffs, the Other at the mouth of the Yazous River which Garrisons if well Man'd Would Effectually put a Check to the Spaniards from sending Arms and Amunition up the River to the different Tribes of Indians on the West Side of the River and Awe the Chickasaw and Choctaw Indians; and be an assylum And place of Retreat to both Inhabitants and Such as trade up and down the River -

We find the disposition of the Chickasaw and Choctaw Indians in a Verry Wavering and Unfix'd State at present Undetermined which Way to place their Affections Either on the faith of the Americans or the Spaniards, they Say they Were Ever the friends of the Virginia people, that being the term Used by them for the Americans, In General, and that they loved them as Brothers But the Great War we had among one Another

General Assembly Sessions
1777 - 1789

devided them, so as to prevent them from Seeing us so long, But now there is peace Come they can Sit down and Make Corn Without any fear of their Enemies And that they were for Gotten by their Old Brothers the Virginians who Never Came to trade among them as they did in the Good Days, Neither do they hear anything from them, But that they still wish to take them by the Hand and to trade with them as they did formerly But on the Other hand they say the Spaniards have sent them Good talks and have sent them Goods when they were Poor and obliged to weare their Own leather, So that I Find that by talking on this manner they seem more Inclinable to favour the Spanish Interest than ours, Yet I conceive That a Genteel present made to them, and a Good Talk from Your Honr. would Entirely Change their Sentiments and Engross Their Good wills to us, As they are frequently Intimating The former Cruelty of the Spaniards, And their hatred to them and the Number of their forefathers, and kindred Who have been by them killed and spoil'd

Every possible method hath been taken by the Spaniards to make those Savages the Inveterate Enemys of all Americans in their talks to both Nations Viz. Choctaws & Chickesaws and also the Creeks, they Ordered And licensed to take all American property brought into their land by any of our Traders and have Even gone So far as to Give directions to them to kill all Such as Should Stand in defence of their property, by which Means they have Engrossed the Whole trade of both nations To themselves and Reduc'd almost all the Traders to take the Oath of Allegence to the King of Spain, so that they Dare not Oppose Any measures the Spaniards Thinks proper to Adopt for the Indians, and have also Sent their Colours into different parts of both nations With Commissions to their Chiefs, Although their is Some of their principle Chiefs Retains the truest friendship For us and is Verry Desirous to have Our friendship and Trade Also Commissions, Colours, Medals, Gorgets, &c, Sent to the Great Chief Friend Anmartubic to be by him Delivered to such of Other Chiefs as he shall think Meritt the same there being by his Account Twenty seven Chiefs besides himself in the Choctaw Nation Who hath Never been prevailed upon to take any Commissions, or Medals, from the Spaniards and Wishes To Continue So, Untill they Receive an answer from Georgia -

Your honour, I hope Will Excuse my Entering into so perticular a detail of those Indian talks, For I Assure you Sir, I think it Highly compatible, With my Duty hear to Mention to you Whatever, I think, Conducive to the public Good, &c -As I cannot think that the Good Disposiyion Of those Numerous and formidable Tribes, is an Object Unworthy the attention our Country, as The Peace, and happiness, of all

General Assembly Sessions
1777 - 1789

Our Western Settlements Depends Upon the Good disposition of those people, and, me thinks that Neither trouble, or Expense, Ought to be considered Adequate, to the Lives, and propertys, of Our fellow Citizens, and the Large fruitful Country belonging to Our Western Teritory, Which is Able to make an ample Satisfaction for all our Trouble -

I beg leave to trouble your patience a little longer to Inform you that in Consequence of my being a Setler formerly at Natchez, they seemed to Claim me as a Spanish Subject, Although, I Had Never taken any Oath &c; to them in any Manner Whatsoever, but always Declar'd myself As an American, for which Reason, I Expect they will Seize my property, in my Absence, in Order To punish me, for being (as they say) the means of the Natchez being Demanded by the Americans at Present &c -

I once more beg that Every method may be taken to Save the friendship of the Chocktaws and Chickasaws as their friendship to us will Strike a Terror to the Creek Indians and be a means of a free passage through their Country As we shall be frequently Under the Necessity Of passing through among them, on our way to the Seat of Government Viz. - Savannah &c.

I hope Your honour will take my Unhappy Situation into your Serious Consideration and begs you Will Give me Every Assistance in Your power by Advice and Otherways for the Protection of my person and property as they have Already hired Some of the Savages to take my Life, &c. What I have Related to your honour in the Inclosed are not mere Suppositions but Are Absolutely to be Depended upon as matters Of fact.

I flatter myself you Will Excuse the prolicity of My Address as the Subject matter is so Capacious That I cannot Comprehend it in a Narrow Compass However Without further apology Shall proceed Viz. I also Recommend to your favourable Notice Mr. John Woods, Mr. Robert Welch, to be Appointed as Officers of the peace in Choctaw Nation in Order to Determine all matters of Controversy Relative to The White people in the said Nation and that a copy of the Laws of the State of Georgia be sent to the sd. Mr. John Woods, and Mr. Robert Welch the better To Enable them to Execute their office, and for the Chickesaw I Recommend Mr. John Jameson and Hardy Perry to be Appointed to the Above mentioned office in that Nation &c -

I further Recommend to your Honr., the Above mentioned John Jameson as a Gentleman Verry Well Qualify'd to Superintend the Choctaw and Chickasaw Nations and to Act as Chief Magistrate With the Other Gentlemen in their Respective Nation he being Universally beloved by all the Good White people in sd. Nations, and also chosen by

General Assembly Sessions
1777 - 1789

Chemastubie and all the Other Chiefs of the Choctaw Nation, and I flatter myself Will fill that post Equal if not superior than most in this Country to the Benefit of and Satisfaction of the public he having always Acquitted himself With honour and Credit both in his public and private Character and hath Ever been a Useful member of Society and always A friend to his country ever Since I have been Acquainted with him which will be a Verry Great Means of keeping them in a peacible Disposition Towards us, &c -

    You Will Receive this by the hand of Mr. Jameson to whome I Refer you further Inteligence and hope your honor will Dispatch him back as soon as possible With such Instructions as you shall think proper, I flatter myself with being able to write you something more Interesting in my next and am in the Interim With Great Esteem

    Your Honrs. Mst Obt. Humbl. Servt.
    Thomas Green

Choctaw Nation
10th Sept. 1785

****

North Carolina State Archives
General Assembly Sessions Records
November, 1786-January, 1787, Box #1

                        Piny Grove   March 1st 1786
Sir,

    On the 11th day of November I had the Honor to address a letter to your Excellency from Augusta informing you that the Creek Indians had not acceeded to the propositions of the Continental Commissioners to Meet them at Golphinton to form a treaty which I presume you have received.

    Since that period the Cherokees, Choctaws, and Chickasaws have met them at Hopewell on Keeowee and formed treaties very prejudicial to the State of North Carolina. That with the Cherokees was completed and signed November the 28th a Copy of which is contained in the Book you will receive herewith as is every other necessary Copy that respects either of the above mentioned treaties.

    I am not able to say the Copy above mentioned is a Verbatim literation as the only means I had to obtain it was to pen it down from the Mouths of the Commissioners when it was delivered to the Interpreters to be explained to the Indians but you may rely that it is substantially a Copy

General Assembly Sessions
1777 - 1789

be explained to the Indians but you may rely that it is substantially a Copy of the Original. Those with the Choctaws and Chickasaws were signed on the 5th and 10th January and are the same as the Cherokee treaty except the third Articles which establishes their respective Boundaries.

I thought it unnecessary to protest against the treaty with the Choctaws because they claimed no part of the lands being within the chartered limits of the State of North Carolina. The State of Georgia appointed three Agents to attend the treaties to be held by the Continental Commissioners of which the present Governor was one and they protested as well at Hopewell as at Golphinton against the right of the Commissioners to treat with any Indians resident within the limits of their State. When I was honored with the Appointment of Agent to attend the aforementioned treaties on the part of the State it was then understood from the letters of the Continental Commissioners to your Excellency that the whole of them might and would probably be completed at so early a day that I might attend them and return Home in two Months and the Council were pleased to advise the issuing a Warrant on the Treasury in my favour as pay for my Service as Agent allowing me the same Sum per day that was allowed the Continental Commissioners by resolve of Congress and as they were not completed before the 10th January I request your Excellency will be pleased to issue Warrants in my favour for such further Sum as will pay me at the same allowance per day to the first day of February, the earliest day that I could possibly have reached Home after the Completion of the treaty on the 10th January. If I had not been engaged in this Business for the Public I should have been in Congress where my Salary would have been nearly the same and the Service much more agreeable.

The Business of the State made it necessary for me to return Via Charleston and there to stay a few days as your Excellency will be informed in my report of my proceedings as a Commissioner for holding a treaty with the Cherokees and thereby the present report has been delayed to this time. I have the Honor to be

                Your Excellencys
                Most Obedient Servant
                Wm. Blount

His Excellency
Richard Caswell Esquire
Governor of North Carolina

H.C. Jan. 6, 1787

General Assembly Sessions
1777 - 1789

Your Committee to whom was referred sundry Papers respecting Indian Treaties and Indian Affairs

Beg leave to report,
That they have examined with Attention the Papers to them refer'd and they find that by the Treaties entered into between the Commissioners Appointed by the United States to treat with the Southern Indians and the Cherokee & Chickasaw Indians at Hopewell on the Keewee.

The Commissioners of the United States have allotted to the said Indians certain Lands as their Hunting Grounds which are obviously within the Jurisdiction of this State being North of the Boundary Established by Law between the Citizens and Indians, and a great part of which is for a valuable consideration sold to our Citizens & some of whom are now Actually Living thereon. Your Committee observe that the Commissioners having only allotted these Lands to the Indians as their Hunting Grounds, the treaty doth not thereby annull the Title of those who hold under our Laws, but have dog'd it in a manner different from the Intentions of the Legislative Rights which is inadmissable.
Your Committee thereupon recommend that the Delegates of this State in Congress be instructed to State our rights to the Lands in Question to the United States of America in Congress Assembled to obtain disavowal of the Treaties so far as they affect the same and if the same should be persisted in, which your Committee cannot Suppose from the known rectitude and Wisdom of Congress that finally they formally Protest against the same.

Your Committee further Reports
That The Honorable William Blount was appointed by the Executive in Pursuance of the Notification from the Commissioners from the United States founded on a Resolution of Congress an Agent on the part of this State to be Present with the Commissioners: And that he has wisely Protested against the said Treaties so far as they affect us. And further that he was Appointed to hold a Treaty with the Cherokee Indians and did attend at the meeting of the Commissioners and Indians and According to the direction of the Governor and Council he shiped to the care of A. Nanderhorst in Charleston the Goods &c. Purchased for that Purpose. That from unavoidable delays in procuring Waggons Colo. Nanderhorst could not send forward the Goods to the place of their

General Assembly Sessions
1777 - 1789

destination until the Commissioners of the United States had Commenced their Negociations with the Indians, the Tenor of which inspired the Indians with an Idea of such extreme advantage that the Agent could not Prevail on them to Treat on Terms Admissable by the State, and was therefore necessitated to sell the Goods for the most that could be obtained which is as follows.

To Bryan Ward one third payable on the first day of April 1786 and the other 2/3s on the first day of April 1787 in Deer Skins Furs and Tobacco. 1,333.3.10

To George Ogg for Clag [**Faded**] & Co. at their Franklin Store kept by said Geo. Ogg   39.15.9

To William Blount   145.9.9
Sterling   1,518.9.4

And the Rum Procured for holding a Treaty disposed of as follows.
To Bryan Ward 1 Hhd. @ 1/4 dollrs. p Gallon
To George Ogg 1 Hhd. @ 1/4 drs. p Gallon
3 Hhds sent to Washington to J.G. & Tho. Blount
1 Hhd lost at Charleston by the head bursting putting it into the Waggon as appears by Colo. Nanderhorst's Letter.
The quantity sold Mr. Ward and Mr. Ogg not shown for want of Gauging rod.

That the first payment being Deerskins an Article liable to damage if not early sent to Market was ordered to be shiped to Philadelphia to Stuart and Barr, and the after payment is Subject to the order of the General Assembly. That on the first payment four thousand Deer skins or thereabout were received by Mr. George Ogg as P Agreement, and in all Probability Shiped to Philadelphia.

Your Committee further Report That it is evident, the Cherokee Indians are much dissatisfied with our disposition of the Land claimed by them within our State, and that Protesting this dissatisfaction may arise from our not having given what they Supposed an equivalent for their Claim: And as our last advices from Congress assure us that the Northern Indians will soon be engaged in a War with us, it may be Prudent to use such means as are in our Power to remove the dissatisfaction in question in a Speedy and Amicable a manner as is practicable. Whereupon, Your

General Assembly Sessions
1777 - 1789

Davidson County to prevent the Indians from taking any Hostile Resolutions, in aid of the Northern Tribes, and that our Delegates in Congress be instructed to lay before the United States of America in Congress assembled the necessity of this Measure, and to obtain leave to continue the same in Service while the necessity exists. And further to establish a good Understanding between the Citizens and Indians. That the skins received on the first aforementioned payment be sold at Philadelphia for Suitable Goods to be given to the Indians to extinguish their Claim as soon as Practicable, and that our Superintendant of Indian affairs be directed to inform them of this benevolent intention of the Legislature.

And we further recommend that the future payments to be made by Mr. Ward be disposed of in a Similar manner and distributed Amongst the Chickasaw Indians for a relinquishment of their Claim to the Lands lying between the Tenesee and Missisippee, a great part of which is sold to our Citizens.

As a further reason why your committee are of opinion that the said Indian treaties are injurious to the citizens within the bounds [Faded] the Indians, your committee refer to the act of Cession to the United States by which alone Congress can pretend any claim to territory within this State one of the conditions in which is, that all grants of land thereto fore [Faded] to any citizen or citizens or any entries made should have the same force and effect as if the Cession had not been made whereas the citizens to whom grants were made be for the cession aforesaid have been left to the mercy of the Indians so that admitting the cession to be valid Congress have not, in this instance performed that condition of the said act.
In the House of Commons 6 January 1787   A Maclaine Ck.
Read and Concurred with as amended
By Order
J Hunt Clk   John B. Ashe S.C.
In Senate 6 Jany. 1787
Read and Concurred with Jam. Coors [Torn]

****

North Carolina State Archives
General Assembly Sessions Records
November, 1786-January, 1787, Box #1
File: Grand Committee & Sub-Committee on Indian Affairs

Alexr. Martin Esqr.

General Assembly Sessions
1777 - 1789

Alexr. Martin Esqr.
Gilford County
North Carolina

Joseph Martin
25th May 1786

Dear Sir)   Smiths [?]   25th May 1786

    Since Closeing my Letters to governor Caswell Mr. Swanson a man of repute who lives in this neighborhood returns from Georgia he assures me the Creek Indians has made a stroke on several parts of Georgia & Killd several people that a party that had Murthered at the Cherokee Corner was follow to the Apelatchicola & there overtaken where two Indians & one whiteman was Killd that the Inhabitants are actually reported sixteen miles in the Country & about seventy in [?]
    You will Lay me under very great obligations if you will be so obliging as to forward the Letters to Governor Caswell under a Cover & inform him of late mischief in Georgia
    I wish you would write to Colo. Evan Shelby your opinion of the new state you will also be pleased to inform me when the anuall Elections are in North Carolina that no mistake may Happen in Sullivan

I am yrs with very great regard
Your Very Humble Sevt.
Jos. Martin

****

North Carolina State Archives
General Assembly Sessions Records
November, 1786-January, 1787, Box #1

No. 209
Joseph Martin
25th May 1786

Alexander Martin Esqr.
Guilford County
North Carolina

General Assembly Sessions
1777 - 1789

Since Closeing my Letters to Governor Caswell Mr. Swanson a man of repute who lives in this neighborhood and return'd from Georgia & assures me the Creek Indians has made a Stroke on several parts of Georgia & Killd several people that a party that had Murthered at the Cherokee Corner was follow to the apalatchicola & there over taken wheare Two Indians & one whiteman was Killd that the Inhabants are actually forted Sixteen miles in the Country & about seventy in length.

You will Lay me under very Great Obligations if you will be so obliging as to forward the Letters to Governor Caswell under a Cover & inform him of the late mischief in Georgia.

I wish you Would write to Col Evan Shelby your own opinion of the new state you will also be pleasd to inform me when the annual Elections are in North Carolina that no Mistake may happen in Sullivan.

      I am with Very Great Regard
      your Very Humble Servt.
      Jos. Martin

****

North Carolina State Archives
General Assembly Sessions Records
November 1786-January 1787, Box #2
Joint Select Committee

Resolution of Congress for raising Troops, establishing Loan Office
& requisition of 30.478 dollars from No. Carolina
20 & 21 Octo. 1786

By the United States in Congress Assembled
October 20th 1786

The Committee to whom was referred the latter from the War Office with the papers enclosed containing intelligence of the hostile intentions of the Indians in the Western Country having reported.

That the uniform tenor of the intelligence from the Western Country plainly indicates the hostile disposition of a number of Indian Nations particularly the Shawanesa Putestamies, Chippawas Trevas and Twightwees.

General Assembly Sessions
1777 - 1789

Nations particularly the Shawanesa Putestamies, Chippawas Trevas and Twightwees.

That these Nations are now Assembling in the Shawanese towns and are joined by a banditti of desperadoes under the name of Mingoes and Cherokees, who are outcasts from other Nations and who have Associated & Settled in that Country for the purpose of War and Plunder.

That they are laboring to draw in other Nations to Unite with them in a War with the Americans.

That it is expected one thousand Warriors will soon be collected in the Shawanese towns from whence they have already dispatched parties to commence hostilities.

That from the Motions of the Indians to the Southward as well as to the Northward and the exertions made in different quarters to stimulate the various Nations against the Americans there is the strongest reason to believe that unless the Speediest measures are taken effectually to Counter-Act and defeat their plans the War will bwcome general and may be attended with the most dangerous and lasting Consequences.

That the Committee therefore deem it highly necessary that the Troops in the Service of the United States be immediately Augmented not only for the protection and Support of the frontiers of the States bordering on the Western territory and the valuable Settlements on and near the margin of the Mississipi; but to establish the possession and facilitate the Surveying and selling of those intermediate lands which have been so much relied on for the reduction of the debts of the United States, whereupon,

Resolved Unanimously That the number of one thousand three hundred and forty Non Commissioned Officers and Privates be raised for the term of three years, unless sooner discharged, and that they together with the Troops now in Service be formed into a Legionary Corps to consist of 2040 Non Commissioned Officers and Privates.

That the Additional Troops be raised by the following States in the following proportions to wit.

New Hampshire	260	}	
Massachusetts	660	}	Infantry & Artillery
Rhode Island	120	}	
Connecticut	180	}	

Maryland & Virginia each 60 Cavalry making 120

General Assembly Sessions
1777 - 1789

That the Secretary at War inform the Executive Authorities of the Respective States in which the troops are to be raised, the number and Rank of Commissioned Officers to be furnished by each State in proportion to the Men.

That the pay, and allowances to the Troops to be raised by this Resolve be the same as established by the Act of Congress of the 12th April 1785.

That the said troops shall be Subject to the existing Articles of War, or such as may hereafter be formed by Congress or a Committee of the States.

That the Board of Treasury contract for a Supply of Clothing and Rations at such places and in such quantities, as the Secretary at War shall judge necessary.

Resolved Unanimously That the States above mentioned be and they are hereby requested to use their utmost exertions to raise the Quotas of troops respectively assigned them with all possible expedition - And that the Executive of the said States be and hereby are requested in case any of their Legislatures Should not be in Session, immediately them for this purpose as a delay may be attended with the most fatal Consequences.

Ordered that the Board of Treasury without delay devise waus and means for the pay and support of the Troops of the United States on the present establishment and report the same to Congress.
Cha Thomson Secy

October 21st 1786

On the Report of the Board of Treasury pursuant to the Orders of yesterday to devise ways and means for the pay and Support of the Troops of the United States on the present establishment.

Resolved Unanimously, That the several States in the Confederacy be and they are hereby required to pay into the Federal Treasury on or before the first day of June 1787 their respective Quotas of the sum of Five hundred and thirty thousand Dollars in Specie which quotas are,

New Hampshire	18.603
Massachusetts	79.288
Rhode Island	11.395
Connecticut	46.746
New York	45.368

General Assembly Sessions
1777 - 1789

New Jersey	29.415
Pennsylvania	72.504
Delaware	7.950
Maryland	49.979
Virginia	90.630
North Carolina	38.478
South Carolina	33.973
Georgia	5.671

Which sums when paid shall be passed to the Credit of the States respectively on the terms prescribed by the Resolve of Congress of the 6th day of October 1779, and that the monies ariseing from the said Requisition be and hereby are appropriated for the pay and Support of the Troops on the present Establishment.

    Resolved Unanimously that the Board of Treasury be and they are hereby authorised and directed to open a Loan immediately to the Amount of Five hundred thousand Dollars at Six P.Cent P. Annum on the Credit of the foregoing Requisition which then are hereby authorised to pledge to the Lenders for the faithfull reimbursement of the monies Loaned with the Interest thereof.
Cha Thomson   Secy.

****

North Carolina State Archives
General assembly Sessions Records
November 1786-January 1787, Box #3
Senate Joint Resolutions

    Part of a Resolution proposed by the Senate regarding Indian Treaty, but rejected by the House of Commons, Jan., 1787

Proceedings of the Senate, 7 January 1787

Resolved, that the General Assembly of North Carolina view a Treaty calculated to deprive a respectable part of her Citizens of their property and to endanger their lives with the Utmost horror and honest Indignation; and that it be represented to Congress in the strongest terms that the late Treaty at Hopewell instead of procuring the blessings of peace to the Citizens of this State, will most likely produce the Contrary effect and involve them in

General Assembly Sessions
1777 - 1789

all the horrors of War, as the Savages appear much more hostile since than before.

Extract from the senate Journal, tho' no part of the Resolution as agreed to by the House of Commons.
Witness S Haywood Clk

Ther part of the Resolution relative to the Indian Treaty held at Hopewell which is contained in this brief was rejected by the house of Commons tho' agreed to by the Senate
Haywood, Clk
Jo. Green Jany 14, 1787

In General Assembly 7th Jany 1787
    The General Assembly having taken into Consideration the late treaty held at Hopewell on the Keewuwe (by Commissioners appointed by Congress for that purpose) with the Cherokee, Chickasaw & Southern Indians whereupon
    Resolved that this General Assembly conceive the said treaty so far as it relates to ceding to the Indians certain Lands within the bounds or limits of this State, is clearly an infringement of the Legislative and territorial rights of the same as set forth in the Constitution of the State and therefore cannot be conceeded to.
    Resolved that it is the sense of this General Assembly that this State has an indefeasible right to a considerable part of the lands ceded by the said Treaty to the Indians, which right was obtained by purchase from the Natives, and that even Congress have not Liberty to dispose of any part of the same by treaty, Sale or exchange.
    Resolved as the opinion of this Genl. Assembly that the exclusive privileges granted by the Consideration to the US in Congress to decide on peace & war, was never meant or intended to authorise the Cession of any part of the territory of the individual States in the Union as described and ascertained by their several ancient charts.
    And whereas many of the Citizens of this State, have obtained from the same titles, lands on the waters of the Missisippi and some of them actually reside thereon, who must necessarily be greatly injured should they be compelled to remove with their families therefrom; And Whereas by the express words of the said treaty they are declared out of the protection of the United States if they do not within the limited time leave their habitations & retire out of the ceded bounds: And whereas the

General Assembly Sessions
1777 - 1789

said treaty should it be carried into effect would deprive the Officers and Soldiers of the late Continental line of this State of a great part of the bounty of lands allowed them by the General Assembly as a reward for Military Services bringing about our Glorious revolution, it was promised to them by a debt of justice and gratitude and almost the only recompense the State had to give to those hardy veterans who spent their time, & shed their blood in the Service of their Country -- the honor of the State was pledged to secure their rights, and it would be highly unjust to snatch the boon from them when no equivalent is obtained to the United States: And whereas it is impracticable for many of the Citizens of this State who have settled themselves within the limits of the said cession to remove agreeable to the tenor of the said treaty and must therefore be exposed to the cruelty and rage of the merciless savages.

Resolved therefore that the deligates from this State in Congress be intrusted to oppose the ratification of the said treaty in the most explicit & [?] terms, and in case the same should take effect (which from the known rectitude and wisdom of Congress cannot be Supposed) to enter thereto the formal protest of this State.

James Coor Spk. Senate
By Order, S Haywood CS

****

North Carolina State Archives
General Assembly Sessions Records
November 1786-January 1787, Box #3
Senate Joint Resolutions

Resolve of the Senate Relative to Indian Treaties &c., Rejected

North Carolina
In Senate Decr. 18, 1786

Resolved, that the Sub-Committee to whom was referred the Papers in Indian Affairs be disolved, and that a special Committee be appointed, whose duty it shall be to form a Resolve expressive of the Sense of the Legislature relative to the late Cherokee and Choctaw Treaties held at Hopewell by the Commissioners or Plenipotentiaries of the United States in Congress; and to form & report a State of the Costs, Charges and

General Assembly Sessions
1777 - 1789

Disposition of the Goods intended as a Present for the Indians by this State, and who shall also report such Measures as they may deem necessary to be adopted in consequence of the Said Treaty & intended Compensation at present not having taken Place on the part of this State.

Resolved further that on the part of this House Mr Stokes, Mr Stone, Mr Galloway, Mr Martin and Mr Lewis be a Committee for the purposes aforesaid.
Jams. Coor S.S.
By Order, J Haywood CS

****

North Carolina State Archives
General Assembly sessions Records
November 1786-January 1787, Box #3
House Joint Resolutions

The Petition of George Lewis and William Price
In House of Commons 6 December 1786, read & referred to the
Committee of Propositions & Grievances
By Order, J Hunt Clk

In Senate December 6, 1786
Read & referred as by the House of Commons
By Order, J Haywood CS

To the General Assembly of the State of North Carolina
The Humble Petition of George Lewis and William Price Sheweth

That Your Petitioners apprehends they have an Equitable right to some Lands lying between the Appalachian Mountains, or Main - Ridge, and French Broad River, which they mean hereby to shew to you how their right Originated; and for the better Explanation thereof, to set forth the same in a Brief Narration the Facts that can now be Collected for that Purpose.

Captain Thomas Price was by License, a Trader several years to the Cherokee Indians; and that a considerable part of the time he Traded with that Nation of Indians he resided in one of their Towns: and in the Course of his Trade, trusted considerable Sums to the Hunting Indians: and finding that his Expectations of Remittances to fail, addressed himself

General Assembly Sessions
1777 - 1789

to some of their Chiefs -- who after a Consultation on the affair, the Indians informed Capt. Price that the Goods were almost wore out, and the Indians were poor; and it was what he would take Land for Pay for his Goods. Capt. Price being in a sad dilemma -- Requested that they would call a Meeting of the Head Men &c. from the several Towns that he had trusted Goods to. They accordingly met, and Capt. Price again addressed himself to then in Plaintiff Terms, told them that his Goods was gone, and he had no skins to pay the great Man, that had the Goods of: They answered they were sorry, but were not able to pay him in skins &c. He must take Land. Capt. Price Concluding that he must comply with their offer, said he would take Lands. After that a large number of the Chiefs and Hunters were Consulted on the Occasion; and by the Solemnity of a Treaty, and Sanction of a Contract, after usual formallities on Simillar Occassions, previous to Confirmations, They Unanimously agreed with, and sold to Capt. Price the Land ascertained by the following Boundaries. Vizt. Beginning at the head of Muddy-Creek, (Water of French Broad River) which takes its rise in the West side of the Main Ridge From thence a due West Course to the said French Broad River. Thence down the said River with the Meander to the Mouth of Ivey-River. Then up Ivey-River, including all the Waters thereof, Joining Capt. Jacob Brown's Purchase. Then with said Purchase to the Boundary line between North Carolina and the Cherokee Indian Nation. Then with said Boundary to the Main Ridge. Thence with the Main Ridge to the Beginning. At the same time they delegated three of their Chiefs to Meet Capt. Price at a certain time on the Premises, to Sign, Seal and Deliver (in behalf of all that claimed the hunting Grounds within the Bounds aforesaid) a Deed of Conveyance of the same. In the Month of November, in the Year of Our Lord One Thousand Seven Hundred and Seventy Five, the Three Chiefs that were delegated met accordingly (One of the Chiefs was Attakullahkullah, or the Little Carpenter) and did Sign, Seal and Deliver a Deed of Conveyance for the same, to the said Capt. Thomas Price, his Heirs and Successors. Before the Land was Conveyed, Capt. Price had advise to consult the King's Superintendant of Indian Affairs; which he accordingly did; and did not Immediately receive an Answer.

    Soon after Capt. Price received a Letter from Governor Wright from Georgia which informed Capt. Price that the Indians had a right to Sell their Lands; and that there was no danger of Obtaining the Royal Assent for the same. Upon which Capt. Price Sent to the Indians for some of them to come to his Dwelling, which was then, on the Waters of Tyger River, near Capt. John Prince's (then a Frontier of South Carolina) to see

General Assembly Sessions
1777 - 1789

the Books which contained the Accounts against them destroyed. At the day appointed for that Purpose, some of the Indians came. Dancing and other Merriments were performed; and in the presence of the Indians, and a Number of White People, the Books were Burned, and a great Rejoicing amoungst the Indians on the occasion.

That George Lewis, one of your Petitioners, as soon as the Titles were confirmed, in Idea of the Purchaser, and the chief Oppinions of the People at large being then into Partnership with Capt. Price in said Lands; and in the Spring following went with Capt. Price and settled on Caney-River near the Centre of the said Purchase, Cleared Ground, and Planted Corn. In the Month of July the Same Year, were Obliged to Move off on Account of Indian disturbances.

In the Year of Our Lord One Thousand Seven Hundred and Sevety Seven Capt. Price and George Lewis, one of your Petitioners, Resumed the Improving the same Place: Built a Dwelling House, Smith Shop &c., and Cleared and Fenced Twenty Acres of Land, Planted and Sowed. At the same time Several Families Setled and Improved under the Idea of the Rights to the same, from Capt. Thomas Price, in Consequence of his Purchase from the Cherokee Indians.

In the Year of Our Lord One Thousand Seven Hundred and Eighty, the said Indians Broke out, and an Open War Ensued. Upon which Capt. Price and his Familly, George Lewis one of your Petitioners, with the others of the Setlers on the said Purchase was obliged to fly in Consternation before the said Indians, leaving their Crops, Tools of Smithing and of Husbandry, and all the heavy part of their Household Furniture; Part whereof is not yet been Obtained, or ever Expected.

Capt. Price and Familly, and George Lewis, one of your Petitioners fled for Refuge to the Turkey Cove, being then the highest place that was Inhabitted, being nearly Thirty Miles. A small time after Capt. Price was Chosen to head a Voluntier Company to Guard against the Indians & Tories, who with George Lewis, one of your Petitioners, was on Constant Duty in their Country's Service.

The same Summer, Major Ferguson, a British Commander, Marched with an Army of Britains and Tories, to the Head of the Catawbey River, in Burke County. Capt. Price and George Lewis, one of Your Petitioners with the others of the Effective Inhabitants, Friend to American Pollicy, who, apprehended themselves not Competant to Attack the Enemy, Fled over the Mountains with, and under that Laudable of Conduct of Col. now Brigadier General Charles McDowell.

General Assembly Sessions
1777 - 1789

After Ferguson was defeated, Capt. Price and George Lewis, one of your Petitioners, being Constant in their Country's Service, not only exposed them to the hardship and danger of War, but the Contagion of onfectious Diseases.

In the Year of Our Lord One Thousand Seven Hundred and Eighty One, Capt. Price fell at the Siege of Augusta, in Georgia; and that William Price, the other of your Petitioners, then in the Sixteenth Year of his Age, was present in the same Engagement. And that George Lewis the other of your Petitioners, was taken with small Pox; and by an uncommon flow of that disease, lost the Sight of both his Eyes.

That Your Petitioner having Shewn by the Facts they now can Collect their Claim to the Purchase aforesaid, do apprehend that they have an Equitable Right to Some, if not all the said Lands -- There being a Precedent of their Case of Henderson and Others, in a Similar Case, that was allowed Part of their Purchase, or some other lands as a Compensation for the same by them paid to the Indians.

That your Petitioners are now Inform'd that it is now Argued that a Purchase then from the Indians, was in the Right of the Crown; and now the Right of the State, of any Lands that was, or may be disposed of by them. Therefore, by the Weight of such Arguments, being Consistant with Reason and sound Policy, Your Petitioners Retracts their Claim to all the said Lands, but hopes that you will Consider their Situation and Circumstances, and Grant them such a Part of the said Purchase, as a Compensation for the Expenditure, or part thereof made in the Purchase.

That Your Petitioners Suggests, that it was not a Voluntary Act of Capt. Price to make the Purchase he did; but it was Imposed on him by the Indians; and that they would Wish to Obviate an affair that they have understood has Militated against the Interest of the said Purchase in a debate in the General Assembly heretofore. That is the great Quantity of Acres included in Forty Miles Square, which the said Purchase is Computed to, which Contains above a Million of Acres. This the Believe may be a Just Computation; But it may be Observed that there is but little of that Purchase Tillable Land. Some has Computed that there is not more than One Acre in a Thousand that is fit for Cultivation. So that when the good Lands by that Computation comes to be Estimated, the Purchase will be Contracted to a small Quantity of Acres..

That your Petitioners has been informed that the Reason why the Petition Exhibited to the General Assembly heretofore by Capt. Thomas and Col. Thomas Wade &c. did not Succeed, was by Imprudent Management and Inattention. Imprudent Management on the part of Capt.

General Assembly Sessions
1777 - 1789

a Gentleman of Fortune -- It was not so much an Object of his Concern. To that your Petitioners cannot Collect any Positive Intelligence, whether the want of Success was Owing to the want of Right, or Imprudent Management.

That your Petitioners being Reduced to very low Circumstances, by Dirt[?] of the late Unatural War -- and losses by the Indians; Especially George Lewis, who is Intirely destitute of Eye Sight, and without hopes of ever seeing light again; and is now chiefly Sustained by the kindness of his Fellow Citizens; and never Expects Some part of the said Purchase can be Obtained.

That your Petitioners do not only mean to shew their Own Circumstances, but that of Sarah Price, Relict of the said Capt. Thomas Price Deceas'd: Who, ever since has remained a Widow, and with hard Strugling has Supported a Familly of Small Children -- One that was born on the said Purchase.

That your Petitioners do not mean to set their present State of affairs before you in that light, as to expect any Redress by what was occasioned by the fate of War, as being Common to many good Citizens; but to show by being driven by the Indians, or their Remote Situation, had not the Opportunity of being informed when the Land Office opened in Burke County, whereby Your Petitioner George Lewis and Capt. Thomas Price, Father to William Price, your other Petitioner might have Entered Some Valuable Tracts -- or Caveated those that did Enter on the said Purchase.

That your Petitioners presumes that Very few of the Citizens had that fair Opportunity when the Office did Open, as the Legislature intended; that all the good Tracts of Land that was not Claimed by Improvements, were Monopolized by a few Gentlemen. So that your Petitioners have lost all means of Obtaining any Valuable Tracts of Land in the Common Way.

That your Petitioners being informed that as the Chief of the Valuable Lands on the said Purchase are Appropriated; and that it will Remain a Difficulty for the Assembly to make Null and Void the Grants already made Out. How that may be your Petitioners cannot Say: Nor do not pretend to Conjecture how their Claims may opperate against the Appropriated Lands; but leaves that to your Wisdom and Goodness.

That your Petitioners are Informed that Six Hundred and Forty Acres of Land including the improvements made by Capt. Thomas Price and George Lewis, one of your Petitioners was Entered by William Sharpe Esqr. and Caveated by Mr. John McDowell of the Pleasant Garden, in

General Assembly Sessions
1777 - 1789

and George Lewis, one of your Petitioners was Entered by William Sharpe Esqr. and Caveated by Mr. John McDowell of the Pleasant Garden, in Burke County; and that the same is yet undetermined. Therefore Consequently the land not yet Granted.

    That your Petitioners presumes that neither of the aforesaid Gentlemen can claim any Equitable Right equal to that of Your Petitioners; and as the affair is Yet undetermined between them, that you by your Goodness will Interfere on Your Petitioners behalf in that case; and Order that the Secretary make out no Grant for either of them Gentlemen, until you have Considered the Merits of this Claim made by Your Petitioners, Or what your Goodness in their Case will Determine.

    That if your Petitioners should only Recover that one Tract of Land, would be of some Considerable help to them; Humbly Submitting the Whole of their affair on the Premises aforesaid to your Consideration. Hoping, Trusting and Confiding that you will Regard the Prayer of your Petitioner as for the nature of their Case, and the Constitution will Admit it. And your Petitioner shall ever Pray

October 20th, 1786

George Lewis & William Price

Sir,

    Relating to the Indian Warriors Elected to the assignment of yr. Land Title on the waters of French Broad river; According to the trust vested in me, I have been faithful, and Succesful without Controversy to your Great Satisfaction -- Yet misfortunately miscarying in [Torn] Design of Effecting the final Discharge of said Engagement, by way of bodily disorder, cutting me Short of the oportunity at present wch mought been the period of this whole undertaking to the last degree of sattisfaction.

    Yet notwithstanding, assuring you that that there is no other [Faded] in view than the final accomplishment thereof at will when proper Chance admits to confirm ye Same without dispute; as already by mutual Consultation agreed upon by the Assembly of Cherrokee warriors Concurred therein Depending &c.

    Which you may depend upon the veracity of your Titles, from what I make [?] to insert

                             Sir, as your friend and Humble Servt.
                                       Hugh Hamilton

Canisega

General Assembly Sessions
1777 - 1789

This Indenture Made this Twenty Second day of November in the Year of our Lord Christ one Thousand Seven hundred and Seventy five Between Ettacullahcullah Chief Warrior and first Representative of the Cherokee Nation or Tribe of Indians and the said Ettacullahcullah and rest of [?] Being the Aborigines and sole owners by Occupancy from the beginning of Time of the Land on the Waters of Tenesy River up to the Virginia North and South Carolina and their Lands Teritories Thereunto adjoining of the one part and Thomas Price and George Lewis of Wattaugah River of the other Witnesseth, that the Said Ettecullahcullah for himself and the Rest of the Nation of Indians for and in Consideration of the Sum of [Torn] [Faded] pounds of good and Lawful money of great Britain to them in [Torn] by the said Thos. Price & Geo. Lewis the Receipt Whereof there the same Ettacullahcullah and his said whole Nation do for themselves and their whole [Torn] people have Granted Bargained and Sold Alliened Enfeoffed Released and Confirmed and by these presents do Grant Bargain and sell Allien Enfeoff Release and Confirm to them the said Thos. Price & Geo. Lewis their Heirs & Assigns all that Land lying and being on the East of French Broad River from the head of Muddy Creek Due West to the West [Faded] Banks of french Broad River and from thence Down to the Northern heads of Ivey River Joining the Wattaugah Line from thence Joining the Carolina Line from thence to the beginning line, And also the Reversion and Reversions Remainder and Remainders Rents and [Faded] thereof and all the Estate Right title Interest Claim & demand whatsoever of Them the said Ettacullacullah and the Aforesaid Whole Band or Tribe of people of in and to the Same premises and of in and to every part or parcel Thereof To have and to hold the said messuage Territory and all and Singular the premises Above Mentioned with the appurtenances unto the said Thomas Price and George Lewis their and assigns in severalty and Tenants in Common and not as Joint Tenants to the only proper use and behoof of them the said Thos. Price and Geo. Lewis their heirs and assigns forever Under the yearly Rent of [Torn] pence or to be holden of the Chief Lord or Lords of the fee of the premises by the Rents and Services therefore due and of right accustomed and the said Ettacullacullah and the Rest of the said Nation for themselves Covenant and Grant to and with the said Thos. Price & George Lewis their heirs and assigns that they the said Ettacullacullah and all the said Nation of people are now Lawfully and Rightfully [Torn] in their own Right of a good sure perfect absolute and Indefeasible Estate of Inheritance

General Assembly Sessions
1777 - 1789

of people are now Lawfully and Rightfully **[Torn]** in their own Right of a good sure perfect absolute and Indefeasible Estate of Inheritance in fee simple of and in all and Singular the said messuage teritorys and premises Above Mentioned and of all and every part and parcel thereof and its appurtenance without any manner of condition Ono**[Torn]** **[Torn]**age limitation of use or uses or other matter cause or thing to alter change or Determine the same And Also that they the Said Ettacullacullah and the foresaid Nation of Indians to Thos. Price & Geo. Lewis heirs and assigns shall and may from Time to Time and at all Times thereafter peaceably and Quietly have hold Occupy possess and Enjoy all and Singular the said premises Above Mentioned to be hereby Granted with the Appurtanenances without the least trouble hindrance Molestation Interuption and denial of them the said Ettacullacullah and the Rest or any of the said Nation their heirs or assigns and of all and Every other person and persons Whatsoever Claiming or to Claim by from or Under them or Any of them and lastly the **[Smudged]** Ettacullacullah and their heirs anything having or Claiming in the said messuage Teritory and premises above mentioned **[Smudged]** **[Whole next line torn and fragmented]** **[Smudged]** and other to Lewis their heirs and assigns make do and Execute or Cause or Procure to be made done and Executed all and every further and other Lawfull and reasonable grants acts and assurrances in the Law whatsoever for the further better and more perfect Granting Conveying and assurring of the said premises hereby Granted with the appurtenances to the said Thomas Price & George Lewis their heirs and assigns forever According to the purported true Intent and meaning of these presents Ratifying Confirming and allowing whatsoever they shall do in the premises -- In Witness Whereof the said Ettakillakullica, Wooea or Pigeon called have thereunto set their hands and affixed their Seals this day and Date Above Written

Ettakilakullica his (🙂) mark
Wooeah his (Ø) mark
Sucky his (ಲ) mark

Signed Sealed and Delivered in the Presents of us
Abednigo Llewelen, Thomas Harris, Jeremiah Harris & Meshack Llewelen

Spartanburg County in the State of South Carolina
 This 14th day of November A:C: 1786 appeared before me James Jordan one of the Justices of the Peace for Sd. County -- The Deponent

General Assembly Sessions
1777 - 1789

Purchasers To Wit   Capt. Thomas Price & George Lewis; and the Deponent called upon to write their names to their marks penn'd down with their own hands And the said Deponent Entrusted then with ye Care of these writings till Called upon -- Thus Declaring and no more.

Given Under my hand}
The day and year Sd. }   Peter Lewis
Jas. Jordan (JP)

Whereas Capt. George Lewis, now of Rutherford County, in the Sate of North Carolina, have informed us the Subscribers that he has some Important Business to be Transacted in that State, that a Character might be of a Considerable Service to Him.

We hereby Certify that we have been acquainted with him from Childhood; That he has Sustained the Character of an honest Person and a good Citizen, Especially during the Time of the late Unatural War Between Great Britain and America, while he was in Our State, the State of South Carolina.

September 20th 1786
Certified Under Our Hands
Thos Brandon, JP, H.M. Hood, JP, Zach Bullock, JP, Thomas Trent, JP
Spartanburgh

House of Commons, Dec. 15th 1786

Your Committee of Propositions and Grievances to whom was referred the Petition of George Lewis and Wm. Price, Report--

That from the Representation of George Lewis, and the several affidavits and other papers laid before them in support of the facts set forth in the said Petition, it appears to your Committee that Captain Thomas Price Father to William one of the Petitioners was regularly licensed to trade with the Cherokee Indians, and that during the time of his trading with them he Credited them for the goods to a Very large Amount. It also appears that George Lewis was in copartnership with said Price while trading with said Indians, and that they from necessity was obliged to accept of a Deed from the Indian Chiefs for a Considerable Quantity of lands as a restitution for the Monies due them from said Indians as they had no other Means of satisfaction for the debts due, It also further appears

General Assembly Sessions
1777 - 1789

that the lands in that part of the Country has since the late War been indescriminately allowed, by the State to be entered, by the Citizens thereof -- That previous to the opening of the Land Office Captain Price was Killed in defense of his Country, and left behind him a helpless widow and Orphans, That George Lewis was at the same time Blind of Both his Eyes in which Situation he now is, and being far distant from the office at which lands in that part of the Country were to be entered, and having as they thought a Right to said Lands as Captain Price in his life time -- and the said George Lewis had made Considerable improvement thereupon, did not avail themselves of the opportunity of entering the said Lands until some time ago, when on attempting to enter them they found it was previously done by a Certain William Sharpe so long before that the said Lewis and William Price was by law excluded from a Right of Caveating.

Your Committee under these considerations, and from the distress'd situation of said Petitioners are of opinion that they are objects Worthy the benevolence of the Legislature, therefore recommend that a Portion of lands in that part of the Country (equal to the sum of money specified in the Deed given by the Indians to Captain Price) be laid off to the said George Lewis and the Widow and Orphans of the said Thomas Price, All which is Submitted -- Hyatt Hawkins Chm

---

A Resolve in consequence of this Report, allowing George Lewis 4000 acres of Land & the Male Heirs of Thomas Price, the same quantity was delivered
M Holland, 26 Decr. 1786
By J Hunt

State of North Carolina }
Rutherford County   } Personally Appeared

Before me A Justice of the Peace for said Capt. Alexander M Daniel Who being Duly Sworn Deposeth & Saith that he the said Depon't in the Year of Our Lord 1769 or 1770 Served as Clerk for Captain Thomas Price in his Store Which Was kept in the Cherokee nation & Upon Posting his the said Capt. Price's Books Perfectly knew that the Indians Were Greatly Indebted to him the said Thomas Price & that While he the said Dept. Continued in the Service of said Price those Indians Never Discharged their Debts but Voluntarily Continued to Involve theirselves Daily Until his the said Capt.

General Assembly Sessions
1777 - 1789

Prices Store was Exhausted, & that he the Dept. never knew Nor heard of any Satisfaction made or Given by the said Indians to Capt. Price Before the Year 1775 Which was As he the Dept. Understood by Disposing of a Quantity of Land Lying on the Western Waters French Broad Cane Creek, Swaneno &c. &c. that he the Dept. is Assured that those Lands Were Disposed of to the said Price in Order to Discharge those Several Sums of Money or trade Due from them the said Indians to him the said Capt. Thomas Price & further the Dept. Saith not.
Alexr. M Donald
Sworn to before me this 30th Day of October 1786
Jonathn. Hampton

State of South Carolina }
Spartanburgh County }

Personally appeared Ephraim Lewis before me and made Oath as followeth, that sometime in the Last of the year 1775 or in the first of the year 1776 being informed by Thomas Price of his purchase of a certain boundary of Land of the Cherokee Indians, on the North side French Broad River &cc being well pleas'd with the same Desineing to be an inhabiter there the Deponent saith he went over with a number of his neighbours to the sd. boundaries being no ways serupelous of the bargain being complete which the deponant saith he saw a deed of conveyance of the same and the deponant further saith that he saw the Indian books burned in the presence of the White folks and Indians. The Deponant firther saith that in the month of May that he was employd by George Lewis to plant Corn on Swannanoe in sd. Purchase
Thus Saith Ephraim Lewis
Given undr my hand this 13th day of Novr. 1786
Jas. Jordan (JP)

State of North Carolina }
Rutherford County }

This is to Certify to all Whom it May Concern that we the Subscribers have been Well Acquainted With Captain George Lewis for several Years & Particularly With his Conduct During the late War, Who has Ever been Esteemed as a Gentleman of Honour Merritting his Country's Applause By

General Assembly Sessions
1777 - 1789

his Valour & Good Services Rendered to his Country being Considered as a Useful Member of Society Deserving the Countenance & Protection that is Due to a good Citizen
Given & Certified This 17th Day of October 1783
By Jonathn Hampton J.P.

Richd. Singleton, HD Graham, Elias Alexander, J Gilliard, J Lewis, James Hothroe[?], Nal[?] Lewis[?]

****

North Carolina State Archives
General Assembly Sessions Records
November 1786-January 1787, Box #4
Bill for Raising Troops for Davidson County

Petition of the Inhabitants of Davidson County
In the House of Commons Novr. 1786 read & Referred
To the Grand Committee on State Papers
By Order, J Hart, Clk
Senate Novr. 29, 1786, read & referred to House of Commons
By Order, J Haywood Clk

Referred to Indian Affairs Commt.
Polk, Maclain, **[Faded]**, Mr Blount

To the Honorable the General Assembly of North Carolina, The Petition of the Inhabitants of Davidson County -- humbly Sheweth

Whereas your Petitioners from their very great and remote distance to any immediate relief or assistance from Government in case of invasions from our natural Enemy the Indians by whom we are almost Surrounded is Such, that it **[Faded]** the **[Faded]** and properties of your Petitioners so precarious & dangerous a State that, unless some speedy assistance from Government can be had we cannot think of living any longer in so hazardous a Situation.
In the first place we beg leave to inform you that our Militia does not consist of more than Six hundred & fifty Men, and that those are settled for upwards of one hundred miles in long which renders us altogether useless in the protection of each other.

General Assembly Sessions
1777 - 1789

We further beg leave to inform you that we are under apprehensions of danger from the Chickasaw Indians for a supposed incroachment on their Lands lying on the South side of the Tenesee River, and as far down the Missisippi River at the Chickasaw Bluff; which Lands have been sold by the State to sundry Individuals, and are now about to Survey by Surveyors by you appointed.

These Indians have ever held this Country and the United States in the highest estimation, but their veneration for us will, cease soon as they perceive their Trees to have been chopp'd, turn to an implacable hatred, and nothing but the blood of innocent inhabitants of this Country will [Faded] their Savage barbarity. We therefore pray that other peace may be made with them, so as to permit Surveyors there to do business, or that you would Enact a Law that none should be permitted to Survey any of the Lands entered in the State entry Office, and thereby free us from any fears from that quarter.

Firther, the late murders committed by Creeks and Celabash Indians in this Country is too certain a proof of what we may expect so soon as Peace may be made with the Georgians and Kentuckians; those places & People being [Torn] times Superior in number to this Country.

Our frontier Settlements are all forced into the interior and there forted; Our Rivers Whereby we may expect both emigration and commerce are blocked up; boats have been Seized & plundered and the Boatman Killed. The pass's to our Country stopped, unless forces by [Torn] together with the almost dayly murdering our Wives and Children calls aloud on You the Guardians of our Lives liberties and property to interfere and provide for our safety.

We beg leave to remind you of our steady and uniform adherence to the Government of this State, when our Neighbours the People of Holsteen withdrew their allegiance, and by whom we were offered [Torn] [Torn] of protection [Faded] we would join [Torn] but we then and now do declare, that nothing can wrest from our Minds that duty & allegiance we owe to Legislative authority.

Your Petitioners have ever held Allegiance and protection reciprocal, and therefore hope from our Candid and impartial representation of Facts that you will take this our Situation under deliberation, and adopt such measures for our defence as you in Your Wisdom shall think most Meet.

****

General Assembly Sessions
1777 - 1789

****

North Carolina State Archives
General Assembly Sessions Records
November 1786-January 1787, Box #5
Senate Bills

Peto. From Inhabitants of Sullivan County
In H Com. 21 November 1786, Read

To the Honourable the General Assembly of No. Carolina

We your petitioners Inhabitants of Sullivan County humbly Sheweth, that we have ever been disposed to have True Allegiance To the State of No. Carolina being Well Attached to her Government & Revere her Constitution, therefore we pray You to Extend to us the benefits Of your Civill Laws & Continue us Under Your protection & Relieve us from those Intestine Broiles that are Aggitated Among us by Wicked & designing Men, Who are perverting Your Laws & Seducing Your Good Citizens to Withdraw Their Allegiance from Your Government as we view our Selves Unequal to the Task of Supporting A Separate Government & are Truly desirous of being Continued under Yours Untill Such Times that we may be seperated With Ease & Convenience With Your Assistance & Approbation--& Should You at any Time hereafter think it Expedient to make A Cession of Any part of Your Vacant western Territory for the payment of the National Debt or Other Imposts, Agreeable to the Requisitions of Congress, We pray you to Continue Your Sovereignty & Jurisdiction over us Untill Such Times that we May be by our Virtue, Wisdom, Experience, Numbers & Wealth Inabled to Conduct the **[Smudged]** of Government, With Credit & Convenience to our Selves, to the honour of the Parent State who gave their assent to Our Seperation, Added Strength to the Union & gave ease to her people; we also pray You to Take into Consideration the Indigence of our present Circumstances, & render to us Every Ease & Indulgence that you in your Wisdom & goodness May think Consistant with the Wellfare & Interest of Your good Citizens In general--& as Sensitive Measures have been Used With those Who have Abused Your powers & Usurped Your Authority, We hope You Will with the Same Spirit of Unanimity Consider the grievances of those Who Ever Strove to Support them--as our Inclinations [?] us to Consult the wellfare of our Country & will Engage us to defend our Rights by a Cheerfull & Steady Obedience to Government & as the Wellfare &

General Assembly Sessions
1777 - 1789

happiness of the Citizens depends on the Wisdom & goodness of government we cannot doubt Your Prudence & zeale to promote them--We also humbly Conceive that when the precepts & powers of Government are Abused her Sovereignty & Jurisdiction discarded her publick Credit Must Sink, & the Private Interest of the Citizens can Share No [Smudged] fate, therefore that peace & Tranquillity may be restored, Publick Credit & Private Interest Revive, We pray you to Inforce Your Laws, & exert the powers of Government, With a feeleing sense of our Sufferings, We Supplicate You to Whome the powers of Government are given & beg Your Paternal Intervention--& Whereas Numbers Among us look upon themselves to be Considerably Injured by the [?] & Injudicious proceedings of the Nominal Courts of the Supposed State of Franklin, many Suites of Law have Commenced & Judgment awarded Against [Torn] & Unlawfully sold to the Greate Injuries of Many Your Good Citizens, We therefore pray You to Extricate us from Every Species [Torn] used Against us; as we have [Smudged] of Society bound our Selves to the [Smudged] of Your Laws, [Faded] we expect to be protected in our Rights; We also beg leave to Recommend to Your Mature Consideration the Vast Extent of the County of Sullivan, Which Must Undoubtly Render Many Inconveniences to the Inhabitants thereof, & for our Ease & Convenience Divide Sd. Counties into Two Separate & distinct Counties as follows (To Witt) Beginning Where the Boundary Line Between the Common Wealth of Virginia & the State of No. Carolina Crosses the North Fork of Holestons River, thence down Sd. Fork to its Junction With the Main Holeston, thence Cross Sd. River Due South to the Topp of Bayes Mountain, thence Along the Topp Sd. Mountain & on the Topp of the dividing Ridge that divides the Waters of French Broad River & Holestons River to French Broad River thence down Sd. French Broad to its Junction with Holeston, thence down Holeston to its Junction With the River Tinisee & thence down the same to the Suck Whare Sd. River Runs through Cumberland Mountain, thence along the Topp of the Mountain to the Afforesaid Boundary Line & thence Along the same to the Begn. & We Your petitioners as In duty Bound Shall ever pray &c.

James Thompson, Stephen Thompson, Elisha Debusk, William Courtney Sr., Willm. Courtney Jr., Wm. Hambleton, Jams. Hambleton, John Carwilies, Wm. Lain, Jos. Pervin, Joseph Cloud, John Crate, Jerem. Cloud, Jasen Cloud, Benjn. Cloud, Christ. Boling, Wm. Boling, Abraham Buie, Thomas Buie, Saml. Smith Sr., Benoni Puriman, Joseph Rogers, Willm Hankins[Hawkins?], Alexr. Donelson, John Crate, Joseph Coale, John

General Assembly Sessions
1777 - 1789

Blackwell, David Blackwell, Wm Davis, John Davis, Jams Davis, Thomas Keff, David Ray, [?] Robbinson, James Daugherty[?], [?] Crabb, Thoms Williams, Zeekel Wray, Bartlett Sims, William Morriss, John Turner, Thos. Midkeff, James Nicholas, Francis Nicholas, Pleasant Duke, Jas. Daniel, Francis Daniel, John Rice, Benjamin Norvell, Joseph Walling, Rolley Dotson, Hutson Johnson, Batlet Sims, William Losson, George Roberds, Lazarus Dotson, Daniel Davis, Andrew Craige, Tollever Dotson, John Asher, Samuel Bayne[?], Jams Manoco[?], Larkin We[Torn], [Faded] Williams, Wm. Nash, John Sims, Ritchard Green Sr., Ritchard Green Jr., Isaac Green, Adam Green, Benjamin Green, Wm. Walden son of Joseph, Elisha Walden, John Walden, Wm. Walden son of Thos., Thomas Walden, John Grubs, John Ray, Henry Rice Sr., Demsey Ward, William Watson, John Golden, Letty[?] Johnson, George Brooks, Reuben Webster, Archer Ficken, John Criner Jr., John Criner Sr., Jos. Criner, Robert Johnson, John McBrune[?], Thos. McBrune, Mark Chambers, Jas Armstrong, Wm Rice, John Rice, John Rice Jr., John Walin, George Heard, Andrew Ingrins, Wm Ingrine, Thomas Murrel, Willm Reed, Wm Armstrong, Wm Armstrong Sr., Robert Stuart, Thomas Stuart, Stokely Donelson, John Rice, Jr., Hutson Rice, John Rice Sr., Wm. Stamps, James Stamps, Robert Staplefield, Hugh Forgey, Thomas Miser, Joseph Edmunds

[Editor's Note: The following petition is also from Sullivan County. It was attached to the above petition. Most of the body of the petition is missing. The names in the petition appear to be intact, but many are faded and unreadable . The rest of the petition may be missing, or may have been misplaced.]

Peto. From Inhabitants of Sullivan County

Thence along the Top of Bays Mountain to the Chimney Top thence a Strait Line to Beens Ford on Watauga Thence up Sd. River to the Iron Mountain thence along the Mountain to the Virginia Line thence Down Sd. Boundary Line to the Beginning--and We Your Petitioners as in Duty Bound shall ever Pray &c.

Jesse Vawter, James Underwood, Philemon Vawter, Daniel Lambert, Jojerin M[?]inse, Jacob M[?]inse, Jacob Thomas, Jno. Sharp, Andrew White, Robert C[?]an, Jacob Gross[?], Gar[?] Gross, Robert Stuart, Thos. Stuart, William McCormick, John Wood, Jacob Mas[?], George Litle, Harter Hirech, Robert Monroe, Frederick Kechlere, John Hommell,

General Assembly Sessions
1777 - 1789

Johnathan Hossell, Thomas Beeler, John Peters, Adam Potter, John Petere, Moses Webb, Michael [?], Theophilus Tucker, James Pemberton, Elzaph[?] Jackson, William Pemberton, Jacob Jackson, John Pemberton, John Gorsuch, Thos. Morrell, Benjamin Webb, Thomas Smalling, James Webb, Lenard Sweet, Wm. Sweet, Wm Scott, Solomin Smaling, Abraham McLelon, John White[?]aff, Joseph Cole Jr., John Miner, David Webb, Joseph Cole, David Lewis, Jno Cole, Solomon Cole, Alisha Cole, Isaac Hicks, Benjamin Webb, Nathan Lewis, Andrew Crockett, Evan Shelby, John Keewood, Stephen Majors, Will. Blevins, John Cas[?], James Hughs, David Hughs, Thomas Hughs, William Hughs, Elijah Cross, William Cross, Ambrose Legg, Griller Cross, Sollomon Cole, Matthew Cole, George Malone, Jehu Hiks, Jonathan [**Faded**], John Webb, George [**Torn**], John McLen, Ritchard Cro[?], Michael Malone, John Malone, Charles Phylips, Isaac Hicks, David Webb, George Webb, George Webb, Asael Cross, Thomas B[**Torn**], Thomas Mos[**Torn**], Samuel Bere[**Torn**], Stephen Hicks, Jaremiah Ha[**Torn**], John Riley, Matthew Plumbly, St[?] Colcock.

****

North Carolina State Archives
General assembly Sessions Records
November 1786-January 1787, Box #5
Senate Bills

To the Honourable the General Assembly of the State of North Carolina
This Petition Humbly Sheweth that your petitioners Inhabitants of the County of Washington sensible of the Great Advantage arising from Every Citizen having an Equal Advantage in the Administration of publick Truste &c and Whereas by the Divition of Washington County into the Counties of Washington and Green the Town Jonesborough where the Courts of Washington for some time past been held is not upon a Direct West Line more than Eight Miles from the Green line which Renders it Very Inconvenient for the Eastern part of the County and the Buildings in the Said Town is at Present held & Occupied as Private property We therefore your petitioners Humbly Request Your Honourable body that you would appoint Commitioners in Order to fix up some Convenient place in the said County for Erecting Publick Buildings for holding of Courts that the Inhabitants of Said County may Reap as Equal an Advantage as their

General Assembly Sessions
1777 - 1789

Local Situation will Admit & your petitioners as in Duty Bound Shall Ever Pray &c

Andrew Taylor Sr., Andrew Taylor Jr., Robert Taylor, Mathew Taylor, Robt. Lusk, Jonathan Tipton, John Campbell, Daniel Moore, Ab[?] Moore, John Hyder, Michael Hyder Jr., Michael Hyder, John Moore Jr., William Foran, William English, John Peoples, Issack Tabour, Robert English, Nathenal Tabour, Henry English, Thomas Brattan, William Daves, Daniel Nichols, Charels Taylor, Solemon Smallin, Samuel Smallin, Isaac Taylor, Jacob Cunningham, Amos Perrimore, James Edon, Austin Edon, Richard Kite, Isaac Kight, John Mattock, John Ceson[?], David Mattock, Solomon[?] Campbell, Issack S. Campbell, Thomas Anderson, J[?] Dugger, John Anderson, Jeremiah Campbell, Peter Parkison, Jo Los[?], Nathan Davis, William Dunkin[**Lunkin?**], Zakeriah Campbell, John Anderson Jr., John Smith, James Jones, Jacob Smith, George Parkeson, Joshua Walker, Josiah Cleark, Isaac Tipton, William Peoples, Risdon Robison, Jacob Wagonner, Thomas Blackwell, Abraham Cooper, Joseph Tipton, John Tipton, William Tipton, Jacob Beyler, John Brown, James Ayres[?], Joseph Hederck, Isaac Lin[?], Howell Ivey, Dawson[?] Rockhold, Jacob Hederck, Lenard Bou[?], Christian Peters, Joell Ivey, George Grear, Isaac Tipton, Jacob Hedrik, Richard Cockes, David McNab[?], Jonathan Pugh, Cottrel Bealey, Jacob Boylor Jr., Abrahan Boyler, Thomas Carder, Elijah Cooper, John Mcentus, Jasper Mcentus, Wm Hammonds, Peter Hammonds, John [**Smudged.**]

****

North Carolina State Archives
General Assembly Sessions Records
November, 1786-January, 1787, Box #1

No. 310
Act of Congress appointing James White esqr.
Superintendant of Indian Affairs
6 Octo. 1786

By

The United States in Congress

General Assembly Sessions
1777 - 1789

assembled   Octr. 6th, 1786

Resolved that Congress now proceed to the election of a Superintendant for the southern district, agreeably to the ordinance for the regulation of Indian Affairs: And that he be directed immediately to proceed to the States of North Carolina, South Carolina, and Georgia, for the purposes mentioned in the said ordinance -Congress proceeded to an election and the ballots being taken-

Mr. James White of North Carolina was appointed.

Chas. Thomson[?]

****

North Carolina State Archives
General Assembly Sessions Records
November, 1786-January, 1787, Box #1
File: Grand Committee & Sub-Committee on Indian Affairs

Nov 20, 1786
List of Papers contained in file No. 4

                         Indian Treaties

No.   161 - a Letter from Mr. Blount
        162 - do from Wm Blount to Comrs. See his Journal pas 19
        163 - do ------do----------do-----   see do--------------   21
        164 - Mr. Blounts protest---------   see do--------------   23
        165 - Treaty with the Cherokees--- see do--------------   55
        166 - Copy Mr. Blounts Letter to the Comrs.-----------   62
        167 - Mr. Blounts protest against Chicasaw Treaty----- 62
        168 - Copy of third Article of Chicasaw Treaty--------   60
        169 - Letter from Mr. Blount
        170 - Extract of Col. Vanderhorst Letter to Mr. Blount
        171 - do-----------do-------------   do-----to----do
        172 - do-----------do-------------   do-----to----do
        173 - Copy of a Letter from Majr. Bowie--to----do
        174 - Account Sale of Indian Goods.

General Assembly Sessions
1777 - 1789

175 - Instructions to Mr. Ogg
176 - Mr. Blounts Letter to Govr. Moultrie
177 - Disposition of the Rum

    See Council Journal Page 47, 48, 49, & 50
    See the Governors Letter to the Delegatee in
    Congress, in Letter Book No. 72.

202 - Letter from Mr. Bloodworth
224 - Letter from Mr. White
196 - Letter fro the Secretary of Congress
197 & 198 - Treaties with the Shawanoes & Cherokees
199 & 200 - do with the Chicasaws & Choctaws
209 - Letter from Joseph Martin
210 - Talk delivered by the Old Corn Tassle
262 - Ordinance for Regulation of Indian Affairs
306 - Letter from Colo. Outlaw
307 - Indian Treaty
309 - Letter from the Secretary of Congress
310 - Appointment of Mr. White Superintendant
311 - directions to the Superintendant
Letter from the Secretary of Congress
Act of Congress for Augmenting the Troops
Intelligence respecting Indians

No. 4
List of Papers
respecting Indian Treaties

The Committee appointed to report on these papers on M. Polk, Mr. Maclaine, Mr. Blount, Mr. McKenzie - you will please to observe that some of the papers mentioned in this list have been taken out & referred to other Committees. Mr. [?]

****

North Carolina State Archives
General Assembly Sessions Records
November, 1786-January, 1787, Box #1
File: Grand Committee & Sub-Committee on Indian Affairs

General Assembly Sessions
1777 - 1789

H.C. JAN. 6, 1787

Your Committee to whom was referred sundry Papers respecting Indian Treaties and Indian Affairs

Beg leave to report
That they have examined with Attention the Papers to them refer'd and they find that by the Treaties entered into between the Commissioners appointed by the United States to treat with the Southern Indians and the Cherokee & Chickasaw Indians at Hopewell on the Tenesee. The Commissioners of the United States have allotted to the said Indians certain Lands as their Hunting Grounds which are obviously within the Jurisdiction of this state being North of the Boundary Established by Law between the Citizens and Indians, And a great part of which is for a valuable consideration sold to our Citizens some of whom are now actually Living thereon. Your Committee observe that the Commissioners having only allotted these Lands to the Indians as their Hunting Ground the treaty doth not [?] seem [?] annull the Title of those who hold under our Laws, but have [?] it in a manner different from the Intentions of the Legislature and which does in effect suppose a right in the United States to interfere with our Legislative Rights which is inadmissable.

Your Committee thereupon recommend that the Delegates of this State in Congress be instructed to State our rights to the Lands in Question to the United States of America in Congress Assembled to obtain a disavowal of the Treaties so far as they affect the same, and if the same should be persisted in which your Committee cannot Suppose from the known rectitude and Wisdom of Congress that finally they formally protest against the same.

Your Committee further Reports

That The Honourable William Blount was appointed by the Executive in Pursuance of the notification from the Commissioners from the United States founded on a Resolution of Congress an Agent on the part of the State to be Present with the Commissioners: And that he has wisely Protested against the said Treaties so far as they affect us. And further that he was appointed to hold a Treaty with the Cherokee Indians and did attend at the meeting of the Commissioners and Indians and according to the direction of the Governor and Council he shiped to the care of A. Nanderhorst in Charleston the Goods [?] purchased for that Purpose. That from unavoidable delays in Procuring Waggons Colo.

General Assembly Sessions
1777 - 1789

Nanderhorst could not send forward the Goods to the place of their destination until the Commissioners of the United States had Commenced their Negociation with the Indians, the Tenor of which inspired the Indians with an Idea of such [?] advantages that the Agent could not Prevail on them to Treat on Terms admissable by the State, and was therefore necessitated to sell the Goods for the most that could be obtained which is as follows.

To Bryan Ward one third payable on the first day of April 1786 and the other 2/3 S on the 1st day of April 1787 in Deerskins Fur and Tobacco. 1,333.34 Pounds

To George Ogg for Clag [?] & Co. at their Franklin Store kept by said Geo. Ogg.   39.15.9

To William Blount-----------------------------145.9.9
                    Sterling 1518.9 Pounds

And the rum procured for holding a Treaty disposed of as follows
To Bryan Ward 1 Hhd. @ 1/4 dollrs p Gallon
To George Ogg 1 Hhd. @ 1/4 dollrs p Gallon
3 Hhds. sent to Washington to IG & Tho. Blount
1 Hhd. lost at Charleston by heads bursting
putting it into the Waggon as Appears by
Colo. Nanderhorst's Letter

  That the first payment being Deerskins an article liable to damage if not early sent to Market was ordered to be shiped to Philadelphia to Stuart and Barr, and the after payment is subject to the order of the General Assembly. That on the first payment four thousand deerskins or thereabout were received by Mr. George Ogg as per Agreement, and in all Probability shiped to Philadelphia.

Your Committee further Report

  That it is evident, the Cherokee Indians are much dissatisfied with our disposition of the Lands claimed by them within our state and that probably this dissatisfaction may arise from our not having given what they Supposed an equivalent for their Claim: And as our last advices from Congress assure us that the Northern Indians will soon be engaged in a

General Assembly Sessions
1777 - 1789

War with us, it may be prudent to use such means as are in our power to remove the dissatisfaction in question in as speedy and amicable a manner as is practicable, Whereupon Your Committee recommend that Troops be immediately raised and stations in Davidson County to prevent the Indian from taking any Hostile resolution, in aid of the Northern Tribes, and that our Delegates in Congress be instructed to lay before the United States of America in Congress assembled the necessity of this Measure, and to obtain leave to continue the same in service while the necessity exists. And further to establish a good understanding between the Citizens and Indians. That the [?] received on the first aforementioned payment be sold at Philadelphia for suitable Goods to be given to the Indians to extinguish their Claim as soon as Practicable, and that our Superintendent of Indian Affairs, be directed to inform them of this benevolent intention of the Legislature.

And we further recommend that the future payments to be made by Mr. Ward be disposed of in a similar manner and distributed amongst the Chickasaw Indians for a relinquishment of their Claim to the Lands lying between the Tennesee and Missisippee, a great part of which is sold to our Citizens

As a further reason why your committee are of Opinion that the said Indians treaties are injurious to the citizens with the bounds adjacent the Indians your Committee refer to the act of Cession to the United States by which alone Congress can pretend any claim to territory within the states [?] one of the conditions in which is that all grants of land theretofore made to any citizen or citizens or any entries made should have the same force and effect as if the Cession had not been made whereas the citizens to whom grants were made before the Cession aforesaid have been left to the mercy of the Indians so that admitting the cession to be valid Congress have not in this instance [?] formed that conditions of the said act

Report Consideration 1787 Indian Affairs
In the House of Commons 6 January 1787 A. Maclaine Ck
read and Concurred with as amended
By Order
  J. Hunt Clk   John B. Ashe. S.C.
In Senate 6 Jany 1787
              read and Concurred with

****

General Assembly Sessions
1777 - 1789

North Carolina State Archives
General Assembly Sessions Records
November-December, 1787, Box #1

Brothers this is to acquaint you of the Circumstance of this Country the Late news from the Creeks which was asserted and the talk Deliverd to Capt. Devenport which was Killd the next Day by them the news from the Creeks is that the head Chiefs of all the nation has held a Counsil of war and is fully Concluded upon throughout the whole nation without Exceptions to Do what mischief they Can to the inhabitance and frontiers as soon as Green Corn Busk is over - and we have Receivd your talk Expecting you would use us as Brothers and not to fail to supply us with Ammonition to keep Ready for any invation that shall happen - the Creeks has Come and Killd our white people before our Eyes and what Can you Expect us to do as we have nothing but Letters passing and no Ammonition to Defend ourselves with Butt [**Faded**] [**Faded**] you by the hand and [**Faded**] and now there is Blood Spilled in our Land but nevertheless I hold you fast by the hand and we Expect our Enemies upon us and without you put something in our hands to Defend ourselves which we shall be made ashamd and not appear Like men it is not for fear of them but it is for want of something to Defend ourselves with I dont want to have all my Warriors killd Up and no Chance to defend myself I have spoke a great Deal with you and this is near the Last week I hope you will not fail to supply us with ammonition as we Expect our Enemies Upon us on both sides and if you will not Listen to our talk we must suffer - I hope you will not see us [?] assistance we must all Die Like old Women When we held the English by the hand in time of war they always sent us ammonition Even at the wrisk of their Lives - and now we hold you by the hand we hope you will Contrive some way to supply us as they used to Do if you hear our talk and will furnish us with ammonitions by any means and Can send us word we will go with horses to the Bluffs to Receive it as we think it the safest way you Can send it to us and if in Case you Send any send it in Bags or Quarter Caskes so that it will be Ready for packing at the shortest notice being given to us being given to us when it Comes - and if any person has goods to sell and will bring them down to Sell for skins or any thing we have they will be very Exceptable from Cumberland Caintucky or Else where - and as we are Red people we wish to have some paint as when we go to war and get Killd we may Die Like Red people and hope you will send us some - we have been

General Assembly Sessions
1777 - 1789

Disputing with the Creeks a Long time and have not Settled it yet have now got the ill will of them more on account of holding you by the hand and if we had ammonition and was to fall on them and Distress them they would become good people and let it Come to the worst we Can only make a peace for a while in order to get a good Chance to breake upon them again for some to make peace and others Stand out and them that makes peace is only a Cloke for the rest till they Can get a good Chance to Strike them again I have nothing more to say at this time only we must Scuffle along as well as we Can and are now thinking about Building a fort to Defend ourselves in from our Enemies and when you send Down the ammonition you must Come Strong handed as we allow it will be Dangerous if you would send a Swivel along with them it might be of great service to them on the River and to us afterwards -- I am your Brother and Friend
Long Town   Mountain Leader Chicasaw Nation July 7th 1787

****

North Carolina State Archives
General Assembly Sessions Records
November-December, 1787, Box #1

Dear Sir/ friends and brothers } 16th July 1787
        New Town
This day god has ordered it so that I Should gave you a Sinceare Answer to your good talk in the presence of all head men and Warriors of my Nation we Sinceerly Wish peace and friendship to Subsist Betwixt us and you my Elder brothers, brothers, god I hope Will gave both of us a heart of Compation towards each other and brighten the Chaine of friendship So that it Neaver Shall [?] any more and not Let any foolish men Spoyle our good talkes.

brothers you Sent me a Longer stran of beads in **[Faded]** to your talke than the one I sent to you Which gave the greatest satisfaction to all our Nation than Ever any thing Could have don it shoed your good will to us Now brother I tell you the Sinceare trooth there is three Very Large towns of the Creek Nation has declared an Open War against your Cuntrey and tree hundred Now at the time Camped on Elke River and goes in Small Parteys to your Settlements Brothers you gave me to understand that no Small

General Assembly Sessions
1777 - 1789

matter Should Spoyl our friendship for which Reason I thinke no more of what has hapened I bury the dead So deepe that We Shall Come no more in Remembrance but brother Lett us With the help of the great being above take Care of the Living of our Women and Children -- from us Tokenliskey and Morter, Little turkey and dragging Canoe} brothers Wee heare in publick meating in presents of all the Representives of our difrent towns doe freely and sincearly Joyne ourselves with one heart and one mind With our Two old Chiefs for to Suporte this good talke and to take up the harmony of peace and Brotherly Love that is Subsisting betwixt us Wee do sincearly determin to do our best indeavors that all hostilitys Shall Sease on our Side brothers our Chiefs mentioned to you that there are those towns of the Creeks declared War against you Wee do not knoe when the War on peace With you there is aboute 300 Now at this time Lying on Elke River [?]idling Loo down and they goes in Small Parteys to your Settlements there has Some has indeavoured to go through our towns but Wee have [Faded] Shall Stop all Wee see but there is Some that Steals through in the Night that Wee knoes nothing of till wee find our Canoes that they Crose the River in you may depend upon us wee Will gave you all the intelagence possable wee Can but at this Wee do not thinke it Safe to Send these to you the Nigh[t] Way Which Wee are Very Sorry for brothers our Sinceare Wishes is for peace and in Conformation [?] Shall wee do send you a national Belt of Wampam the names of the head men and Warriors at this great meeting at New town.

two head Chiefs } Tokenlisky and Morter

Little Turkey the draging Canoe and Wilskunney from Chote Clanose from high wasse Taquatche from lookout Mountain the duke of Chatenoga Chaldo of Eastenora Tonoya of the Spring Escholato of Niccoracke ------ and Tossels talke.

      Twelve prinsable Chiefs and Warriors to Colo. Jas. Roberson of Cumberland.

****

North Carolina State Archives
General Assembly Sessions Records
November-December, 1787, Box #1

                  Chickasaw Nation Septr. the 6th 1787

Sir,

General Assembly Sessions
1777 - 1789

      This is to inform you that the Hair Lip King & head men of this Nation Desires that you will not Let your People be Settling or moving on any Lands this way that is to say any more than was allowed at the meeting with the Red King of this nation who is now been Dead some time past you have Seen but one of our head men that is Pyomingo or the Mountain Leader who has promised you Land in many places however this to Desire that you may not think any thing of them promises as none of the Rest of the head men will hear to any thing of that kind but desires you to Set Still in the bounds that was first Agreed on, therefore I hope you will not think this any thing but a friendly warning from us that you may not be Scatter'd Up & Down the Country you Live in as you must Certainly Know the Danger you are in by being Scatterd, not only of the Creeks but many Other nations that are Daly Killing you However this nation never desires any thing but peace & friendship with you & to be at a good Understanding with you & all nations, is our real Desire. We hope that you may not Depend on Supplying this Nation any more with Goods as the trade is now opened at Mobile which is much nearer & Cheaper than you Can possibly Supply Therefore if you know of any Coming this way with goods your best way is to prevent them that they may not Come hear to be Left as the mountain Leader has Left Capt. Bushears to himself & Gone to war against the Hossews What has been Said on the other Side of this Leaf is by the King of this Nation now the Beloved man Speaks I must Imagine that Pyomingo must have been a Little in Drink when he made you all them promises of Lands and gave Such Strong invitations to bring your people to this Nation, for my part I never was Desirous of Settling near where my Brothers the white people had Stocks of Creatures or hunting near them this is therefore my Brothers to Desire you hereafter not to think of making plantations any nearer than you are none to our hunting Grounds as it is our whole Dependance for to ourselves & families and as we are neighbors & our Houses near Each other, I write you this my Brother to Let you know that we are Desirous of being good neighbors & not encroach on Each other, & I must inform you that it is dangerous for your people to be Coming here Backward & forward as the Creeks are often here & them & you are at war, you are our Brothers they are Likewise so that I would not wish to See you or they hurted in this nation this is the talk & Desire of the whole nation, tho only we two writes to you its in behalf of all & hopes after you Receive this & Read it you'll Send the talk to the falls and Kentucky that all your head men may See it & hear it & after you have all Read it & heard it our Desire is that you will Send us an answer we are Brothers your Friends

General Assembly Sessions
1777 - 1789

Hair Lip King, Macklassawtuskau, Tuskau Potapo, Wm. Glover, Fanny Mingo

****

North Carolina State Archives
General Assembly Sessions Records
November, 1786-January, 1787, Box #1

[Editor's Note: It is not known from the records who wrote this letter. It is unsigned.]

List of Kill'd & wounded
Thomas Knowling Kill'd at Bartons
John Maloogen wounded at Do.
Stewart Kill'd at Big sink spring
Jesse Martin & son Do. at Do.
Jeans Kill'd at Big Baron River
a stranger wounded at the Roaring Spring on Monday last.
a young Man wounded at Bledsoes Station, & several others fired upon but not hurt.
Thos. Hickman & two men ware out a Surveying upon Duck River & ware drove in.
This has been done since I came here

Novr. 10th 1787

****

North Carolina State Archives
General Assembly Sessions Records
November - December, 1787, Box #1
Joint Papers

By
The United States in Congress Assembled
October 26th, 1787
On a report of a Committee consisting of Mr. Kean, Mr. Clarke and Mr. Grag for to whom was referred a Motion of Mr. H: Lee with directions to

General Assembly Sessions
1777 - 1789

report Instructions for holding treaties with the Northern and Southern Indians--

Resolved that the Executive or Legislature if they be in Session in the States of North Carolina, South Carolina and Georgia be and they are hereby authorised to appoint each of them one Commissioner, who shall in conjunction with the Superintendant of Indian Affairs for the southern department, or in his absence, by themselves negotiate a treaty for the establishing peace between the United States and the tribes of Indians in the southern department: And any two of the Commissioners to be appointed as aforesaid in conjunction with the Superintendant, or in case of the absence of the Superintendant, any two of the said Commissioners, agreeing, their decision shall be final & conclusive: And that the said Commissioners shall each be allowed five dollars a day for the time they shall be employed in that business in full for their services and expences, exclusive of their expences at the place or places where the treaties shall be held.

That the sum of five thousand dollars, being a part of the sum appropriated by the resolution of the twelfth of the present month for holding Indian Treaties in addition to the goods in the hands of the former commissioners for holding a treaty with the Southern Indians be applied to holding the said treaty at such time & such places as shall be appointed by the Superintendant of Indian Affairs for the Southern department in conjunction with the executive of the State of North Carolina for the treaty with the Cherokees, and with the executive of Georgia for that with the Creek Nation; or in case of the absence of the Superintendant, then the time and place to be appointed by the Executive of each State in manner aforesaid. The aforesaid Sum to be in full for all charges of whatsoever nature they may be relative to the said treaty, including the pay of the Commissioners and Militia: And that the States of North Carolina, South Carolina and Georgia be called on to furnish the aforesaid sum in equal proportions, to be credited on requisitions of Congress

That the Commissioners aforesaid be and they hereby are authorised to apply to the States of North Carolina, South Carolina and Georgia for any number of men nor exceeding one hundred of their Militia for the purpose of guarding & protecting the Stores and goods necessary for carrying the said treaty
Cha Thomson [?]

General Assembly Sessions
1777 - 1789

By
The United States in Congress assembled
October 26th, 1787

Instructions to the Commissioners for Negotiating a Treaty with the tribes of Indians in the Southern department, for the purpose of establishing peace between the United States and the said Tribes.

Gentlemen,

Several Circumstances rendering it probable that Hostilities may have commenced, or are on the Eve of Commencing between the State of North Carolina and the Cherokee Nation of Indians, and between the State of Georgia and the Creek Nation of Indians -- you are to use every endeavour to restore peace and harmony between the said States and the said Nations on terms of Justice and humanity.

The great Source of Contention between the said States and the Indian tribes being boundaries -- you will carefully enquire into, and ascertain the boundaries claimed by the respective States, and altho' Congress are of opinion that they might constitutionally fix the bounds between any State and an Independent Tribe of Indians, yet unwilling to have a difference subsist between the general Government and that of the Individual States, they wish you so to conduct the matter that the States may not conceive their Legislative Rights in any manner infringed, taking care at the same time, that whatever bounds are agreed upon they may be described in such terms as shall not be liable to miscontruetion and misrepresentation -- but may be made Clear to the Conceptions of the Indians as well as Whites.

The present treaty having for its principal object the restoration of peace -- No Cession of land is to be demanded of the Indian Tribes.

You will use the utmost Care to ascertain who are the leading men among the Several Tribes -- the real headmen and warriors -- there you will spare no pains to attach to the interest of the United States -- by removing as far as may be all causes of future Contention or quarrels -- by kind treatment and assurances of protection -- by presents of a permanent Nature -- and by using every endeavour to conciliate the affections of the white people inhabiting the frontiers towards them.

You will encourage the Indians to give Notice to the Superintendant of Indian Affairs of any designs that may be formed by any Neighbouring Indian Tribe, or by any person whatever against the peace of the United States.

General Assembly Sessions
1777 - 1789

You will insist that all prisoners of whatever age, Sex or complexion be delivered up, and that all fugitive Slaves belonging to the Citizens of the United States be restored.
Cha. Thomson sec[?]

****

North Carolina State Archives
General Assembly Sessions Records
November-December, 1787, Box #1
Joint Papers

Acct. Sale of Deerskins
Shipped from Georgia
By order W. Blount esqr.

By John Ramsay
New York 10th May, 1787

Sales and returns 4 Hhds Deer Skins paid by Bryan Ward for ap of Goods purchased of Col William Blount Commissioner of Indian Treaties for State of No. Carolina, May 10th 1787

3 Hhds Sold by John Ramsay of New York   £187 " 9 " 2

Return 7 Chests Hyson   }
[?] in hands of H. Tooner   }
esqr. of Wilmington   }

June 8th
1 Hhd Sold by ditto   £44. 10
Returns 12 ps Linnen Viz.
4 Ps.   97 yds   2/10   13.14.10
4 Ps.   98   3/   14.14
4 Ps.   99   3/2   15.13.6
                    £44.2.4
in hands of W.A. Neale at New Bern

General Assembly Sessions
1777 - 1789

Sales of Three Hhds Deer Skins shipt by Mr. Robert Montfert in the Sloop Julia Capt. Latham from Savannah On Acct of the State of North Carolina Pr Order of William Blount Esqr.

1 Hhd 400 skins ind. Drest	993	
Tare	155 838 @ 22d	£76.16.4
1 Hhd 230 skins inhair Nett	677 @ 18d	50.15.6
58 Ind drest	121 @ 22d	11.1.10
1 Hhd 252 skins inhair	841 @ 18d	63.1.6
Charges Viz		£201.15.2
Cash pd Fse. 3d Cash	£3.12	
Cast[?] Cooperge & Weigh Master	12.3	
Comm'n & [?] 5p	10.1.9	14.6
Nett Sale		£187.9.2

New York 10th May 1787
Errors Excepted
John Ramsay

****

North Carolina State Archives
General Assembly Sessions Records
November-December, 1787, Box #1
Joint Standing Committees

State of North Carolina
Kinston, May 1787
Richard Caswell Esquire Governor and Commander in Chief in and over the said State.

To the Inhabitants of the Counties of Washington, Sullivan, Greene & Hawkins, Geetings
Friends & Fellow Citizens
I have received information that the former Contention between the Citizens of those Counties respecting the severing such Counties from this State and erecting them into a separate Free and Independent Government, hath been again revived notwithstanding the tenetive and Salutary Measures held out to them by the General Assembly in their last Session, and some have been so far Misled as openly and avowedly to Oppose the

General Assembly Sessions
1777 - 1789

due operation and executor of the Laws of the State Menacing and threatening such as should adhere to the same [Faded] violence, and some Outraged on such Occasions, have been actually Committed whereby Sundry of the Good Citizens of the said Counties have been induced to Signify to Government their Apprehensions of being obliged to have recourse to Arms in order to support the Laws and Constitution of this State. And notwithstanding the conduct and Behaviour of some of the refractory among might Justify such a Measure, Yet I am willing to hope that upon reflection and due consideration of the dreadfull consequences which must ensue in case of the Shedding of Blood among yourselves, a momemts thought must evince the necessity of Mutual Friendship and the Test of Brotherly love being strongly cemented among you, You have or shortly will have, if my information is well Grounded enemies to deal with **[This line completely Faded]**
Your whole force may become necessary to be exerted agt. The Common enemy, as'tis more than probable they may be assisted by the Subjects of some Foreign power, if not Publicly, they will furnish Arms & Amunition privately to the Indian Tribes, and will be made use of against you and when your neighbours are so Supported, and Assisted by the Northern & Southern Indians, if you should be so unhappy as to be divided among yourselves, what may you not then Apprehend? I dread the event.

  Let me entreat you to lay aside Yoyr Party disputes, they have been , as I conceive, and yet believe, will be if Continued, of very great disadvantage to your public as well as Private concerns, whilst those Disputes last, Government will want that energy which is necessary to Support her Laws and Civilize her Citizens, in place of which Anarchy and confusion will be too prevalent and of Course private Interest must suffer.

  It certainly would be sound Policy in you for other reasons to Unite, the General Assembly, have told you that whenever your Wealth and Numbers so much increase as to make a Seperation necessary they are willing the same shall take place upon Friendly & reciprocal Terms, is there an individual in your Country who does not look forward in expectation of such days Arriving? If that is the case, must not every thinking Man believe that this seperation will be soonest & most effectively obtained, by Unanimity, let that carry you to the quiet Submission to the Laws of No. Carolina, till your Numbers will Justify a General Application and then I have no doubt but the same may be obtained upon the principles held out by the Assembly, nay tis' my opinion that it may be obtained at an earlier day than some imagine, if Unanimity prevailed amongst you Altho this is an Official Letter, yet you will readily

General Assembly Sessions
1777 - 1789

see that it is Dictated by a Friendly and Pacific Mind, don't neglect my Advice on that account, if you do, you may repent it when tis' too late When the Blood of some of your dearest and worthiest Citizens may have been Spilt and your Country laid Waste in an Unatural and cruel Civil War and you Cannot Suppose, if such an event should take place, that Government will Supinely look on & See you Cuting each others throats without interfering and exerting her powers to reduce the disobedient.

 I will conclude by once more intreating You to consider the dreadful Calamities & Consequences of a Civil War, Humanity demands this of me, Your own good sense will Point out the propriety of it, At least let all Animosities and disputes Subside till the next Assembly, even let things remain as they are without pursuing Compulsory Measures until then and I flatter myself that Honorable body will be disposed to do what is Just and right and what Sound Policy may dictate.

 Given under my hand & Seal at Kinston
 The 31st day of May 1787
 Rd. Caswell

****

North Carolina State Archives
General Assembly Sessions Records
November, 1786-January, 1787, Box #1

To the Honorable the General Assembly of North Carolina
The underwritten Representatives of the County of Davidson and the County of Sumner beg leave to represent That the Inhabitants of the western Country are greatly distressed by a Constant War that is carried on against them by Parties of the Creeks and Cherokees & some of the Western Indians, that some of their horses are dailey carried off secretly or by force and their own Lives are in danger whenever they leave sight of a station or stockade, that in the course of the present Year thirty three of their fellow citizens have been Killed by those Indians a list of whose Names is hereto Annex'd and as many more have been wounded, that by original Letters or Talks which are herewith submitted to your consideration from the chiefs of the Chickasaw Nation it will appear that they also are jealous and uneasy lest Encroachments should be made on their hunting Grounds & that unless some assureance is given to them that these Lands shall not be touched there is much reason to believe that they will Shortly be as hostile as the Creeks or Cherokees, that these Counties

General Assembly Sessions
1777 - 1789

have been settled at great Expence and personal Danger to the underwritten & their Constituents that by Such Settlement the adjacent vacant Lands have greatly increased in Their Value whereby the Public have been enabled to sink a considerable Part of their domestic debt, that they and their Constituents have cheerfully endured the utmost difficulties in settling the western Country in full confidence that they should be enabled to send their Produce to market through the River which waters their Country they now have the Mortification not only to be excluded from that Channel of Commerce by a foreign Nation but the Indians are rendered more hostile through the Influence of that very Nation probably with a Vow to drive them from the Country as they claim the whole of the Soil. The underwritten now call upon the Justice and Humanity of the State to prevent any further Murders or Depredations on their Constituents or themselves, they claim that, Protection of Life and Property which is due to every Citizen and they beg leave to recommend as the most Safe and Most convenient Means of Relief that the General Assembly Would be pleased to adopt the Resolutions of Congress of the 26th of October last. This Relief they trust will not be refused especially as the United States are pleased to interest themselves on this Occasion and are willing to bear the Expence.

Anthony Bledsoe, Jas. Robertson, Robert Hayes, Robert Ewing, Jas. Sanders

The following are the names of Several persons Inhabitants of Davidson & Sumner Counties who have been Killed since the first day of January 1787 by the Indians, Cornelius Ridle, Eneas & James Thomas, Wm. Price & Mrs. Price, Mrs. Bowman, Wm. Bush, Major Wm. Hall and two sons Richard and James Hall, John Buckanan, Abner Bush, Dunham Mark Robertson, Josiah Renfro, Thomas Hickman, Calep Wallis, Thomas Ramsey, Mr. Staton, James Biswell, Wm. Smothers and a Frenchman, Thomas Nowlin, Wm. Hayes and five others in Company Samuel Lewis, William Colyears and three others Killed since the Representatives left home as they are informed by Letters.

****

North Carolina State Archives
General Assembly Sessions Records
November-December, 1788, Box #3
File: 1788 Joint Papers
Petitions Rejected Or Not Acted Upon

General Assembly Sessions
1777 - 1789

State of North Carolina We the subscribers being
Green County present when the old

Tasel and old abraham and the Dark Night Was Kild Doth solemnly sware that It was Contrary to John Surviers Orders and that it Was Don by a sertain John Cirk Who had his Mother and six brothers and sisters Kild a few Days before Who Was protected by a party that rose Contrary to the sd Surviers Orders and Directed the sd Cirk to Do as he pleased and that the sd John Survier Was Near a Quarter of a mile from the place at the time (and that the inhabitance Involved and Concluded to atact the towns With Out the sd Surviers Knowing any thing of it and then sent the Distance of Twenty Miles for the sd Survier to Command them and that When he Came Down he advised the peopel to pass the [?] towns and go against Chickamaga and the high wassey Indians Which Was Don and one town Destroyed and a Number of Indians Kild that When he Returned to the Inhabitance they had got satisfactory accounts that it Was Chil howe Indians that Kild Cirks family and so purvaid on him to go against the sd Chilhowe Indians, Which Case the above Indians Was Kild (all which Was Don after the Report of Browns family being Kild at Nick a Jack and Inglish and a young Woman being Kild his wife and four Children taken prisoners and three young men on bever Creek and McCarbeneys Wife Was Kild on the North side of holston And Kirks family Kild on the south side of holston and french Broad sworn to before me this 25th of Octr 1788

A. Cullan JP   Nathaniel Evins
                          James Hubbert
Depositions given
by Col. Hardin
    &
Mr. Outlaw

****

North Carolina State Archives
General Assembly Sessions Records
November-December, 1788, Box #3
House Joint Resolutions

North Carolina

General Assembly Sessions
1777 - 1789

In the House of Commons, 6th December 1788

Whereas Sundry of the Inhabitants of the Counties of Washington, Sullivan, Greene and Hawkins, were called into actual Service in defence of the Frontier Inhabitants of this State against the Indians agreeable to orders issued by his Excellency the Governor with the advice of the Council of State,

And whereas no provision hath hitherto been made for the Settlement and liquidations of the Claims for such Services, nor for the necessary Supplies furnished.

Therefore Resolved, that Landon Carter, John Scott & John Blair be appointed a Board of Auditors for the Settlement and liquidation of all claims in consequence of Such Service, and that the board shall make allowances for all articles of provision furnished agreeably to the then Cash prices for all and every of Such Article & articles and in no other manner whatsoever, and for the actual Service of the People called out agreeably to the Militia Law.

Resolved further that the said Board shall lay the whole of their proceedings before the next General Assembly.

Resolved further that the said Auditors previous to their entering into the duties of their office shall take the following Oath. I AB do solemnly & sincerely Swear, that I will do equal Justice between man and man, the State and Individuals and to the best of my skill and abilities, So help me God.

And State auditors shall be all owed for their Services at the next General Assembly
Jno. Sitgreaves Spk.
By order, J Hunt CHC

****

North Carolina State Archives
General Assembly Sessions Records
November-December, 1788, Box #1
Joint Standing Committees, Indian Affairs

State of North Carolina
   By his Excellency S.J. Esquire, Governor, Captain General and Commander in Chief in and Over the said State - A Proclamation.

Whereas it hath been represented to me that certain ill disposed persons within the District of Washington have been guilty of committing Outrages

General Assembly Sessions
1777 - 1789

against the Indian Inhabitants, and have in a most cruel and unjustifiable manner put some of those people to death. I do therefore by and with the advice & consent of the Council of State strictly injoin all the Citizens of this State from going on the Territories assigned to the Indians or committing any Hostilities against them without the express order and Permission of the Commanding Officer of the said District.

Given under my hand & the Great Seal of the said State at Hillsborough this 29th day of July 1788.

****

North Carolina State Archives
General Assembly Sessions Records
November-December, 1788, Box #1

The Petition of Sundry the Inhabitants of French Broad River, in the House of Commons 14th Nov. 1788 read & referred to the Committee on Indian Affairs
By Order, J Hunt CHC

In Senate 14 Novem, 1788 read & referred as by the House of Commons
J Haywood CS

      We the Inhabitants Living south of french Broad River on the frontiers of Green County Within the Bounds of this Teretorial Jurisdiction of No. Carolina Being assembled under the Constitutional Bill of Rights held out in this constity of sd. State to the Citizens thereof for Instructing the Representatives in petitioning to this Honourable the General Assembly for the Redress of grievances &c. We your petitioners Humbly Sheweth to Your Honourable Body that we were settled on Land afterwards allotted for the Cherokee hunting ground Before the Lines were Extended Between the Whites & Indians by the Treaty at **[Faded]** after which time the Indians Gave us free Liberty to live and Enjoy our Livings on Sd. lands peaceably and unmolested, But contrary to their agreement, we suffered many miseries and losses By sd. Indians Which we Bore Without Resentment untill they Began to murder and had actualy murdered and taken Seventeen persons and finding them made no Difference Between persons Settled on lands Claimed and sold By the State of No. Carolina and those on the Unapropriated lands We were at length oblidged to Raise arms in our own Defence or otherwise Submit to the Bloody Hatchet We therefore hope that you will take these Matters into

General Assembly Sessions
1777 - 1789

Consideration and Extend your Linative[?] arms of protection around us and as a number of our Citizens fell Victoms to the savage Barbarity in Defence of the Counterey Whose Widows and fatherless Children Calls Loudly to Heaven and you to Consider their Case and Extend Mercy Being Reduced to so low a Circumstances as to have no other Alternative to Support their families But their Small Claims of land or Improvement and those Who have Escaped their Bloody fingers are Reduced By Loss of stock of all kinds and Crops that they must take up with hunger for their Companion and familiarly shake hands with the cold hand of poverty.

We would allso shew to your Honerable Body that the Inhabitants adjacent to us have formed and prescribed to themselves Bounds Sufficient for a County and have petitioned your Honourable Body for the Same Which Boundaries Leaves us out and should we be Successful in obtaining protection of Government We assure your Honours that the Bounds Below Sd. Boundary line, already settled, is fully sufficient for a large County We therefore hope that you in your Wisdoms will Redress these our Grievances By granting us a County Bounded as followeth Viz. On the N. West by Hawkins Line untill opesite the head of Beaverdam Creek then a direct line to the Ridge Dividing Little River and Plat Creek watters thence along Sd: Ridge to Robert Poors on the Little East fork of pigeon then South to the mountains we therefore Submit this our Information and petition to your Honours Wise Consideration Hoping that you will fulfill these our petitions and When your Wisdoms see Convenient to open a land office that You would grant the settlers some preferance of thei Improvements and in such a manner as to enable the Inhabitants to secure their Claims and we your petitioners as in Duty Bound Shall Ever pray.

Wm. Hamilton, Wm Stephens, [?] Duggan, James Okern[?], James Wilson, Joseph Woods, Tobias Wilhelm, Anthony Lawson, John Woods, John Kennedy, Samuel Moore, James Stevenson, James Dicson, James Woods, Patrick Woods, James [Care?], Samuel Cant[?], Wm. Price, John Duggan, Joseph Dickson, John Dickson, John Reno, George Hallsmark, Richard Shields, Wm. Simpson, William Moon, Jesse Moon, John Manning, Benjamin Manning, Job Manning, Jos Manning, Elijah Royers, Robt. Shields, James Shields, Da:d Stocton Shields, John Shields, Wm. Shields, Thos. Shields, James[?] Smith, Joshua Tipton, Mordec Tipton, Meshack Tipton, Iaian Edwards, Joshua Simpson, John Lovlaty (his mark,) Reuben Simpson, Adam Wilson, Richard Manos, Isaack[?] Hamilton, W. Wallace, Saml Thompson, T. Wallace, Robert Thompson Junr., Robert Thompson Senr., Olover Wallace, [?] Wallace, James Thompson, John

General Assembly Sessions
1777 - 1789

Johnson, George [?]enerd, Thos Wallace, Joel Wallace, Martinno Atchley, James Tylor, Thomas Paite, John Tiler, James Tiller, Laden Romins.

****

North Carolina State Archives
General Assembly Sessions Records
November-December, 1788, Box #1

State of No. Carolina   }
Cumberland County   }

This Day Came James Robertson before me -- Justice of the peace for this County & made oath that Col. Anthony Bledsoe or his heirs with himself the said Robertson Doth Stand bound Unto James Horket[?] & Allexr. [?]er in the Just & full Sum of two Hundred pounds Currency for their Service Performed in Going to & Returning from Allexander Mc Giliverey in the Creek Nation to Nashvile Sworn to before me this Day of Novemr. 1788   Jas. Robertson
Fayetteville Novr. 20th 1788
Jas Porterfield

****

North Carolina State Archives
General Assembly Sessions Records
November-December, 1788, Box #1

Chickasaw Nation - 1788
Mountainleader
To   } Letter
C. Robertson

Long Town Chickasaw Nation May the 30th 1788

Well my oldest Brother I Expect to come and see you Before Long I am going into the Settlement and I will Call and See you. I have sent a Letter to Congrass, I desire you would Loock at it and if you think well of it Seal it and send it on its way to Congrass. I wish you Could send one of your young men with it to Congrass and then to Pitts Burgh wheare I will be to

General Assembly Sessions
1777 - 1789

Recive from Congrass what the will said. I would have Rit More But I Expect to be in my Self in about Ten or Twelve Days and when I come in I Shall Call at places princeble houses on my Way till I Come to the place apointed so no more at present But Remain your Brother in Love and peace

C. Robertson

his
Piomingo X Moutainleader
Mark

****

North Carolina State Archives
General Assembly Sessions Records
November-December, 1788, Box #1

At a Counsel held at Long Town Chickasaw Nation

May of the 30th, 1788 Resolved that theare Should be a question asked Congrass & that is To Wit ------

Whereas about Three years ago at sineco in Georgia theare was a Treaty held Respecting a sartain Track of Land granted by the inglish to the Chickasaws and at the Trety above mentioned we the Chickasaws did apoint a sartain man to finnish our Bargin and Bring the goods to the Long Ile of holeston wheare we Might Receive them ---- Now our Brethering we have waited a Long Time and has not Received an answer theare fore we know not what to loock for and we no not the Reson we thearefore will wait four Months Longer in which we desire you would Consider in your Selves what you will do and in that Time send an answer to Pitts Burg wheare Piomingo otherwise the Mountain Leader will be to Receive your resolves we Expect acording to your promis you will pay us --- we have Nothing More to informe you But we Still Remain your Brothers in peace and Love and Subscribe our Names.

   His   His
John X Brown Thomas X Brown
Mark   mark

       His
Piomingo X Mountain Leader
    Mark

General Assembly Sessions
1777 - 1789

****

North Carolina State Archives
General Assembly Sessions Records
November-December, 1788, Box #1

The Petition of Mary Bledsoe

In the House of Commons, 12 Novr. 1788 read & Referred to the Comt. On Indian Affairs
By Order J Hunt, CHC

In Senate 12 Nov. 1788 read and referred as by the House of Commons
By Order J Haywood CS
Rejected

To the Honorable the General Assembly
    The Memorial of Mary Bledsoe relict of the late Col Anthony Bledsoe, Sheweth
    That her late husband as commanding Officer of the County of Sumner in concert with the commanding Officer of the County of Davidson, did agree and engage with Capt. James Hocket, and Capt. Alexander Erwing to go with a Flag to the Creek Nation of Indians, that in consequence of the Said Service being faithfully performed by said Hocket and Erwing, your Memorialist's late Husband & said commanding Officer of Davidson County did contract to pay to each the Sum of one hundred pounds and became jointly and Severally bound for the same, that the Service was faithfully performed by said Erwing & Hocket, as will appear by Letters which they brought from Mr. McGillivray, the tenor of which your Memorialist trusts will justify the measure and prove Satisfactorily to the honorable Assembly, that public good has been effected thereby.
    Your Memorialist further Sheweth, That the Mountain Leader and fourteen Men of the Chickasaw Nation (who have ever been friendly to our people, having never Aided the British Enemy, nor treated with the Spaniards) on their way to Congress to obtain some reward for their fidelity and peaceable demeanor, being Met by your Memorialist's late Husband, and the commanding Officer of Davidson County, of whom they demanded an escort and Money to bear their expences, but they thinking it more advisable and perhaps attended with less expence, prevail'd on them to Accept of some presents and to return to their Nation, thereby flattering

General Assembly Sessions
1777 - 1789

themselves with holding said Indians in friendly confidence towards this State in particular and with the United States in general, and which your Memorialist trusts and verily believes has Succeeded agreeably to their most Languin hopes and wishes, the presents made on this Occasion were 6 Guns, Viz, 1 at the price of £20, 2 at £16 each, 1 at £14 & 2 at £12 each, Cloth trimmings and making a Coat for the Mountain Leader £21 & ammunition purchased of Erving & Gillespie £40 making in the whole £151 -- which added to the foregoing £200 -- makes the Sum of Three hundred and fifty pounds, for which the estate of your Memorialist's late husband, jointly with the commanding Officer of Davidson County is bound and liable, Your Memorialist therefore humbly conceives that (as the Services rendered and contracts entered into were for the benefit of the State at large, and as from the frontier situation of her late husband's settlement he was Subjected to many disbursments, hardships & Services, of which she makes no Account but which nevertheless has considerably contributed to leave his estate involved) she will not be considered as importunate by praying the General Assembly to take this matter into their Serious consideration, and to grant a Sum of Money adequate to the discharge of the foregoing contracts, or such other relief in the Premises as in their Wisdom they shall deem just and equitable, And Your Memorialist shall pray &c.

****

North Carolina State Archives
General Assembly Sessions Records
November-December, 1788, Box #1

Petitions from Greene County

In the House of Commons read & referred to the Committee on Indian Affairs
By Order, J Hunt CHC

In Senate 20 Nov. 1788 read & referred as by the House of Commons
By Order J Haywood CS

To the Honorable the General Assembly of the State of North Carolina,
    The Petition of Sundry Inhabitants of Green County Humbly Sheweth, That we Labor under Great Disadvantages and difficulties by

General Assembly Sessions
1777 - 1789

Reason of the great distance we lie from the Courthouse it being Att least Ninety miles from our lower Settlements and no Civil Officer Residing in less than forty miles by Which means Vilany often goes unpunished and the Honest and Good Citizens Wronged of their Right.

It is therefore our Earnest Request that your Honourable body would take into consideration our distressed Situation and grant us Relief by laying us off a County and Appointing Officers for the Administration of Justice by which means the Benefits and Blessings of Government may be Extended to us.

It is also the Earnest prayer of your petitioners that the County be bounded as follows (Viz) Beginning att the main Dividing Ridge or Apalachain mountainswhere the Waters of little Pidgeon and little Rivers Interlocks from thence along the Divide between Sd. two Rivers to the Waters of Boyd Creek Thence Along the Divide between Boyds Creek and Little Pidgeon to the uper point of a large Island in French Broad Known by the name of Seviers Island Thence a N West Course to the Hawkins line, which Bounds Would Include a Compact County and large as necessary and Good Ways may be had for the most Distant Settlers to Attend at Courts and other public meetings which would be much to our Advantage & Satisfaction

---

Petitions of Inhabitants of Greene County & South of French Broad River, In the House of Commons 20 Nov. 1788 read & referred to the Committee on Indian Affairs
By Order, J Hunt CHC

We your Petitioners Are now Sufferers by a Most Cruel and unhappy War with the Cherokee Indians, We have been Closely Confin'd in forts these six months past, and many of our people Barbarously Massacred, our farms not Attended our Horses and Cattle Drove from our Stations and often We are not able to do more than Defend ourselves from our Walls under these distresses. We have been often without assistance from the more Secure parts of the District, the Divisions and contraversies among the people Render'd it often out of the power of the Militia Officers to Assist us. And also some of your petitioners are Settled on unapropriated land and it is our Earnest Desire to be Conformable to your Government and laws, We have Defended our Contry as far as in our power, att the Risque of Both life and Property.

General Assembly Sessions
1777 - 1789

It is therefore the Earnest prayer of your petitioners that your Agust Body would take our Distressed and local Situation under your Wise Consideration and grant us a preference to our Claims to land when a land Office shall be opened for that purpose of Entring such lands, that is to Each settler or Resi'd enter a Survey of Six Hundred and forty Acres att as low Rates as possible Not Incompatible with the Interest of the Community at large.

These our Complaints and Reasonable Requests we hope you will acquiesce with as far as you in your Wisdom may Judge Convenient, And your petitioners as in Duty Bound Do Ever Pray.

John Gillespie, Jas. Ewing, Thos. Dison, William Gillespie, John Gillaspie, John Hanna, William Hanna, John Liddy, James Witherspoon Senr., David Loveless, James Witherspoon, Nicholas Bartlet, James Gillespie, George Zindel[?], John McAlister, Robert Daniel Pearcy, John Hanna, William Woods, Robert Hanna, Joshua Hanna, Calvin Jonsten, Ephraim McDowell, Wm Hanna, Wm Woods, Ephram McDowell Junr., Thos Brown, John Thompson, Jacob Riffe, William Hanvy, Robert Hanna, Alexr Ewing, John Kelley, Thomas Colewell, James Beard, Andrew Giffin, John Lowry, George Ewing, George Berry, Thos. McColough, **[Faded]** McColough, James Alexander, **[Next five names faded]**, William Reagan, Robert McMurray, Samuel McMurray, William McManos[?], James Donohen, Charles Reagan, Peter Dosher, Jacob Thomas, Henry Thomas, Joseph Rosson, Jonathan Cunningham, Levy Jones, Alexr Kelley, Wm Gillesty, Wm Henderson, Jas Gillespy Junr., Stephen [?], Saml Newell Junr., Saml Newell Senr., Jas Black, Jas Bogle Junr., Wm Houston, Matthew Houston, Saml Topton[?], John Carr, Adam Dunlop, John Dunlop, Littlepage **[Smudged]**, Benjamin Tipton, John Coats, John McCain, Amos Byrd, Jas Caldwell, John Hicklen, Alexr Milligan, John Chambers, John Byrd, Ferins Conner, Humphrey Montgomery, Amos Byrd Junr., John Walker.

****

North Carolina State Archives
General Assembly Sessions Records
November-December, 1788, Box #1
Governor's Messages

To the Honorable the General Assembly

General Assembly Sessions
1777 - 1789

Gentlemen,

In Pursuance of your Message of Yesterday I herewith send you such of the Publick dispatches & Documents, as appear to me of importance & claim your immediate attention.

The first object which calls for your serious Attention, is the Proceedings of the late Convention of the People at Hillsborough, and the situation into which the State will be cast on the Meeting of the Congress of the United States, under the new Federal Constitution, as this State will not be represented in that Congress & her Interests may be eventually affected by their Proceedings, you will consider of the best method to obviate any inconvenience which may arise from the particular circumstances of our Situation, & direct such mode of Communication as may appear most eligible, untill the New Constitution is altered, so as to meet the approbation of the People of this State, & they become United with the other States.

You will Perceive from the Papers I now lay before you the unsettled & unhappy Situation of the Inhabitants of this State on the Western Waters, the outrages & Hostilities which have been Mutually committed between them of the Neighboring Tribes of Indians, have greatly alarmed not only the Neighboring States, but the United States in general insomuch that Congress have ordered Troops to be in readiness to Protect the Indians from Insults in future & the more effectually to secure the Peace of the United States.

I submit to you the expediency of enacting such Regulations as may be effectual to settle such disputes as may unfortunately hereafter arise, between the Citizens of this State and the Neighbouring Tribes of Indians, in such manner as to avoid Bloodshed and effectually bring to immediate Punishment, all who shall Presume to Violate the Treaties subsisting between the United States & the Indian Nations.

I declined appointing a Commissioner to Treat with the Indians in Conjunction with the States of South Carolina & Georgia, in Pursuance of the resolve of Congress, observing that by the Instructions from Congress it was intended these Commissioners, were to Settle the Boundary between this State & the Indians, a Power, which appeared to me improper to be entrusted in any Persons but such as were Appointed by the Legislature.

I submit to you the necessity of enacting a Law for the Punishment of Piracy & Robberies at Sea, to give power to apprehend & secure Subjects & Citizens of other States & Kingdoms Guilty of Crimes, who are fugitives from Justice & take up the residence in this State, and

General Assembly Sessions
1777 - 1789

also Prevent the importation into this State, from other Kingdoms & States, Convicted Felons.

You will receive an Act of the Virginia Assembly, similar to one which was before the last Assembly held at this Place and laid over for Consideration, for cutting a navigable Canal bwtween the Waters of Pasquotank in this State, and the Waters of Elizabeth River in the State of Virginia, to take effect whenever the General Assembly of this State, shall pass an Act for that Purpose. There is likewise a Resolve of the Virginia Assembly respecting the Boundary Line between the two States which requires your immediate Consideration, that I may be enabled to return an Answer to the State of Virginia.

I forwarded the Resolve of the last Assembly respecting the Navigation of the River Mississippi to your Delegates in Congress, who have Obtained an explicit Declaration of Congress avowing the undoubted Right of the Citizens of the United States to the Navigation of that River.

Fayette Ville
November 5th 1788

Saml. Johnston

****

North Carolina State Archives
General Assembly Sessions Records
November-December, 1788, Box #1
Governor's Messages

By the United States in Congress Assembled
September 1st 1788

Resolved, That the Secretary at War be, and he is hereby directed to have a Sufficient number of the Troops in the Service of the United States in readiness to march from the Ohio, to the protection of the Cherokees, whenever Congress shall direct the same, and that he take measures for obtaining information of the best routes for troops to march from the Ohio to Chota, and for dispursing among all the white inhabitants settled upon or in the vicinity of the hunting grounds Secured to the Cherokees by the Treaty concluded between them and the United States, November 28th 1785, the Proclamation of Congress of this date.

Resolved that Copies of the said Proclamation and of these Resolutions be transmitted to the Executives of Virginia & North Carolina,

General Assembly Sessions
1777 - 1789

and that the said States be and they are hereby requested to use their influence that the said Proclamation may have its intended effect to restore peace and Harmony between the Citizens of the United States and the Cherokees, and to present any further invasions of their respective rights and possessions, and in Case Congress shall find it necessary to order troops to the Cherokee towns to enforce a due observance of the said Treaty, that the said States be, and they are hereby requested to co-operate with the said troops for enforcing such observance of that Treaty

Resolved That Papers which have been transmitted to Congress concerning certain hostilities alledged to have been committed by John Sevier and others on the Cherokee Indians at Chota, be referred to the Executive of North Carolina, and that the said Executive of North Carolina, and that the said Executive be, and they are earnestly requested to cause inquiry to be made into the said hostilities and to take measures for having the Perpetrators thereof apprehended and punished.
Chas. Thomson Secy.

****

North Carolina State Archives
General Assembly Sessions Records
November-December, 1788, Box #1
Petitions Rejected or not acted on

Memd. Of Circumstances respecting the Cherokee War. At Hawkins Court on the 2d. day of the Court being the 3d. day of June, Martin Calld a Council of the officers & Agreed to Carry on a Campaign against the Cherokees and was to rendevous at Whites Mill on the 23d. of same month and Gave outlaw[?] orders as Commissary to provide provision for 800 men.

Three weeks before this Council was Held, a party of Martins Men Stationed at Whites Mill and some of the Neighbours Destroyed Coratee town at the Mouth of Holeson, & Kill'd a Squaw & Indian Lad, or boy at the same time.

On the Seventh day of June Sevier went first against the Indians on Highwassee River. On the Ninth day of June James Lackky went in with a flagg to Chilowa, and was here informed that on the 4th day of June thirty three Indians had went out against wears Station, from Chilowa. On the Eleventh day of June Sevier went and destroy'd the town of Chilowa

General Assembly Sessions
1777 - 1789

At a public talk held in Chota on the 5th day of June, the Indians told the White people, that the Tassell had removed to Chickamauga and was not to return Under five Moons.

55 persons had been Killd before Sevier would agree to go against the Indians - Elis Hasting[?] told Sevier before he went out at Taylors ferry that it was the Chilhowa Indians that Killed Kirks family & that they intended War.   Joseph Harden present

---

State of North Carolina }
Green County   }

We the Subscribers being present When the Tasel and Old Abraham and the Dark Night was kild Doth Solemnly Sware that It was Contrary to John Sevier's Orders and that It Was Don by a sertain John Cirk Who had his Mother and Six brothers and Sisters kild a few Days before Who was protected by a party that Rose Contrary to the Sd. Seviers Orders and Directed the Sd. Cirk to do as he pleased and that Sd. John Sevier Was Near a Quarter of a Mile from the place at the time (and that the Inhabitance Involved and Concluded to atack the Towns With Out the Sd. Seviers Knowing any thing of it and **[Faded]** the Distance of Sixty Miles for the Sd. Sevier to Command them and, and that when he Came Down he advised the people to pass the N[?] towns and go against Chicamauga and the Highwassee Indians Which Was Don and One town Destroyed and a Number of Indians Kild, that When he Returned to the Inhabitance, they had got Satisfactory accounts that It Was Chilhowa Indians that Kild Cirks family and so purvail'd on him to go against the Chilhowa Indians Which Case the above Indians Was Kild (all Which Was Don after the Report of Browns family being Kild at Nuk a Jack and Inglishes and a young Woman being Kild his wife and four Children taken prisoners and three young men on Bever Creek and McCarbrneys Wife Was Kild on the North Side of Holston, and Kirks family Kild on the South Side of Holston and French Broad Sworn to before me this 25th of Octr. 1788.
D Outlaw JP
Nathaniel Evins & James Hullest

North Carolina }
Green County   }

General Assembly Sessions
1777 - 1789

Personally appeared before me, Joseph Hardin Esquire Justice of the peace for Sd. County, Capt. James Mauher[?] and Mr. Benjamin Mooney, And made Oath that they were present at the town of Chilhowa under the Command of Governor Sevier, that when the Tassell & Old Abraham Were taken prisoners, that they heard Sevier say that it was a Very lucky Circumstance, that he hoped by having them Warriors prisoners, that a peace Could be easily Negociated, and he now hoped that peace and Quietness would soon take place in the Country, and Urged how Necessary it was to keep those Indians Safe, in order to bring about such a desirable end[?], and heard the said John Sevier order Major Craig to place the foot Men as a Guard or the Indians [Faded] and society the Number of foot men the deponant says Consisted of forty odd Men, after the same being done Sd. Sevier Went Away in order to have the enemy Collected together; in his Absence, the Guard Let a Certain John Kirk into the house among the Indians, who were soon all massacred by Sd. Kirk, after some little time they see said Sevier returning Riding very fast Whom Coming Up Complained very Much at the inhumanity and Barbarity of the People Massacreing the Indians [Faded] Submitted to their Mercy Appeared to be Much effected and Concerned, And exclaimed Much against Such inhuman Conduct and Said was afraid Such Unmerciful treatment Would bring a Curse Upon the Country - Soon after a Certain Charles Murphy a half breed Was Brought in as a prisoner, Who informed the Army that the Indians that lived in Chilhowa was the people that killd Mr. Kirks family and massacred Several of the fellows [Faded] that did the Murder , Also Old Abrahams Wife gave the information, And both of them gave information that there was thirty three Warriors Who had went out of that town Some few days before against the people Who lived on Pidgeon River, the deponants also Sayeth, that a number of the Army Wanted to Kill the said Charles Murphy, and on their being About to do it, John Sevier Came riding Up and beged for God sake, they would not Kill him & said that he hoped that every person Who had any regard for him, meaning himself, Would interfere and save Murphy: Also ordered some of the Men to take Murphy out of the Army Who was afterwards by said Sevier ordered to be Set at full Liberty, which we have great Reason to believe was done to Keep the said Murphy from being Killd; We the deponants farther Sayeth that we heard John Sevier Esquire say that he was Sick at seeing so Much Blood Spiled and he appeared to be Extremely Sorry for the prisoners that Was Killed.

    The deponants farther sayeth, that they were with the said John Sevier at the taking of the town of Highwassee, and See in the town House

General Assembly Sessions
1777 - 1789

yard Several White people's Scalps hung Upon a pole, the same happening a few days before they went against the town of Chilhowa: The deponants farther say that the said John Sevier dureing Several towers[**Tours**] they were out with him, that He Always gave orders to the Men by no means to Kill Women or Children, Also Maketh Oath that said Sevier Would not Consent to have any of the Near towns destroyed til after he was fully Satisfied, these Indians had Killed kirks Family & Also had Went out against the people who lived on Pidgeon River, and farther Sayeth not.
James Mahan & Benja. Mooney
Sworn to this 25th day of October 1788
Joseph Hardin J:P

State of North Carolina }
Green County   }

John McMahen being of full age came before me Joseph Hardin Esquire Justice of the peace for said County and after being Sworn on the Holy Evangelist of Almighty God deposeth and saith that he was one of the party that went under the Command of John Sevier Esq. Against the Indian town Calld Chilhowa after being at the same place Some Short time, The deponant See some of the party firing some Guns at some Indians across the River at a house which the deponant was inform'd Old Abraham lived on which the Indians hoists a flag and after some little time two Indians Got into a Canoe and was a coming across the River, the deponant asked Which Was Old Abraham and being told the deponant said he thought he would die Very Quick, John Sevier Riding Up at that time said Spe[**Faded**] not, would you be so cruel as to Kill any person that Submitted to our Men: he the deponant further saith that when Old Abraham came over he see the said John Sevier Shake him by the hand and after some little time the Canoe was sent back to Old Abrahams house, and brought over the Tassell and one other Indian, he heard John Sevier order Major Craig to put them into a house, place the foot Men as a Guard over them and not Suffer them to be hurt by any Means, the deponant saith that the Number of the foot men Consisted of about forty or fifty men: The deponant further Saith that after the Indians Was put into the House and the Guard placed for their Safety that John Sevier then Rode away to Collect Some of the Army together; The deponant then went to the door and told Craig to Stand one side that he Wanted to have a Crack at one of them Meaning the Indians, Mr. Craig told him he must not, that it was the

General Assembly Sessions
1777 - 1789

Governors orders that none of the Indians Should be hurt, then a Cartain Robert Pearce Came Up with a Cocked Gun and told Craig to Clear the way or he would make daylight Shine through him, on that Craig Complained that it was very hard, that he was Ordered there by the Governor and must be drove away, Contrary to his Orders the deponant told Craig to go after the Governor and he would see that the Indians Should not be hurt provided he did not stay too Long, on which Craig went after Governor Sevier but before either Craig or Sevier Returned the Guard give way and and John Kirk went into the house and Killd the Indians, Soon after Governor Sevier came riding up very fast at which time the said Kirk was going to Kill some Indian Wemans, the Governor then spoke and Complained and mentioned how disgratefull and inhuman it was to put prisoners to death after Submitting to Mercy, that it Scandalized a Christian People and would bring a Curse Upon a Country, It would be Guilty of Barbarity; and spoke much to the like Effect [?] to be Very much against Such inhuman Conduct: Soon after a Certain Charles Murphy a half breed Indian was brought into the Army a prisoner and a number was going to Kill the said Murphy, on which the said John Sevier Rode Up and said for Gods Sake for them not to Kill him that there was blood enough allready spilled, that said Murphy, in Consequence of Which was said and Sit at his full Liberty by the said Sevier which seemed to give great umbridge to the whole Army, and some said it would be well done to Kill any man that would save an Indian further Saith not, Sworn to this 25th Day of October 1788   John McMahan
Joseph Hardin JP

State of North Carolina }
Greene County   }

John McMahan being of full age, Came before Me Joseph Hardin Esquire, Justice of the peace for Sd. County and after being Sworn on the Holy Evangelist of Almighty God deposeth and Saith, that he was one of the perty that went under the Command of John Sevier Esqr. Against the Indian town Call'd Chilhowa, after being at the same place some short time, the deponant See a white flag some of the party fireing some Guns at some Indians across the River at a house which the deponant was informd Old Abraham lived in on which the Indians hoisted a flagg, and after some little time two Indians got into a Canoe and was coming across the River; the deponant asked Which Was Old Abraham, and being told, the deponant

General Assembly Sessions
1777 - 1789

said he thought he would die Very Quick -- John Sevier Riding Up at that time said Shurly Not. Would you be so Cruel to Kill any person that Submitted to our Mercy: he the deponant further Saith, that when Old Abraham Came over, he see the said John Sevier Shake him by the hand, and after some little time the Canoe Was Sent back to Old Abrahams house, and brought the Tassell, and one other Indian, he heard John sevier order Major Craig to put them into a House, place the foot Men As a Guard over them, and not Suffer them to be hurt by Any Means. The deponant Saith, that the Number of foot men Consisted of about forty or fifty Men . The deponant further Saith, that after the Indians Was put into the House, and the Guard placed for their Safety, that John Sevier then Rode away to Collect some of the Army together; The deponant then went to the door and told Craig to Stand one Side, that he Wanted to have a Crack at one of them, Meaning the Indians. Mr Craig told him he must not, that it was the Governors Orders that None of the Indians should be hurt: Then a certain Robert Pearce Came up with a Cocked Gun, and told Craig to Clear the Way or he would Make daylight Shine through him, on that Craig Complained that it Was Very hard, that he was ordered thereby the Governor, and must be drove away Contrary to his orders. The deponant told Craig to go after the Governor, and he would see that the Indians should not be hurt provided he did Not Stay too long, on which Craig Went after Governor Sevier, but before either Craig or Sevier Returned, the Guard give Way and John Kirk went into the house and Killd the Indians. Soon after Governor Sevier came riding up very fast, at which time the Sd. Kirk was going to Kill some Indian Woman, the Governor then spoke, and Complained and mentioned how disgracefull and in human it Was to put prisoners to death, after Submitting to Mercy: that it Scandalized a Christian People, and he doubted would bring a Curse Upon a Country that would be Guilty of such Barbarity: and spoke Much to the like Effect, Seemed to be very Much effected and Concerned, and Complained Much against Such inhuman Conduct. Soon after, a Certain Charles Murphy a half breed Indian Was brought into the Army a prisoner and a Number Was going to Kill the said Murphy, on which the said John Sevier Rode Up and beged for God Sake for them Not to Kill him, that there Was blood enough Already Spilled, that the said Murphy in Consequence of which was saved, and Set at his Full Liberty by the said Sevier, which seemed to give great umbridge to the Whole Army, and some said it would be Well done to kill any Man that would save an Indian, further saith Not, Sworn to this 25th day of October 1788   John McMahan
Joseph Hardin JP

General Assembly Sessions
1777 - 1789

[Editor's note: The first part of the following affidavit could not be located or it is missing from the records.]

Riding in Company with John Sevier & others then going Against Chilhowa heard Sd. sevier Direct the people Not to Kill Women nor Children, Likewise heard David Craig say that when the Tasel, Old Abraham & the Dark Night was taken prisoners that him the Sd. Craig Went to Sevier & asked him what would they do with the prisoners (Ading) some of the people Would Kill them If they was Not taking Care of. That him the Sd. Sevier directed them the Sd. Craig to put them in a house & sett a gard on them, , of the foot men that March'd over the Mountains with him Sd. Craig & that John Kirk (who had Lost his Mother brothers & Sisters by the Indians) being encouraged by a party Contrary to sd. Seviers Orders Came in & Killed them.

Sworn to before me this 25th of Octr 1788 James Lackey
A Outlaw JP

****

North Carolina State Archives
General Assembly Sessions Records
November-December, 1788, Box #1
Petitions Rejected or not acted on

The Comity reports that it ordered by government they shall be pay by our own tax

In Senate read and laid over untill the next General assembly
By Order

To the Honorable the General Assembly of the State of North Carolina
      We the Subscribers members of Washington District beg leave to inform your Honorable Body that the General for the said District is not a Residenter thereof as the Law directs and that he is also Agent for the Indians which appears to be inconsistent of itself to Command on one side and advise and direct on the other which we think a great injury to the District and not consistent with the Law of the State or Common Justice, We Therefore beg your Honorable Body to take our Situation under your

General Assembly Sessions
1777 - 1789

consideration and give us such relief as you in your Wisdom shall think right.
Thos. Ervine[?], Jas Reddy, Wm. Cocke, Joseph Hardin

****

North Carolina State Archives
General Assembly Sessions Records
November-December, 1788, Box #1
Petitions Rejected or not acted on

The Honorable the General Assembly of the State of North Carolina

The Memorial of Daniel Kennedy Most Humbly Sheweth, That Notwithstanding the many petitions the Cherokee Indians have lately Made that their Utmost Wishes are to Enjoy Peace at their Old Towns, Yet those perfidious Wretches After some of their Chiefs holding a Friendly Talk With General Martin at Keowee, and there Promising that None of their Warriors Should go Out any More to War, have Lately On the Warm Spring Road About thirteen Miles from Greene Courthouse, After taking a Certain Aaron Bowman and his Son Captives, & Leading them Back One Mile and a half One of the Indians Enquired at them how far it was to the first houses &c. An Indian Came Behind said Bowman, Struck at him With his Tomahawk, and at the third Stroke Killed him, in Sight of his Son about 13 or 14 Years old, they then Scalped, and Striped him Naked, then Turned to the boy, Tomahawked Scalped, Striped and left him also for Dead, the Boy lay from 10 O'Clock in the Morning of the 19th of November Instant, Until Near Night, When some measure Come to the use of his Reason, and removed from that place which was Very Rocky, to Ground Covered with Leaves, hoping thereby to Alleviate the pains of Death, Which he Expected Shortly to Encounter. But he Lay on that Place Until the Morning, Being Still Alive & Capable of Reason, Inspired With the hopes of Life he Endeavoured to Travel to a house Which was only three Miles Distant, he performed it (Which hath Enabled me to Give this Detail, But Died on the Night of the 21st Instant

Your Memorialist Begs Leave to Remark, that the Murder Aforesaid was Committed at a Time when, and place Where, the Inhabitants Considered themselves in some Measure Secure, having Rec'd Copies of the Friendly Talk held at Keowee Aforesaid, & Being Within the lands purchased from Government Near thirty Miles.

General Assembly Sessions
1777 - 1789

By Express from the Frontiers, this Moment Came To Hand. The Indians have On Saturday Night Last, Wantonly set fire to Houstons Station On Nine Mile Creek, Burnt some Stocks & Grain and Drove off the remainder of the Stocks of Cattle and Horses from Those Distressed people Who are Now Reduced to the Necessity of Staying to Endeavour to Support their Families, Being destitute of property to purchase the Necessaries of Life in the Interior parts, Neither is Your Memorialist of Opinion, that there is Sustenance for them in the Secure parts, as there is a Considerable Number of Emigrants Also to Support.

Your Memorialist Begs Leave to Suggest that it is Not Within the Design of this Memorial, to Enumerate the many Unprovoked and Barbarous Murders, and Outrages, Committed By the Sd. Indians on the Citizens of this Country. But Only to shew, That they have Actually Violated their promise Notwithstanding the Gracious Overtures that have been Made to them By Your Agent the Honourable General Martin, for Which Your Memorialist Begs Leave to refer you to Genl. Martin aforesaid, if present, and the Members from this Country.

Your Memorialist further Observes that By Advice from Capt. Davidson On Sawannano, the Middle Settlements & Valley Towns have Taken the Bloody Hatchet. The Creeks have Also Joined with them in the War, probably Under an Apprehension (Which is But Too Well Founded) that the Citizens of this Country are Under the Frowns of Congress for Encroaching on their Territory - What then Will Be the Consequence? Will They Not Continue the War here in Order to Enrich themselves By the Sport, Whilst they Directfully Affirm that their Wishes are for Peace and are Endeavouring to Cultivate a Friendship With Our Neighbouring Counties and States in Order that We may Be Denied of any Assistance from any Quarter.

Your Memorialist Humbly hopes that Your Paternal Bosoms Will Burn With Resenrment on the Recital of these Facts, as Ours Did for you in the Darkest Times of the Conflict, With that Daring and Formidable host Great Britain, and her Allies (the Savages) When the People of this Country Cheerfully Yielded Not Only her Proportion of Men to Relieve the Wants and Distresses of Our Brethren on the Eastern Side of the Mountains, But Voluntarily stood forth in Your Cause when many Sunshine Patriots Shrunk from the Service of their Country.

With the Greatest Submission, Your Memorialist Begs Leave to Remind You of the Gracious promises of Friendly protection You made to Us in the Time of Disorder in this Country, for Which In Your Senate Journal of the 14th of December 1786 Which had its Effect in Uniting the

General Assembly Sessions
1777 - 1789

people of this Country Back to Your Government -- Your Memorialist Submits the Whole of these Considerations to Your Great Wisdom & Shall Ever Pray
Dan Kennedy, Lieut Colo Comd.
Greene County.

****

North Carolina State Archives
General Assembly Sessions Records
November-December, 1788, Box #1
Messages Regarding Balloting

North Carolina
    In the House of Commons 28 Novr. 1788
Mr Speaker & Gentlemen
    We agree to ballot at the line by you proposed for the Officers mentioned in your Message of this Day, approved of your Nominations, and have added thereto for an Agent for the settlement of the Accounts, Mr. Abishai Thomas, and for Commissioners for holding a Treaty with the Indiand, Mr McDowell junr. and General Caswell.
Jno. Sitgreaves, Speakr
By Order, J Hunt CHC

****

North Carolina State Archives
General Assembly Sessions Records
November-December, 1788, Box #2
Senate Joint Resolutions

Resolves on Indian Affairs

North Carolina
    In the House of Commons 28 Nov. 1788
Mr Speaker & Gentlemen
    We have appointed Mr Cock and Mr Person to Act with General McDowell for the purpose of Confering with His Excellency the Governor, on the Subject of Sending a Talk or Talks to the Indians &c.
Jno: Sitgreaves Speakr

General Assembly Sessions
1777 - 1789

By Order, J Hunt CHC

North Carolina
        In Senate 28 Nov 1788
Resolved that General McDowell be appointed by this House, to act with such person or persons, as the House of Commons may appoint, to confer with His Excellency the Governor, on the Subject of sending a Messenger with a Talk or Talks to the Indians, and to advise and inform the Governor of the Nature and Value of such Service.
Alexr. Martin SS
By Order, J Haywood CS

In the House of Commons 28 Nov 1788
Read & Concurred with
Jno: Sitgreaves Speakr
By Order J Hunt CHC
Mr Cock & Mr Person

****

North Carolina State Archives
General Assembly Sessions Records
November-December, 1788, Box #2
Senate Joint Resolutions

Resolution, the Govr to issue a Proclamation requiring Persons to remove off Indian hunting grounds &c
Rejected.

North Carolina
        In Senate 26th Nov. 1788
Resolved that His Excellency the Governor be directed to issue a proclamation requiring all Paersons to withdraw themselves immediately from their Settlements unlawfully made on the Lands allotted by the State of North Carolina to the Cherokees for their Hunting Grounds.
Alexr. Martin SS
By Order, J Haywood CS

****

General Assembly Sessions
1777 - 1789

North Carolina State Archives
General Assembly Sessions Records
November-December, 1788, Box #2
Senate Joint Resolutions

       Resolve Indian Affairs

North Carolina
  In Senate 18th Nov. 1788

  Whereas it may be necessary to send a Talk or Talks at or before the resting of this General Assembly to the Cherokees Chickamauga & Creeks with a view to obtain a Cessation of Hostilities between the said Indians and the Citizens of this State, until a Treaty can be effected; and as there is a certain Mr Alexander Drumgoole now in Town who can safely and expeditiously communicate Intelligence to the said Nations of Indians or either of them -- Resolved that a joint Committee of both Houses be appointed to confer with said Alex. Drumgoole and receive his proposals on this head and Report thereof.
Alex. Martin SS
By Order, J Haywood CS

****

North Carolina State Archives
General Assembly Sessions Records
November-December, 1788, Box #2
Joint Select Committees

North Carolina
  In Senate 18th Nov. 1788
Mr Speaker & Gentl.
  The Subject matter of a Resolution of this House herewith Sent you we propose shall be immediately reported on by a joint Committee and have appd. For this purpose on our part Mr McDowell, Mr Jones & Mr Ben Williams   Alexr. Martin SS
By Order, J Haywood CS

North Carolina
  In the House of Commons 18 Nov. 1788

General Assembly Sessions
1777 - 1789

Mr. Speaker & Gentlemen
    We have appointed Mr Outlaw, Mr McDowell, Mr Cabarrus, Mr Person and Mr Phifer to Act with the Gentlemen by you appointed to confer with Mr. Drumgoole on the propriety of Sending a Talk to Certain Indian Tribes &C.   Jno. Sitgreaves Speakr.

North Carolina
    In Senate 21 Novem. 1788 the Within Report was read and concurred with   Alex. Martin SS
By Order J Haywood CS

    Report of the Committee appointed to confer with Mr. Drumgoole
Your Committee appointed to confer with Mr. Alexr. Drumgoole & Report

That Mr. Drumgoole is willing to wait for some days until the General assembly shall come to some determination on the Subject of Indian Affairs, and to carry any Talk or Talks, which they may think proper to send, to the Cherokees Chickemaugaws or Creeks, provided the Assembly will make a reasonable Allowance for his Delay while here. -- Mr. Drumgoole has a wagon & four Horses in Town & three persons, to maintain; therefore your Committee are of Opinion that Mr. Drumgoole be allowed the Sum of four pounds Pr. Day, while he remains here waiting the Orders of the Assembly commencing the 17th day of Novr.
Submitted   Thomas Person

In the House of Commons 21st November 1788 read and concurred with
By Order J Hunt CHC   Jno: Sitgreaves Speakr.

North Carolina
    In Senate 21 Novemr. 1788 the within Report was read and concurred with
Alex. Martin SS
By Order J Haywood CS

Report of the Committee appointed to confer with Mr. Drumgoole
Nov. 1788 a Resolution to the effect of this Report & made by the Senate enabled Mr Drumgoole to Draw the Amt so that no thing is to be done on this report   J Hunt

****

General Assembly Sessions
1777 - 1789

North Carolina State Archives
General Assembly Sessions Records
November-December, 1788, Box #2
Joint Standing Committees

Petition of the Sundry the Inhabitants of the Western Country

In the House of Commons 7 Nov. 1788 read & referred to the Committee of Propositions & Grievances
By Order, J Hunt CHC

In Senate 7 Nov. 1788 read & referred as by the H Commons
By Order, J Haywood CS

Report of the Committee on the Petition of Sundry the Inhabitants of the Western Counties. Report on the Petition relative to the Price of Vacant Lands, Novr 1788

The Committee to whom the Petition of Sundry Inhabitants of the Western Counties on the Subject of Lands & the price of entering the same was refered

Report that the rates already established by Law for the Entry of Vacant or unappropriated Lands are Sufficiently low & Cheap, they therefore beg leave to recommend that the said Petition be rejected.
All which is Submitted
Thomas Person Clk. 11 Novr. 1788

In the House of Commons 10 November 1788, The House taking this Report into Consideration Concurred therewith
Jno: Sitgreaves, Spkr
By Order J Hunt CHC

North Carolina
    In Senate 11th Nov 1788, Read and Concurred with
Alex. Martin
By Order J, Haywood CS

General Assembly Sessions
1777 - 1789

To the Honourable the General Assembly of the State of North Carolina
The Petition of the back Inhabitants of this State Humbly Sheweth That there are many small Pieces of Land in the upper or Back parts of this State now Lieing Vacant; and the price of Entering of Land being high, and the Inhabitants in General in low Circumstances Causes many families to live on rented Lands, whereas if the price of Entering was Reduced they might be in a Capacity of Getting Land of their own.

We therefore Your Petitioners do Humbly pray that you Would reduce the price of Entering of Land so as to put poor men in a Capacity of getting Land to maintain their families on: and Your Petitioners as in duty Bound will ever pray.

Benj: Herndon, Cha. Jordan, Richard Ferguson, Daniel Culbreath, Andrew Woods, Ze[?] Jessop, Benjamen Jonson, S[?] Blackburn, Spill Trible, John Busby, Sadrack Hanick[?], Samuel Walker, Alexander Gilreath, David Grant, Joseph Herrison, Joel Cofey, Timothy Chandler, Jos. Douste[?], John Robins, Danl Vannoy, George Graham, Wm. Lands[?], Isaac Parlier, Edmun De[?]se, Rowland Judd, Gabriel Smothers, John Gilreath, John Jones, William Elson, John Hageler, [?] Johnson, James Fletcher, Benj Johnson, Elisha Heddin, John Prophet, Pleasant Profitt, George C[?]eacy, Charles Jordon, Thos. Witherspoon, Ben Watson, William Tribble, Russel Jones, Ambrose Hamons, Wm. Nall, Benjamin Ro[?], Job Cole, David Beas[?], James Jackson, [Faded], Peter [Faded], William [Faded], [Faded], Benja. Greer, Eliga Calloway, Joseph Calloway, Wm. Walter, John Doss, Henray Mullens, John Greer, Wm Farmer, Robert Walters, Champ [?], Cannet Oens, Joseph Suiet[?], Joseph Toppins, Robert Judd, Dosson Suiet[?], Henry Chambers, Samuel Styers, James Chambers, James Chambers Senr., Benjamin Brown, Joseph Dyers, Aaron England, Joseph Brown, Daniel Chambers, James Weatherspoon, Daniel Eggers, Jesse Councill, Wm. Mullin, Benjamin Culbrith, John Wilcockson, [Faded] McNiel, Wm. Brown, John Lips, Joshua Storie, James Tompkins, John Cargill Senr., William Jackson, Samuel Allen, Robart Shepard, David Hickason, Jesse Alexander, Thomas Powers, Ahab hamilton, Robert Chandler, George Hulme[?], John Triplet, George Brown, Edwin Brown, Jno. Lovelace, Daniel Holman, Robert Cleveland, Richd. Allen, Robert Nall, Silas Tomkins, Jonathan Torryppens[?], Francis Vannoy, Jacob Hamton, Elisha Reynolds, Solloman Davids, Isaac Norman, James Williams, James Profitt, David Proffit, Andw. Baker, George Gordan, Ichabod Black[?], John Tunnliff, John Shepard, Rheuben Johnson, Alex.

General Assembly Sessions
1777 - 1789

Smith, Thos. Weatherspoon, Micajah Penington, Benj. Penington, John Ayers, Wm. Allen, Wm. [?]be.

****

North Carolina State Archives
General Assembly Sessions Records
November-December, 1788, Box #2
Joint Standing Committees

      Petition of the Inhabitants of French Broad Settlement

In Senate 7 Nov. 1788 read & refer'd to the Committee of Propositions & Grievances
By Order, J Haywood, agreed

In the H. of Commons 10 Nov. 1788 read & Refd. As by the Senate
By Order, J Hunt CHC

To the Honourable the General Assembly of the State of North Carolina
      The Petition of those whose Names Are hereunto subscribed humbly sheweth that your petitioners having settled themselves within the Chartered limits of your State but without Limets prescribed by law for Extending the Settlements of this Commonwealth; have from painfull Experrance felt the inconvenience of living without the protection of the Laws - we therefore beg you would include all that tract of Country on the East side of Tinnasee River within your Government, and if you find it convenient to Open An Office; to dispose of those lands that you would giev the Settlers a Pre-Emption for their settlement at a moderate price or Compensation, And a time to make up the money as we have been and still are greatly distressed by an Indian War; many of us having had all Our property plundered by the Enemy; and as the poor and distressed are Our General Carractors we hope that your Honourable Body will Considar us in Opening the Office On this side the Mountain. We hope that Our having settled Ourselves Contrary to the Authority of Government will not Operate Against us as thos prohibatory Laws are Never Sufficiently promulgated and have Never hither to been put in Execution. Permit us then to implore you not to suffer us to be the Objects of the Resentment of Government; as we did not transgress your laws from a Refractory disposition, but only allowed the practice of the different States; who had

General Assembly Sessions
1777 - 1789

confirmed the actual settlers in their Settlements upon their paying the price settled by Law: We hope your Honourable House will take the premises under your serious consideration And Your Petitioners shall pray &c.

George McNutt, Geor. Jordan, Evan Morgan, John Shavas, Henry Welkertson, Mathew Matthews, James Turman, John Cordar, William Thrift, C[Faded] Bright, John Huff, John Nav[?] Senr., Charls [Faded], John Wagner, Wm. Thornten, Richard Gros, John Tylor, [Faded] Groce, Jas. Sedus[?], Robt. Henry, Wm. Stuart, Jacob Woodward, Geor. Henry, Edward Stephenson, Daniel Quarrels, Edward Clingan, Benjamin Odell, Robt. Taylor, Wm. Bell, John McFarland, George McFarland, Hes[Faded] Rodgers, [Faded] Campbell, Samuel Tal[Faded], [Faded] Horn, [Faded] Huff, Joseph Henrey, Jas. Nicholson, James Morris, Benj. McFarland, Alexr. Campbell, David Henderson, Moses Ashbrook, T Ashbrook, Samuel Wilson, Ephraim Manning, Richard Maning, [Faded] Brown, Thomas Christian, Anthony Christian, Abijah Fewter[Fenter?], Leonard Huff, Peter Huff, David Stourt, Thomas Fowler, La[?] Armstrong, Hennery Jones, Jonnuthan Wood, George Adams, Reubin Pridus[?], David Johnson, George Chivenor, Michal Yocome, Jonah Denton[?], Richd Pryer, Daniel Mees, John Denton, Philip Chavis, Gilbert Chavis, William Pryar, Joseph White, Edward C[?]day, James Ashworth, William Chavis, Philip Chavis, Thomas Gooing, James Dial, John McKissick, Calep Odle, Isaac Odle, John Evins[?], Jos. Inglish, Jas. Stater, Wm Sims[Tims], William Henery, George Henery, Joseph Inglish, John Brickny, Jesse Nilson, Joseph Preyer, John Tulley, Wm Deere, John Williams, Thos. Williams, Ja. Williams, John Keeney, Thomas Keeney, fredrick McCarrey, John Moon, James Turner, John Siscoe, John Parker, John Davis, Joseph Lovlady, John Webb, John Layman, Mikel Houk, John Whiteford, Capt. Robertson, John Mannering, Tobias Wilhelm, Benjemen Manning, John Nulley, Ab[Faded] [Faded], John Anderson, William Inglish, John Inglish, James Inglish, Spence Graham, Joseph Sharp.

****

North Carolina State Archives
General Assembly Sessions Records
November-December, 1789, Box #1
Committee of Indian Affairs

Information of Anthony Foreman 26th Jany. 1789

General Assembly Sessions
1777 - 1789

I heard John Sevier, at a Public Gathering of people on French Broad Stand up and Inform the People, that he had received a Letter from Col. Body & also one from Colo. Outlaw, Informing him that the assembly of North Carolina had now thrown the People of the Country from under their Protection, and that they had no other way now but to Stand in their own defence, and Mr. Sevier Further said you all well know, that the Cherokees have Refused Selling their lands to us from time to time, and we have no Other way now but to take it by the Sword by going into their Nation Killing, and taking their women and Children, destroying their Provitions, and by these means we will Compell them to give up their lands to us

At the same time it was mentioned that Colo. Outlaw had Offered his Service with Two Hundred men to Assist in the above Plan to Carry an Expedition against the Cherokees, and they said they Ware determoned to Stop the Treaty Ordered by North Carolina agreeable to the requisitions of Congress.

Creek Nation 14th March 1789

Received a letter from Alexander Dromgoole directed to his Excellency Alexr. McGilvary sent by said Dromgoole from the Governor of North Carolina Given under my hand the Day above Written
Danl. McGillivray for Alexr. McGillivray

North Carolina
    In Senate 7th Novem. 1789, Mr Speaker & Gentl.
We have added Mr. Sevier to the Committee appointed to report on Indian Affairs   Chas. Johnson Sp. Protem
By Order, J Haywood CS

To the Honorable the General Assembly, Gentlemen,
    I herewith send you a Packet which I have received this Morning from Mr. Alexander McGillivray Chief of the Creek Nation of Indians, and other Papers which I Submit to your Consideration
                                           Saml. Johnston
Fayette Ville, 16th November 1789

General Assembly Sessions
1777 - 1789

North Carolina
In the House 23d Nov 1789

Mr Speaker and Gentlemen of the Senate,
    We herewith send you a Message this day received from his Excellency the Governor enclosing papers from the Chief of the Creek Nation and others, together with the papers therein referred to which we propose referring to the Committee on Indian Affairs
S. Cabarrus SHC
By Order J Hunt CHC

North Carolina
In Senate 24 Nov. 1789

Mr Speaker & Gentl.,
    The Message from His Excellency the Governor of today, Letter from the Chief of the Cherokee Nation and other Papers accompanying them we agree with you in referring to the Committee on Indian Affairs.
Chas. Johnson Sp.
By Order, J Haywood CS

A Message from His Excellency the Governor & a letter from Bennett Bellew.

In the House of Commons 4 Decr. 1789 read & referred to the Committee on Indian Affairs
By Order, J Hunt CHC

In Senate 4th Decem. 1789 read & referred as by the House of Commons
J Haywood CS

The Honorable the General Assembly
    Gentlemen,
Considering it my duty to communicate to your Honorable every information respecting Indian Affairs which comes to my knowledge, I do

General Assembly Sessions
1777 - 1789

myself the Honor to Send you a Letter which has this moment come to my hands
Fayette Ville, 4th December 1789

Saml. Johnston

His Excellency
Governor Johnston
Hon'd by Mr McBride   }No. Carolina

Eastonoley Oct. 30th 1789

Sir/ to his Excellency the Governor No. Carolina
  Being Sensible of your good will & friendly Disposition towards the Cherokees I am en coriged to say before your Excellency a Breef account of the Cituation of Both white People & Indians, on my Return from Congress I Passed through the inhabetants of the Western Countrey which I found in great Confusion, some Short time Before I Ereve in that Countrey thare was an Indian Killed by som of the inhabetants, the Indiand as well as the White People are very much Desturb'd on the Occasion, it is a Pity the Poor inhabetants should Suffer in general for a few individuals which will Ever be the Case while the western Countrey Stands as it is at Present, Promit me Sir to take the Liberty to appolegise for som fals Representations that I make no Doubt have Been Layed before your Excellency affirming that I Persuaded the Cherokees to with hold their Lands from No Carolina, I am not astonished to heare Reports knowing that thare is a Nomber of People who Reside in that nation whose Principles are Base Enough to encorage a Savage War in order that they may inhance the Plundered Property taken from the unwary travelors & Defenceless Fameleys Residing on the frontiers when they found I was Likely to Bring about Peace & tranquility between the Contending Parties, they then Perceiving such a measure would Disconcert their Diabolecal Plans, However I hope I shall be Excused when I inform your Excellency that at the Request of Som Gentlemen in this Countrey I have Consulted a Nomber of the Chiefs of the Cherokees in Respect to their Lands now inhabited By white People & I am induced to believe that the Lands Conditionally given up to General Sevier might be obtained Could he make the Compensation good he Promised them, at the Treaty the Indians as they seem to think they are Bound to him Shold he Comply, Shold such a Measure meet your Excellencys Apprebation I shall be hapy in my endeavours to Bring about a Cession of those Lands & for Ever shall look

General Assembly Sessions
1777 - 1789

upon my self in Duty Bound to use Every Exertion in my Power for the entrest of No Carolina & shall for Ever be Hapy in a friendly intercourse & Candid correspondence with your Excellency, I have the Honour to Remain with Due Respect, Sir your most obedient & most Hble. Sarvt.
Bennett Ballew.

Nov. 25th 1789
Committee on Indian Affairs
State of North Carolina in account with John Steele, agent for Indian Treaty

In House 25 Novr 1789 referred to the Committee on Indian Affairs
By Order, J Hunt CHC

In Senate 25th Nov. 1789 referred as by the House of Commons
J Haywood, CS

Gentlemen
      Having had the honour to be appointed by the last general assembly, Agent of Indian affairs for this State, and under that Appointment having received from the public Treasury a considerable Sum of money -- I conceive it my duty to inform your honorable body in what manner I have discharged this important trusts.
      The Accompt of my disbursements will accompany this letter, to which for full and further information I beg leave to refer.
      I have the Honour to be, Gentlemen, Your most Obedient Humble servant   John Steele
Fayetteville, Novemr. 25th 1789

Dr The State of North Carolina, 1789

Cash paid for Merchandizes & receipts	}	1048.57.3
Cash paid Military department P pay rol -2	}	107.53
Cash paid Commissary Dept. -3	}	65.16
Do for Wagg. The goods from Fayetteville to Salisbury -4	}	44.10.6
Ditto for transporting the same from Fayetteville to Salisbury to Warford		

General Assembly Sessions
1777 - 1789

6 waggs.	}	92.0.0
paid several expresses Pr. -5	}	28.2.0
paid Robt Morgan a soldier -6	}	3.0.0
paid for an Express to Governor	}	15.0.0
paid one of the waggoners as extra	}	1.0.0
paid for Sundry articles in Fayette while purchasing the Goods	}	6.7
paid for carrying a Letter to Genl. & Colo. McDowell	}	0.10
paid by Genl McDowell for Genl Winns Express	}	1.0.0
Pd. Housekeeper 41 days	}	16.8.0
Paid Danl Alamong att the Store after the Troops were dismissed	}	<u>8.8</u>
		£1438.11.9
To Balc. Due P Keel in Currency	}	105.5.1
18 days personal Service at Ninety six in February last at 5 dollrs. P Day	}	36.0
81 days personal service transacting the business of the Commission	}	162.0

Fayetteville 29th Novemr. 1789, This day appeared before me the Subscribing Justice John Steele, who made oath that the above acct. of Monies paid out and services performed as Commr. Is just and true to the best of his knowledge, Sworn to before [?]

By Cash from the public treasury P Governors Warrt.	1333.6.8
By Balc. Due J.S. in Currency	<u>105.5.1</u>
	£1438.11.9

Errors Excepted, 25 Nov 1789, Fayetteville
Jno. Steele, Commr. Indian Affairs.

Memorial of John Sevier

In Senate 20 Novem. 1789 read & referred to the Committee on Indian Affairs
By Order, J Haywood CS

General Assembly Sessions
1777 - 1789

In House 24 Novr. 1789 read & referred by the Senate
By Order, J Hunt CHC
Carter

To the Honble the General Assembly Now Siting
    The Memorial of John Sevier Humbly Sheweth
Your Memorialist begs leave to inform Your August and Honorable body that in the Month of May in the year one thousand seven Hundred and Eighty five; at the Request of the people Settled and inhabited on the West Side of the Appalachian Mountains, Did in fair & Open Treaty Held with the King and a number of the Warriors and Chiefs of the Cherokee Nation, Stipulated, agreed for, & obtained all the lands lying within the Chartered limits of this State, running as far So. As the dividing Ridge between Little River & the Great Tenasee, and South of the Great Rivers Holeson and French Broad,
    Your Memorialist Humbly Conceive, that he was not only Authorized by the people of the Western Territory alone, but was Vested with a full and ample power from the Executive of North Carolina, to Negotiate the treaty aforesaid, which will more fully and at large Appear on the examination of the direction & instructions Received from his Excellency Alexander Martin Esquire, then Governor of this State.
    Your Memorialist begs leave to Suggest that if the Treaty aforesaid be properly Attended by the legislature that the same May be of very Great importance and Utility to the State.
    Your Memorialist therefore humbly pray that the same may be taken Under your consideration, and in duty bound Will pray &c &c.
John Sevier

****

North Carolina State Archives
General Assembly Sessions Records
November-December, 1789, Box #1
Committee of Propositions & Grievances

Public Service
To the Honourable the General Assembly of the Sate of North Carolina

Fort Johnston October 12th 1789

General Assembly Sessions
1777 - 1789

Mr Speaker and Gentlemen,
    Agreeable to an Act of Assembly passed last Session impowering the Commanding Officers of Washington, Sullivan, Greene and Hawkins Counties to fix a Station with thirty three men on the north side of Tenasee to guard the frontiers. I was appointed by the Officers, to take the Command of said Station; Who Instructed me to Indeavour to raise thirty three men by voluntary Inlistment for the term of one year if not sooner discharged by the Governor, and erect a Station at the most suitable place near the junction of Holstein and Tenasee River. But if I found I could not Inlist the men to report to them and they would raise them by drafts - agreeable to my Instructions I indeavoured to raise the men but found I could ingage but a few. I then made Application according to my directions informing the Officers that I would proceed with the men I had collected to take possession of some suitable post to Strengthen and incourage the frontiers and expected they would send men to fill the Company as soon as possible. I Immediately came to the frontier and set about erecting a Strong Station, but the men were not sent agreeable to my expectation; and as the Indians seemed very Insolent and the frontier people much discouraged I again made application representing the situation of the frontier and praying an answer wheather the men would be sent or not; or directions wheather I should continue with the few I had, but I have never received neither men nor answer. I still continue to keep possession of the Post with the few men I collected.
    At the request of the frontier Inhabitants I lay this before you.
I am Mr. Speaker & Gentlemen your very Humble Servant.
David Campbell

David Campbell, Representative
In H Com 6 Nov 1789 read and referred to Committee of Props. & Griev.
By Order
In Senate 6th Novem. 1789 read & referred as by the House of Commons
By Order, J Haywood CS

****

North Carolina State Archives
General Assembly Sessions Records
November-December, 1789, Box #1
Petitions Rejected or not acted on

General Assembly Sessions
1777 - 1789

To his Excellency Samuel Johnson Esqr. Govr. Com. And Chief in and Over the State of No. Carolina and the Honourable Council of State the Petition of Sundry inhabitants of the Indian territory Humbly Sheweth,
That fully Sensible we are that we have been the Objects of the Just displeasure of the State of North Carolina by Violating her laws and Rejecting her just Injunctions in not removing ourselves agreeable to the laws of Our Country but having long Experienced the Clemency and parental Tenderness of a Parent State whose interest we have Ever held as Sacred to us. We are thereby Encouraged to Address a patriotic Chief Magistrate and an inlited Council to take us under their protection and deliver us from the Hands of those who by their Rebellion and unjust Revolt from the tenderest of parents Justly merits the frowns of Government, at least we humbly pray that we may not be Considered Eaders or incouragers of Revolt and Rebellion against the Just Authority of No. Carolina and altho it is with the Greatest pain **[Torn]** consider ourselves destitute of the benefits of Civil Government we are ready with ourselves and fortunes to Support her laws and Constitution looking with an assured hope that we shall meet with a most Grecious and unmerited Reception into the Bosom of Civil Government at which time we Shall Consider Ourselves as the most distinguished objects of the Clemancy and unbounded liberality of a free and independent State, and Shall Consider ourselves doubly bound to Reverence her laws and Support her interests.

John Ward Junr., John McFarland, James Nickels, Thomas Keeny, George McNutt, Mical Yockam, James Turman, Samuel Wilson, Peter Huff, Adam Scott, Thomas Rogers, Seth Rogers, Thomas Giffy, Benjamin Allen, Solomon Allen, Frederick Mayberry, Thomas Little, Moses Ashbrooks, Samuel Dorn, Richard Manning, Andrew Horn, Ephraim Manning, Gesper Manning, William Horn, Thomas Moon, William Thornten, John Campbell, Alexr. Rodgers, John Calfer[**Coffee?**], John Nane[**Lane?**], Alexr Ward, David Stuart, John Shever, Alexr. Campbell, James Campbell, David Tate, John Keeny, John Ward Senr., John Cordar, Henry Neightherton, Benjemine McFarland, George McFarland, George Ashbrook, Francis Rowan, Jonathan Wood, John Denton, Daniel Ma[**Faded**], John Evans, Isaac Odell, Calleb Odell, Simon Odell, Richard Gross, Wm. Di[**?**], Thomas Wall[**?**], G McCown, Daniel Luttrel, Wm Goff, Samuel Job, Joseph Whit, Richard Price, David Fine, Spencer Coleman, Jacob Job, John **[Faded]**, Jonah **[Faded]**, Samuel Odell, John Brickey, George Adams, Spencer Geahorn[**?**], William Whitson, Thomas

General Assembly Sessions
1777 - 1789

May, Simon Odell, Thomas Davis, Thomas Abell, Thomas Stephens, Nehemia Odell, Benedick Lore, William Pryor, John McKissack, Philip Chavis, John Stephenson, John Oston, Nicholas Woodfin, Ritchard Lotral, James Graves, Joseph Pryor, Edward Loveday, Philip Chavis, William Mac Kea, Jeremiah Denton, Dunkun Mkea[?], John Odell, William Inglish, James Mc[?], Thomas Mc [?], David Mc [?], Lenky[?] Jones, John Denton, James Storles, William Fortner, Joseph English, James Inglish, John Keeney, James Whitson, Isaac Job, Thomas Evins, John McCown, G McCown Junr., Edward **[Faded]**, Benja. McFarland, George Parkes, Geo. McFarland, Saml. Jack Junr., Isham Harris, George Douglas, John McCallie.

****

North Carolina State Archives
General Assembly Sessions Records
November-December, 1789, Box #1
Committee of Propositions & Grievances

Fort Johnston, October 12th 1789

Public Service
To the Honourable the General Assembly of the State of North Carolina.

Mr. Speaker and Gentlemen,
    Agreeable to an act of Assembly passed last session impowering the Commanding Officers of Washington, Sullivan, and Hawkins Counties to fix a Station with thirty three men on the north side of Tenasee to guard the frontiers. I was appointed by the Officers, to take the Command of said Station; who Instructed me to endeavour to raise thirty three men by voluntary Inlistment for the term of one year if not sooner discharged by the Governor and erect a station at the most suitable place near the junction of Holstein and Tenasee Rivers, but if I found I could not Inlist the men to report to them and they would raise them by Drafts - agreeable to my Instructions I endeavoured to raise the men but found I could engage but a few; I then made Application according to my directions informing the Officers that I would proceed with these men I had collected to take possession of some suitable post to strengthen and encourage the frontiers, and expected they would send men to fill the Company as soon as possible. I Immediately came to the frontier and set about erecting a Strong Station,

General Assembly Sessions
1777 - 1789

but the men were not sent agreeable to my expectation, and as the Indians seemed very Insolent and the frontier people much discouraged I again made application representing the situation of the frontier and praying an answer wheather the men would be sent or not; or directions wheather I should continue with the few I had, but I have never received neither men nor answer. I still continue to keep possession of the post with the few men I Collected.

At the request of the frontier Inhabitants I lay this before you. I am Mr. Speaker & Gentlemen your very Humble Servant.
David Campbell.

In H Com 6 Nov 1789, read to Commt. Of Prop & Grievances
By Order

In Senate 6th Novem 1789 read & referred as by the House of Commons
By Order, J Haywood

****

North Carolina State Archives
General Assembly Sessions Records
November-December, 1789, Box #1
Committee of Indian Affairs

The Honorable the General Assembly, Gentlemen,

Considering it my duty to communicate to your Honorable Body every information respecting Indian Affairs which comes to my Knowledge, I do myself the Honor to Send you a Letter which has this moment come to my hands.
Saml. Johnston

Fayetteville, 4th December 1789

****

North Carolina State Archives
General Assembly Sessions Records
November-December, 1789, Box #1
Committee on Indian Affairs

General Assembly Sessions
1777 - 1789

Gentlemen,
    Having had the honour to be appointed by the last general assembly, Agent of Indian Affairs for this State, and under that appointment having received from the public Treasury a considerable Sum of money --- I conceive it my duty to inform your honorable body in what manner I have discharged this important trust.
    The accompt of my disbursements will accompany this letter, to which for full and further information I beg leave to refer.
    I have the honour to be, Gentlemen, Your most Obedient Humble Servant
Fayetteville, Novemr. 25th 1789

The State of North Carolina in acct. currt. With John Steele

Dr.

To Cash paid for merchandizes pau[?] & receipts	1048.57.3
Cash paid Military department p pay rol	107.13.00
Cash paid Commisarys dept.	65.16.00
Do. For Wagg: the goods from Fayetteville to Salisbury	44.10.6
Do. For transporting the same from Salisbury to Warford, 6 Waggs.	92.00.00
paid several expresses pr.	28.2.00
paid Robt Morgan a Soldier	3.00.00
paid for an express to the Governor	15.00.00
paid one of the waggoners as extra Att.ec	1.00.00
paid for sundry articles in Fayetteville while purchasing the Goods	6.7.00
paid for carrying letter to Genl. & Col. McDowell	00.10.00
paid by Genl McDowell for Genl Winns express	1.00.00
pd. 1 Housekeeper 41 days at/ p day	16.8.00
paid Danl Alamong attng the Store after the troops were dismissed	8.8.00
	1438.11.9
To balc. Due P Steel in Currency	105.5.1
18 days personal Service at Ninety Six in February las at 5 dolls p day	36

General Assembly Sessions
1777 - 1789

81 days personal Service transacting the business of the Commission	162
Cr	
By Cash from the public treasury P Governors warrt.	1333.6.8
By Balce. Due J.S. in Currency	105.5.1
	1438.11.9

Errors Excepted, Fayetteville
November 25th 1789
Jno. Steele, Commr. Indian Affairs

Fayetteville 29th Novemr. 1789, This day appeared before me the Subscribing Justice, John Steele, who made Oath that the above acct. of monies paid out and Service performed as Commr. Is just and true to the best of his knowledge, Sworn to before [Faded] Jno. Steele.

The State of North Carolina in A/ C with John Steele, Agent for Indian Treaty. In Hcom 25 Novr 1789 referred to the Commt. On Indian Affairs. By Order, J Hunt CHC

In Senate 25th Nov 1789, referred as by the House of Commons.
J Haywood, CS

****

North Carolina State Archives
General Assembly Sessions Records
November-December, 1789, Box #1
Committee of Propositions & Grievances

The Petition & Memorial of Colo. James Miller

In Hcom 24 Novr. 1789, referred to the Comt. Of Prop. Grievances
By Order, J Hunt CHC

In Senate 27th Nov. 1789 read & referred as by the H Commons
By Order

To the Honorable the General Assembly of the State of North Carolina

General Assembly Sessions
1777 - 1789

The petition & memorial of Colo. James Miller of Rutherford County Humbly Sheweth, That in the faul of the year 1780 he your memorialist was on Command on the frontier of this State against the Indians and Lord Corn Wallace was marching through this County at the same time, that provitions for the troops was Difficult to procure.

At which time a Mrs. Widdow Mary Potts Stood Indebted to a Certain John Goodbread a Sum of money (on a bond) upeards of thirty Pounds, Your Memorialist at that time being Commissioner of Confiscated Property for said County and the said John Goodbread being Considered to have forfeited his Property by his Joyning the Enimy taking Arms &c and as Also by the Judicial Proceedings of said County Court was induced to believe that it woud be no violation of Justice to the State on Mrs. Potts giving to the Public Use beef Cattle to the value and full ammount of the bond Afforsaid that she Shou'd be exonarated from her bond, Your Memorialist Humbly Sheweth that the said Mrs. Mary Potts did furnish to the Public the value of said bond in [?] and that Your Memorialist Did give a receipt against said bond.

Your Memorialist further Sheweth that John Goodbread has recovered his property & has brought Suit against Mrs. Potts recovered the Amount of his bond notwithstanding the Afforsaid receit, your Memorialist further Sheweth that Mrs. Potts has Also recovered of him your memorialist the full amount of Said bond: Your Memorialist persumes as he was totally influenced from a principal of Justice together with the Public Intrist that you in Your wisdom and Goodness will give such relief as the nature of his peculiar Case may require -- And your Petttioner as in Duty bound shall ever Pray.
James Miller

State of No. Carolina }
Rutherford County } July Court 1788

No. 24 John Goodbread
      Vs
Mary Potts Admr of John Potts Decd

Thereupon **[Torn]** Jury (to Wit)
1. Jesse Melton, 2. John Elans, 3. Henry Killy, 4. John Taborn, 5. John Whiteside, 6. Elias Morgan, 7. **[Smudged]** Tipton, 8. Samuel Thompson,

General Assembly Sessions
1777 - 1789

9. Stephen Willis, 10. Daniel Madden, 11. William Robinson, 12. Francis Brown.

Jury impanneled & duly sworn do find : For the Plantiff & Assess damages to forty three Pounds Nineteen Shillings.   £43.19.0
Clerk fees   2.4.3
Sheriff & Government Tax   0.0.18
[Smudged]   1.5.0
[Smudged]   48.8.3

State of North Carolina }
Rutherford County   } [Torn] Court 1788

Mary Potts Adm. Of John Potts decd
 vs
James Miller

Jury impanneled & being duly sworn do find for the plantiff & Assess damages to forty eight pounds six Shillings & three pence
    £48.6.3
Cost and Charges in Suit   3.9.10

The above suit was instituted for the recovery of a Number of Cattle taken & made use of for the Public servise &c

Extract from Records
RT [?] Clk.

I do hereby Certify the foregoing to be true Copys taken from the Record in Witness Whereof I have affixed the Public County [Smudged] Office this 15th Day of Oct. 1796[?]

****

North Carolina State Archives
General Assembly Sessions Records
November-December, 1789, Box #2
Committee of Propositions and Grievances

General Assembly Sessions
1777 - 1789

To the Honorable the Genl Assembly of the State of North Carolina,
   The Petition of Elisha Hadden Humbly Sheweth that in the year 1788 bring called out by Order of John Tipton Lieutenant Col. Commandant of the County of Washington to Serve in the Militia on the Frontiers of Washington District in Order to prevent the inrodes of the Savage Tribes of the Cherokees and others which they were daily making into the Said Frontiers, Your Petitioner had the Misfortune to Receive a Dangerous Wound in his Leg and arm by Some of the aforesaid Indians which Reduced your Petitioner to close confinement for upwards of Sic Months and still incapable of performing any kind of Bodily Labour for the Support of his Family, most part of which Time your Petitioner was under the care of a Surgeon who makes Demands of Your Petitioner for the Sum of Fourteen Pounds which was his charge for the time he had the care of me which charge your Petitioner will be Reduced to the necessity of Paying in his distressed Situation if your Honourable Body do not Take his Case into your serious consideration and Grant him the aforesaid Sum which he is compelled to pay and Your Petitioner is in duty Bound &c
Elisha Hadden

Petition of Elisha Hadden, Report thereon Delvd. , Mr Blair by J Hunt

Petition of Elisha Hadden In House 1 Dec 1789, referred to Comt. Of Props. And Grievances
By Order, J Hunt CHC

In Senate 2d Decr. 1789 read & referred as by the H Commons
J Haywood CS

****

North Carolina State Archives
General Assembly Sessions Records
November-December, 1789, Box #2
Committee of Propositions & Grievances
Petition Rejected

To the honourable the General Assembly of North Carolina, The Memorial of Robert Hays Humbly Sheweth,
   That the people of Miro District when they knew a treaty was about to take place last Spring with the Southward Indians, being Sensible

General Assembly Sessions
1777 - 1789

how much to the advantage of that part of the State it would be to have Some person present, who could point out, the many Instances wherein the Indians had been guilty of a violation of the treaties made heretofore, and also State many facts interesting to the Commissioners to know. These people I say did unanimously make choice of your Memorialist to go to the treaty and render them what Service he could.

That your memorialist was farther induced to undertake this business because a Chief of the Chickasaws and his son had just then arrived in our Settlement intending to go to the said treaty on business of importance and could not go on without some white person to assist him. That as your memorialist was on his way to the said treaty he was attacked by a large party of Creek Indians; who killed the two Chickasaws, two white men, and wounded others. The rest of your Memorialists party being driven off naked, and with the loss of every thing they had along with them. Your Memorialist therefore Submits his Case to your honourable body, trusting you will give him some relief proportionate to his loss and Sufferings. & your Memorialist as in duty bound will be impressed with the highest feelings of gratitude accordingly
Robert Hays

The Committee to whom the Memorial of Robert Hays was referred, Report, That it appears to your Committee that the said Robert Hays was not employed by the Agent for holding the treaty with the Indians, But that he undertook to attend the said Treaty voluntarily, or at the Instance of the Inhabitants of Mero District.

Therefore your Committee are of opinion as Mr. Hays undertook said business of his own accord, that he is not entitled to have any allowance made him for the losses he sustained in going to said treaty, and Reject the said Memorial, Which is Submitted.

H. Hill CSA
In Senate 22d Decr. 1789, read & Concurred with, Chas. Johnson, Sp.
By Order, J Haywood CS

****

North Carolina State Archives
General Assembly Sessions Records
November-December, 1789, Box #2

General Assembly Sessions
1777 - 1789

House of Assembly
Saturday the 24th January 1789

Mr Sullivan from the Committee to whom was referred the intercepted letters of Joseph Martin Esquire Agent to the Cherokee and Chickasaw Indians appointed by Congress which were laid before this house by General Mathews -- brought in a Report, which being read, was agreed to by the House and is as follows.

Your Committee report that whatever reasons and Advantages the said Joseph Martin may have for carrying on a correspondence of a private nature with Alexander McGilveray, yet while this State is at war with the Creek nation, and the said Joseph Martin being in the Service of the United States, Your Committee are of opinion that the conduct of the said Joseph Martin is culpable and reprehensible - and Your Committee request that His Honor the Governor do transmit to Congress a Copy of the intercepted letter of the said Joseph Martin to Alexander McGilveray of the Creek Nation, and also copies of the said resolutions to His Excellency the Governor of North Carolina; he the said Joseph Martin being an Inhabitant of that State. And that His Honor the Governor do in his communication to Congress and the Governor of the State of North Carolina impress them with the designs of the said Martin of removing himself and property from without the reach of the law, seeking the protection of the Creek Indians and how impossible it is for the State of Georgia to expect Peace whilst the very officers of the United States are treacherously leagued with the Savage Tribes.

Your Committee can not but further observe that this letter and the resolution of Congress were found in the possession of men of the most infamous character living in the Creek nation, and who, at this time had in their possession a considerable share of Plunder, the property of George [Torn].

Extract from the Minutes of the Governor of Georgia -- Jas. M Lumm[Torn]

****

North Carolina State Archives
General Assembly Sessions Records
November-December, 1789, Box #2
Reports and Papers

General Assembly Sessions
1777 - 1789

George Brooks depo. Vs. Joseph Martin
Sundry Depositions from the Western Country

In Senate 5th Decemr. 1789 read and referred to the Committee on the representation respecting General Martin
J Haywood CS
Sevier

October the 13th 1789
This day George Brooks Came before me Benjamin Murrell one of the Justices of the Peace for the County of Hawkins and made Oath that about the year one Thousand Seven hundred and Eighty as well as he remembers in the month of Aprill the then Colonel Evan Shelby [?] General Shelby Commanded a number of men and was carrying on an Expedition against the Chickey Moggey Indians that the said Shelby applied to this Deponant & the present Colo. Elijah Robertson to go to the Cherokee nation and let the present General Joseph Martin know and Inform him that it was Colo. Shelbys Orders for Martin to meet him at the mouth of Little River and to direct Martin to keep the Expedition against the Indians a profound Secret and to meet Shelby at the mouth of Little River to go with him and the troops under his Command against the Indians, Colo. Shelby had before sent one Hudson with Secret intelligence for Martin who By Accident got drowned in the River which detained the Army some days & this deponant and Colo. Robertson in order that the Indians might not mistrust the business they went on took a letter from Shelby pretending as if Shelby had something to do about tradeing with them and mentioned Something about Skins but this Deponant & Robertson was directed to make Martin fully Acquainted with the Expedition and to pointedly Charge him to keep to keep the matter Secret & to meet Shelby at the place above mentioned which this Deponant Sayeth they did but Martin said he Could not go with them then as Shelby had directed but said he would meet Shelby & the troops at the mouth of Holson this deponant & Robertson then went as they ware ordered Expecting to meet the troops at the mouth of Little River whare they Staid five days without any provision and was Oblidged to return to the nation whare they was Charged by the Indians as having acted as[?]es and was Informd by the Indians that Martin had told them of the Expedition & found Martin then in the Indian Town Contrary to the Expectation of this Deponant and then was Informd by the traders that Martin and the Raven One of the head Men among the Indians had been

General Assembly Sessions
1777 - 1789

gone two days to the mouth of the River to see if the troops had passed & this Deponant heard Martin say at that time in presence of the Indians & Traders that he thought it was his duty to let the Indians Know of the Expedition & that his talks should be always Strait and true, Some time after this Deponant heard that an Expedition was Ordered Out against the Cherokee Indians to be Commanded by Colo. John Sevier and the present General Joseph Martin in presence of this Deponant Applied to two of the Hunnicuts two noted Torys to go with them to the nation and after they Refused he the said Martin promised this Deponant that if he would go with him he would get this Deponant a Horse he had Lost which the Indians had taken from him and when they had Crossed French Broad River Martin told this Deponant that his business to the nation was to Inform the Indians that the white people was going against them after which Conversation they met some Indians and Martin Told them of the Campayne and one of the Indian fellows and Martin Set Out Appearrantly in grate haste to Inform the towns when this Deponant got to the towns he saw Martin in the Town house Councelling with about a hundred Indians Expresses Ware Concluded to be sent to all the towns & Spies was Sent to See what Rout the Army took and about four Hundred Indians and Tories was gathered and Set to way lay the Different fords the tories & some Indians this Deponant understood was Commanded by one McDanniel and while this Deponant was in the towns the Indians brought in an account that Sevier had marched against the Over hill Indians and had killd one Indian, after this Deponant returned home he was Informd that the Indian was killd by John Hill which may better Serve to Identify the time that he is at present able to do by Memory and Further Saith not, Sworn to and Subscribed the day & date above written. Before me
Benjm. Murrell JP
George Brooks

August the 15th 1789

Ms. Gillaspie, Ms. Hanah, Ms. McDowell & her Daughter late prisoners With the Cherokee Indians, Voluntarily Declared Before Us, Wm. Lowery & Olipher Alexander Two of the Justices of the Peace, Ms. Gillaspie & Ms. Hanah Saith that they Heard General Martins Letter read, Which He Had Sent to the Indians In the Turkey Town, Which Inform'd the Indians that he did not Mean to Hurt them In the War. Reason Might Teach them so as he had Twelve Children In their Station, and that He Did Not Blame

General Assembly Sessions
1777 - 1789

them for what they Were a Doing to the people for he had often Told them to Remove off the Lands But they were a Head Strong Disobedient people & Would Not Mind what he said, Ms. McDowell & Daughter Saith, that Mr Hughs a White man that is now Husband to the squaw Martin formerly kept Told them that if Martin Had Been a friend to the White people that he Might have Let them know when the Indian Campaign Was a coming As he New of it Before it Started & further Saith not
Declared Before Us
William Lowry   JP
Olipher Alexander   JP

19th Octo. 1789 Hawkins Cty.

This day Colo. Hutchings Came before me & made Oath that some time in the year 1779 a Certain James Trainer applied to Sd. Deponant to Know if a person Who had taken the Oath of Fedility to the States was not in Consequence there of Bound to give information of any Treaterous Conspiracies that came Within his knowledge. Sd. deponant told Sd. Trainer he thought it the Most Essential part of that Oath, upon Which Sd. Trainer presented to this deponant a letter Which he Sd. he had Copyed of From a Letter Wrote by Capt Martin Now General Martin to Mr. Steward the British Agent Which Sd. Trainer had Copyed a part of Sd. Letter but Was prevented fully Copying it, A paragraph in the Letter this deponant Remembers thus (in answer to Mr. Stewards Letter he Informd Sd. Steward that he had Sent him the Rattle Snake warrior & Nineteen Fellows & should he have Any Further Commands to Let him Know it & he Was all Obedience -- this deponant being Much Surprised at Such a piece, With Several other paragraffs Not so Well Remembered handed it back & Informd Sd. Trainer he would upon Sight make it Known to Genl. Martin, & accordingly did so, in a Friendly manner He informd Sd. deponant that he Wrote Such Letter by the Advice of Gouvernor Henry; in Order to discover the Movements of Mr Steward, & **[Smudged]** & demanded Sd. Letter & told him if he did Not Immediately Give it up he would throw him into the Fier upon which Sd. Trainer Gave it up to Sd. Martin & Further this deponant Saith not
Thomas Hutchings
Sworn to before me & Subscribed Before me the day & date Above Written,   John Cox JP

General Assembly Sessions
1777 - 1789

Colo. Robertson's Deposition

State of North Carolina Hawkins County
This day Colonel Elijah Robertson came before me and made Oath that in the year 1779 He was imployed by Colonel Shelby to go to the Cherokee Nation to discover the disposition of the uper Cherokees Colonel Shelby being then at the head of a Number of troops going against the Chickamaugah Indians and apprehensive the uper Towns were also for war he was Directed to go to their Towns if thought practicable but by no means to discover the intended expedition to any one but the present General Joseph Martin, also tell Martin he was directed to meet the Troops at the mouth of Little River being the place this deponant was directed to meet Colonel Shelby, according to orders this deponant denyed to the Indians he knew any thing of an expedition going against Chickamaugah but informed Martin Shelby's orders and request that he should meet him at the Mouth of Little River, Martin told this Deponant that he could not go then, But said he would meet the Troops at the Mouth of Holston, this deponant saith that he then left the Towns in order to fulfill his orders but being disappointed in meeting with the troops was obliged to return back to the Nation where he was informed that Martin had given inteligence to the Indians of the expedition, this deponant went to see Martin in order to get Martin to tell the Indians he had been mistaken and did not understand this deponant to which Martin replyed that he dare not deny what he had told them, this deponant further saith that the Indians abused him very much and told him they had then ketched him in a lye and had got him and Martin face to face, Martin then told the Indians that they would always find his talks strate and this deponant saith that he told no other person in the Nation but Martin of the Troops being on their way against Chickamaugah and further saith not.
Elijah Robertson
Sworn to before me, Willm. Reed, Octr. 10th 1789

North Carolina
    In Senate 7th Nov. 1789
Mr. Speaker & Gentlemen
    We propose that a joint Comt. Be appointed to take under their consideration and Report on the Letters and Papers now before this Assembly relative to the conduct of General Joseph Martin for which

General Assembly Sessions
1777 - 1789

purpose we have apptd. Mr Blount, Mr Smith, Mr Skinner, Mr Montgomery & Mr Mayo, who will act with such Gentlemen as you may think proper to name for this purpose.
Chas. Johnson Sp. Pro tem.

North Carolina
    In the H Comm. 7 Novr. 1789
Mr Speaker and Gentlemen
    The House concur with the senate in referring the papers relative to the conduct of General Martin to a joint Committee and have on our parts appointed Mr Davie, Mr Blount, Mr Williams, Mr Stokes, Mr McDowall and Mr Wilson
S. Cabarrus S.C.
By Order, J Hunt CHC

Resolve Congress
14th August 1788

By the United States in Congress assembled
August 14, 1788

In the report of a Committee to which was referred a Letter from the War Office with papers from the Superintendant of Indian Affairs for the Southern Indians.
    Resolved, that a further sum of four thousand dollars or so much as may be found absolutely necessary, be allowed in addition to the six thousand dollars granted by a resolution of Congress of the 26th October 1787, for defraying the expence of the Treaty intended to be made with the Southern Indians and that the States of North Carolina, South Carolina, and Georgia be required to furnish the same in equal Sums to be credited on their respective quotes of Specie requisitions of Congress. That it be earnestly recommended to the State of North Carolina, to furnish without delay, her quota of the six thousand dollars before granted, as well as the four thousand dollars granted by this resolution, that no misfortune may happen from the want of sufficient funds to bring the treaty to a happy issue. And that the Executive thereof, to appoint a Commissioner if possible, in time, to assist at the said treaty.
    Resolved, That if any of the States shall furnish more than its quota of either of the before mentioned sums, such State, shall have a

General Assembly Sessions
1777 - 1789

credit for the whole sum furnished, in like manner, as expressed in the preceeding resolution.
Signed   Chas Thomson Secy.
Certified to be a true Copy by Wm Knox

By the United States in Congress Assembled
August 20, 1788

Resolved, That Joseph Martin esquire be, and he is hereby appointed Agent for the Chickasaw Nation of Indians, together with the Cherokees, with the powers that are described in the act of the 19th of June last,
Signed, Chas. Thomson, Secy.
Certified to be a true Copy by Wm. Knox

War Office September 4, 1788

Sir,
    In the absence of the Secretary at War, I had the honor to write you on the 22d. ultimo, at the same time enclosed you a Resolve of Congress of the 20th Ultimo appointing you Agent to the Chickasaw Nation of Indians, the first was addressed to the care of, and to be forwarded by the Post Master at Richmond and a duplicate to Hillsborough North Carolina with similar directions.
    I now transmit you a Resolve of Congress of the 1st instant accompanying a proclamation of the same date which is intended to have an extensive circulation, and therefore I take the liberty to enclose you ten copies.

I have the honor to be, Sir, Your Most Ob. Servt.
Wm Knox

Colo. Joseph Martin
Agent for the Cherokee & Chickasaw Nations of Indians.

Resolve of Congress
1st September 1788

General Assembly Sessions
1777 - 1789

By the United States in Congress Assembled
September 1st 1788

Resolved, That the Secretary at War, be, and he is hereby directed to have a sufficient number of the Troops in the service of the United States in readiness to march from the Ohio, to the protection of the Cherokees, whenever Congress shall direct the same, and that he take measures for obtaining information of the best routs for troops to march from the Ohio to Chota, and for dispersing among all the white inhabitants settled upon, or in the vicinity of the hunting grounds secured to the Cherokees by the treaty concluded between them and the United States, November 28th 1785, the proclamation of Congress of this date.

Resolved, That copies of the said proclamation, and of the resolutions, be transmitted to the Executives of Virginia and North Carolina, and that the said States be, and they are hereby requested to use their influence that the said proclamation may have its intended effect, to restore peace and harmony between the Citizens of the United States and the Cherokees, and to prevent any further invasions of their respective rights, and possessions; and in case Congress shall find it necessary to order troops to the Cherokee Towns to enforce a due Grievance of the said treaty, that the States be, and they are hereby requested to co-operate with the said troops for enforcing such observance of that treaty

Resolved, That the papers which have been transmitted to Congress concerning hostilities alledged to have been committed by John Sevier and others on the Cherokee Indians at Chota, be referred to the Executive of North Carolina and that the said Executive be, and they hereby are earnestly requested to cause enquiry to be made into the said hostilities and to take measures as having the perpetrators thereof apprehended and punished.
Signed, Chas Thomson, Secy.
Certified to be a true Copy by Wm Knox.

****

North Carolina State Archives
General Assembly Sessions Records
November-December, 1789, Box #3
Committee on Indian Affairs

General Assembly Sessions
1777 - 1789

The Honble. The General Assembly Now Siting,

The Memorial of John Sevier Humbly Sheweth,
  Your Memorialist beg leave to inform Your August And Honourable body, that in the Month of May in the year one thousand seven hundred and Eighty five; at the request of the people Settled and inhabited on the West side of the Appalachian Mountains, Did in fair & Open Treaty Held with the King and a Number of the Warriors and Cheifs of the Cherokee Nation, Stipulate, agreed for, & obtained all the lands lying within the Chartered limits of this State, Runing as far So. As the dividing Ridge between Little River & the Great Tenasee, and South of the great Rivers Holeson and French Broad.

  Your Memorialist Humbly Conceives, that he was not only Authorized by the people of the Western Territory Alone, but was Vested with a full and ample power from the Executive of North Carolina, to negotiate the treaty aforesaid, which will more fully and at large appear on the examination of the direction & Instructions received from his Excellency Alexander Martin Esquire, then Governor of this State.

  Your Memorialist beg leave to Suggest, that if the Treaty aforesaid be properly Attended to by the legislature, that the same May be of very Great importance and Utility to the State.

  Your Memorialist therefore humbly pray that the same may be taken Under your Consideration, and in duty bound Will ever pray &c &c
John Sevier.

In Senate 20 Novemr 1789 read & Referred to the Committee on Indian Affairs.
By Order, J Haywood

In H Comm 24 Novr 1789 read and referred as by the Senate.
J Hunt, CHC

****

North Carolina State Archives
General Assembly Sessions Records
November-December, 1789, Box #3
Committee on Indian Affairs

General Assembly Sessions
1777 - 1789

Creek Nation, 14th March 1789

Received a letter from Alexander Dromgoole directed to his Excellency Alexr McGilvary sent by said Dromgoole from the Governor of North Carolina, given under my hand the Day above written.
Danl. McGillivray for Alexr. McGillivray

Information of Anthony Foreman 26th Jany. 1789

I heard John Sevier, at a Public Gathering of People on French Broad Stand up and Inform the People, that he had received a Letter from Col. Body & also one from Colo. Outlaw, Informing him that the Assembly of North Carolina had now thrown the People of the Country from under their Protection, and that they had no other way now but to Stand in their own defence, and Mr. Sevier further said you all well know, that the Cherokees have Refused Selling their lands to us from time to time, and we have no Other way now but to take it by the Sword by going into their Nation Killing, and taking their Women and Children, destroying their Provitions, and by these means we will Compell them to give up their lands to us
At the same time it was mentioned that Colo. Outlaw had Offered his Service with Two Hundred men to Assist in the above Plan to Carry an Expedition against the Cherokees, and they said they were determined to stop the Treaty Ordered by North Carolina agreeable to the requisitions of Congress.

North Carolina, In Senate 7th Novem. 1789. Mr. Speaker, We have added Mr. Sevier to the Committee appointed to Report on Indian Affairs.
Chas. Johnson, Sp. Pro tem
By Order, J Haywood, CS

****

North Carolina State Archives
General Assembly Sessions Records
November-December, 1789, Box #3
Committee on Indian Affairs

To the Honorable the General Assembly

General Assembly Sessions
1777 - 1789

Gentlemen,
      I herewith Send you a Packet which I have received this Morning from Mr. Alexander Dromegoole, enclosing a Letter from Alexander McGillivray Chief of the Creek Nation of Indians, and other papers which I submit to your Consideration
Fayette Ville, 16th November 1789
Saml. Johnston

North Carolina
In the Hcom 23d Nov 1789
Mr Speaker and Gentlemen of the Senate
      We herewith send you a Message this day received from his Excellency the Governor enclosing papers from the Chief of the Creek Nation and others, together with the papers therein referred to which we propose referring to the Committee on Indian Affairs
S. Cabarrus S.H.C.
By Order, J Hunt CHC

North Carolina
In Senate 24 Nov. 1789
      Mr Speaker & Gent.
The message from his Excellency the Governor of today, Letter from the Chief of the Cherokee Nation and other papers accompanying them we agree with you referring to the Committee on Indian Affairs.
Chas. Johnson Sp.
By Order, J Haywood CS

****

North Carolina State Archives
General Assembly Sessions Records
November-December, 1789, Box #3
Draft Bill, Not Introduced

A Bill to Conform & Carry into Effect a Treaty enter'd into in the year 1785 between John Sevier Esqr. on the part of the State of No. Carolina and the head Men & Warriors of the Cherokee Indians and for the Relief of the Inhabitants on the South Side of French broad River.

General Assembly Sessions
1777 - 1789

Whereas John Sevier Esquire under the authority of the State of North Carolina did on the 31st day of May in the year 1785 actually hold a Treaty in a fair open & public manner with the Cherokee Indians and thereat purchased for a Sum not expressly stipulated all the lands on the South side of French Broad River between Big Pigeon & the ridge which divides Tennessee & Little River.

Be it therefore enacted by the General Assembly of the State of North Carolina and it is hereby enacted by the authority of the same: That the said Treaty shall be and is hereby confirmed and to the end that the same may be carried immediately into Effect, a Commissioner for that purpose shall be chosen by joint Ballot of both Houses -- And the Commissioner so chosen shall be & he is hereby authorized and empowered to draw from the Treasurer or the wa[?] the Sum of six hundred pounds which he shall lay out to the best advantage for suitable Goods to be by him delivered as soon as possible in a fair open & public manner to the Head Men & the Warriors of the said Cherokee Indians as a compensation for the aforenamed ceded territory.

And be it further enacted, That each and every person residing within the territory aforesaid shall be entitled to a preemption, agreeably to a Law passed in the year 1779 "declaring what shall be considered Occupancy," not exceeding Six hundred & forty Acres of Land which they shall enter within twelve Months from the passing of this Act & not till after the said Cherokee Indians shall be fully paid & satisfied, with an Entry Taker to be appointed by joint Ballot of both Houses - who shall give Bond with sufficient Security to the Governor for the time being for the Sum of five thousand pounds & hold his office at Morganton in the County of Burke and the Entry Taker so appointed shall for all Lands entered in his office aforesaid receive for the use of the State of No. Carolina Eight Shillings in Money & Ten pounds in Specie Certificates for each & every hundred acres - and for himself the fees usually allowed to other Entry Takers -- And the Surveyor of Greene County is hereby directed to Survey all such Entries in the manner prescribed by Law for other Public Surveys.

And be it further enacted, That all the territory below Big Pigeon & between French Broad & the ridge which divides Tennessee & Little Rivers shall be and the same is hereby annexed to the County of Greene and the Inhabitants of said territory shall be formed into a separate Battalion of Militia & called by the name of the Western Battalion of Greene County in the same Manner & under the same regulations as the second Battalion of Rowan County -- And the said Battalion **[Faded]** called on for a General Muster shall meet at Newels Station any Law or

General Assembly Sessions
1777 - 1789

custom to the contrary notwithstanding - provided always that the Benefits of this Act shall not extend to the Settlers on the South Side of French Broad River until the Conditions of the Treaty aforenamed shall have been fully complied with.

And be it further enacted, That all Laws or parts of Laws which may come within the purview & in[?] of this Act are hereby repealed annulled & made void to all intents & purposes as if the same had never been made.

****

North Carolina State Archives
General Assembly Sessions Records
November-December, 1789, Box #3
Messages

The Bill to discharge the expenses of an Expedition against the Indians & to Bill County Treasurers of Washington &c. to receive in payment of Taxes &c. Referred to the Commt. On Mr. Outlaws Warrants.

North Carolina
In Senate 27 Nov 1789
Mr Speaker & Gentl.
   We propose that the Bill to discharge the expence of an Expedition against the Indians, And the Bill to empower the County Treasurer and Collectors on the several Counties in the district of Washington to receive from any Person or Persons in payment of their Public taxes any Accts &c be Submitted to the consideration of the Committee appd. To Report on the Warrants laid before the Assembly by Mr. Outlaw. John B. Ashe Spk. P Tem
By Order, J Haywood CS

****

North Carolina State Archives
General Assembly Sessions Records
November-December, 1789, Box #3
Senate Bills

233

General Assembly Sessions
1777 - 1789

A Bill to repeal part of an Act Intituled An Act Once More to extend an Act Intituled An Act to Pardon & Consign to Oblivion the Offences & Misconduct of Certain Persons in the Counties of Washington, Sullivan, Greene & Hawkins.

  Be it enacted by the General Assembly of the State of North Carolina & by the Authority of the same that all & every part of the last providing Clause in the above Mentioned Act be & the same is hereby repealed & made Void.

In Senate 9th November 1789, read the first time & passed
By Order, J Haywood CS
Mr Willis, Mr Mkennie

In the House of Com 9 Nov 1789 read the first time & passed
By Order, J Hunt CHC
Mr Crecy & Mr McCowan

In Senate 10th Novem. 1789 read the second time & passed
By Order, J Haywood CS

In the Hcommons 10th Novr 1789 read the second time & passed
By Order, J Hunt CHC
Mr Grove & Mr McCowan

In Senate 12th Novem. 1789 read the third time & passed
By Order, J Haywood CS

In Hcomm 30th Nov. 1789 read the third time & passed & ordered to be engrossed
J Hunt CHC

Committed to a Comt of the House, Mr. Person, Mr Smith, Mr Rhea, Mr Stokes & Mr McDowell

---

Report on the Pardon Granted John Sevier, Esquire, 1789

General Assembly Sessions
1777 - 1789

The Committee to whom was referred the Bill to repeal part of an Act Intituled an Act Once More to extend an act Intituled an act to pardon and consign to oblivion the offences and misconduct of certain persons in the counties of Washington, Sullivan, Greene and Hawkins.
Report:
      That on examining sundry papers and hearing oral testimony it appears that John Sevier Esqr. together with sundry other persons in the said counties, did in the years 1785, 1786 & 1787 in a great measure [Smudged] the peace and good order of the Government of the State of North Carolina; That their conduct was in many particulars highly reprehensible. Your committee further report that at the time the people in those counties first attempted to subvert the Government of North Carolina the said John Sevier Esquire did oppose them in such a manner as actually to prevent elections from being held under their new government in two of the counties, and when he at last joined them it was in obedience to the entreaties of several of the most influential persons in that part of the country.
      Your Committee therefore conceive that the offences of all the citizens of said counties have been pardoned and consigned to oblivion, that the said John Sevier Esquire ought to be placed in the same situation; it appearing to your Committee that he was not as highly reprehensible as many others, all of which is Submitted.
John Rhea

In Hcom 30th Nov 1789, read and concurred with.
By Order, J Hunt CHC
S.Cabarrus S.H.C.

Message - Pardon Bill
Committed by the H Commons
Rejected

North Carolina
In the Hcomm 13th November 1789
Mr. Speaker and Gentlemen
      We propose that the Bill to repeal part of an Act Intitled an Act once more to extend an Act to Pardon and to consign to Oblivion the Offences &c of certain Persons in the Counties of Washington, Sullivan, Green and Hawkins be referred to a joint Committee who are to examine into the propriety of passing the same and make report thereon for this

General Assembly Sessions
1777 - 1789

purpose we have on our parts appointed Mr. Davie, Mr. Hawkins, Mr Person, Mr Spiller & Mr Hamilton of Edenton
By Order
J Hunt CHC
S. Cabarrus S.H.C.

Senate Message
Washington, Sullivan, Greene &c Bill not refd as proposed by the Hcommons, 1789
North Carolina
In Senate 13 Nov 1789
Mr. Speaker & Gentlemen
    We have received your Message proposing that the propriety of passing the [?] to repeal part of an Act to Pardon and consign to Oblivion the offences and misconduct of certain Persons in the Counties of Washington, Sullivan, Greene and Hawkins be reported on by a joint Committee to which we cannot agree from these principles, that the Bill has already had a third reading in this House of course its Utility fully investigated and that now to commit it would be contrary to all rule heretofore observed
Chas. Johnson Sp.
By Order, J Haywood CS

****

North Carolina State Archives
General Assembly Sessions Records
November-December, 1789, Box #3
Senate Bills

A Bill to repeal part of an Act Intituled an Act for appointing an Agent & holding a Treaty with the Cherokee Indians & for other purposes.

Be it Enacted by the General Assembly of the State of North Carolina & it is hereby enacted by the Authority of the same that so much of the before recited Act as relates to the appointment of an Indian Agent his duty & pay be & the same is hereby repealed & made Void.

In Senate 8th Dec. 1789 read the first time & Passed
J Haywood

General Assembly Sessions
1777 - 1789

In Hcomm 10th Decr 1789 read the first time & Passed
By Order, J Hunt   CHC
Mr Hamilton & Mr Pride

In Senate 21st Decr. 1789 read the second time & Passed
J Haywood CS

In House Com. 21st Decr. 1789 read the second time and Passed
By Order, J Hunt   CHC

Mr Snead & Mr Spiller
In Senate 21 December 1789 read the third time & Passed
J Haywood CS

In the House of Commons 21st Decr 1789 read the third time & Passed
Ordered to be Engrossed
By Order, J Hunt   CHC

****

North Carolina State Archives
General Assembly Sessions Records
November-December, 1789, Box #3
House Bills

A Bill to Extend the Civil and Millitary Authority of this State to the Inhabitants South of French Broad & Holstein River.

Whereas it Appears to this General Assembly that a number of the good Cittizens of this State by & with the Consent of the Cherokee Indians have Settled Themselves on the south side of French Broad & Holstein Rivers & thereby are destitute of the Benefits of Government.

Be it therefore Inacted by the General Assembly of the State of North Carolina & it is heareby Inacted by this Authority of the same that from and After the Passing of this Act the Civil and Millitary Authority of this State is Heareby declared to have as full power & Lawfull Authority on the South Side of sd. River as in Any Other part thereof and the Officers of Each department In the County of Green are heareby Required and

General Assembly Sessions
1777 - 1789

Commanded to Execute the Law in as full and Ample a manner as in Any Other part of this State and the sd. Inhabitants are hereby Declared to be part of Green County, And be it further Enacted by the Authority Afsd. - That all Laws or parts of Laws in this State Contradictory to this Laws are Hereby Repealed & made Void, any Law, Usage or Custom to the Contrary Notwithstanding.

In the Hcom 10th Novr. 1789 read the first time and passed
By Order, J Hunt CHC
Mr. Grove & Mr. Baker

In Senate 12th Novem: 1789 read the first time & passed
By Order, J Haywood CS
Mr Clay & Mr Payne

North Carolina
In the House of Commons 26 Novr 1789
Mr Speaker and Gentlemen
  We propose that the Bill herewith sent you to extend the civil and Military authority of this State to the Inhabitants South of French Broad & Holstein Rivers be referred to the Committee on Indian Affairs.
By Order, J Hunt CHC
S. Cabarrus, S.H.C.

North Carolina
In Senate 26 Nov 1789
Mr Speaker & Gentl.
  We agree that the Bill for extending the Civil & Military authority of this State to the Inhabitants South of French Broad and Holstein Rivers be ref'd as by your proposed.
John B. Ash Sp. P Tem

****

North Carolina State Archives
General Assembly Sessions Records
November-December, 1789, Box #3
House Bills - Rejected

General Assembly Sessions
1777 - 1789

A Bill for defraying the expences of an Expedition carryed on against the Cherokee Indians, and other necessary expences thereon accruing.

Whereas in the year one thousand seven hundred and Eighty Eight, the Militia under the command of Brig. Genl: Joseph Martin in the district of Washington were called out on actual service against the Chicamoga Indians, who are part of the Cherokees, who at that time were plundering and killing the inhabitants on the frontiers of said district -- also, men, who by the orders of the said Brigadier General Joseph Martin, were drafted for the protection of the said district; and no compensation being hitherto made for the services of the said Militia, in remedy Whereof:

Be it enacted by the General Assembly of the State of North Carolina and it is hereby enacted by the Authority of the same, that a board of Auditors, consisting of shall, and is hereby appointed to sitt in the district of Washington, to liquidate and adjust according to Law, all accompts of the said expedition, and other necessary expences thereon accruing in defence of the said district.

And be it further enacted, that the said Auditors shall take the following oath or affirmation before they enter upon the duties of their Office, that is to say, "I AB Auditor for liquidating and adjusting the Accompts of an expedition carryed on against the Chicamoga Indians do swear that I will, faithfully, and to the best of my knowledge discharge the trust reposed in me."

And be it further enacted by the Authority, aforesaid that the said Auditors shall issue specie certificates for all claims by them so adjusted; which specie certificates shall be received by the several sheriffs in the said District, and by the treasurer of this State, in payment of public money due from said district an no other, untill the whole be paid.

And be it further enacted by the authority aforesaid that the aforesaid board of Auditors when convened, shall appoint a clerk, and shall liquidate and adjust the claims as abovementioned, and shall lodge or cause to be lodged in the Comptrollers Office, the check books and all other papers relative thereto at or before the meeting of the next General Assembly.

And be it further enacted by the Authority aforesaid, that each of the said Auditors, shall be allowed **[Blank]** Shillings for each and every day they shall be travelling to and from and performing the duties by this Act directed, And the Clerk shall in like manner be allowed **[Blank]** shillings in currency certificates as abovementioned.

General Assembly Sessions
1777 - 1789

In Hcom 12th Novr 1789 read the first time & Passed
By Order, J Hunt CHC
Mr Anderson & Mr Alderson

In Senate 14th Novem: 1789 read the first time & Passed
By Order, J Haywood CS

In the House of Commons 25 Novr 1789 read the Second time & Rejected
By Order, J Hunt CHC

****

North Carolina State Archives
General Assembly Sessions Records
November-December, 1789, Box #4
House Bills - Petition

To the Honerable the Commisners Apointed on behalf of the United States to treat with the Cherekee Indens

    The memorial of the Inhabitatents So, Of French Broad humbly sheweth that your memorialists being indused by the Laudable Intention alone of promoting publick as Well As private Intrust and Inergized by the uniform liberil Conduct of States holding Vacant teretory to Words the first Adventurers taking pesession Of the same have Immigrated from Different quarters Of the Empier And Settled Our Selves in the teritory above Mentioned as we beleave not Only With the Countenance and protection but Even upon the Satie[?] of Government so far as gives Our Settling here to us Every Appearance of being Strictly legil the Salletary Effects of Which has Been felt by us and Observed by forenors And as Our Settlers had the Appearance Of legality so Our Conduct to wards the Cherecees has been Just and Agreable we have had their Consent for Settling the land Repeatedly the price And purcheses being by boath parties Referred to the futer Determination Of government but as Events unfore seen by youre Memorialists have taken place Which Renders Our lives And properties unsecure and government Rather Seems to frown on us than to Extend protection in our Distreses which have given us a great alarm As fully Sensible of Our precarious situation we now Gentl'men Turn Our attention to you knowing you to be Vested with Ample power to Release us from Our present Dificulties and Dangers that is to have the line

General Assembly Sessions
1777 - 1789

deviding the Citizens of the United States from the Cherecee Indens Extended so far as to take in the Settlements by which means we will againe become Orderly Citizens and be set in a Sittuation in which government will take notis Alas and give us the protection of those very laws under Whose Influence and Instruction we Expect to be Secure And hapy youre Memorialists beg leave to inform you that from youre humble and patriot carecters we have the most flatring Hopes of Releaf from Our present distreses Well Assured that no Exartion on youre part Will be Wanting in Our faver knowing that Virtue is its Own Rewarder and no Action is More Meretorious than to Releave a Multitude Of the humen famely from distress And Ruin the purity Of Whose Intentions what Ever may be their mistakes will plead for them the Justice to Rest Assured that they Repose an unbounded Confidence in youre Integrity and Atatchment to their Intrust - And as in duty bound Shall Ever Pray

Alexr Mt. Gomery, [?] Cox, Fred Ja[?], Edmund Vanois, Isaac Skilman, Alexr McGlalin, Barefoot Aransjon[?], John Hiser, Benjamin Fanshire, Richard Fanshire, David Fanshire, George Hallmark, David Horton, William Smallwood, Alexr Meglalin Junr., Joseph Tayeler, Fl oyd Nichols, William Patihes[?], Jas Walker, John McLellan, John Mabary, Burlen Price, Anthony Lawson, Jesse **[Faded],** John Parker, James Hanby, Woolsey **[Faded],** Hugh Johnson, Scott Magills, Valentine **[Faded]**, James Oldam, John Brian, Wm Miller, John Moon, Jos Parker, James **[Faded], [Name Faded],** John Menis, Joseph McReynolds, Enos Bowman, John Alexander, Alin Alexander, Ebin Alexander, John Dunkin, James Maginly, John Jackson, James Tedford, **[Faded]** Tedford, James McKenny, John Tedford, Barcly McGhee, **[Name Faded], [Name Faded], [Name Faded],** Joseph Tedford, Samuel Jackson, James Houston, Matt Houston, Samuel Henery, James Houston, Patrick Young, Alexander McEwen, Samuell Houston, John Houston, Robt Wilson, David Caldwell, Thomas Dickson, John Kelly, Thomas Caldwell, Alexander Ewing, James **[Faded],** John Cloid, Matthew Russell, Ezekiel Cloyd, John Singelton, John Thompson, Robert Hanna, Joshua Hanna, James Gillespie, Thos Brown, Calvin Johnson, James M: Alester, **[Name Faded],** Jas. Gillespy, John McCain, John Coats, John Clack, W. Wallace, Wm. Henderson Senr., Joseph Beavers, John Henderson, Thomas Henderson, Wm. Henderson Junr., Robert Henderson, Meshak Tipton, James Magers, David Emmens, James Rodgers, henery Rodgers, Robert Carr, Ollipher Wallace, John Wallace, Samuel McClelan, Saml Thompson**, [Faded]** Thompson, J

General Assembly Sessions
1777 - 1789

Wallace Senr., Robert Thompson, James Thompson, Joel Wallace, John Beavers, Elige Rodgers, James Bevers.

****

North Carolina State Archives
General Assembly Sessions Records
November-December, 1789, Box # 4
House Bills - Petition

To the Honourable the General Assembly of the State of North Carolina the Petition of Sundry inhabitants South of French Broad river humbly Sheweth

      That amongst the repeated depredations Committed on us by the Chirokee Indians within these months passed thare has been a great number of horses Stole; It is therefore the earnest Prayer of your petitioners that if a Treaty is [Faded] that nation and a purchase made of the lands we reside on; that a deduction be made from the sum promised them for their lands to the Amount of the value of the horses that they have taken from theWhite people and that each person may receive a Certificate for the value of their horses thus lossed which will be received by government in the purchase of lands, yet to be entered in this State And your petitioners as in duty bound shall ever Pray.

Saml Newell, Wm. Upton, Wm. Houston, John Kerr, Mathew Houston, Jos. Black, Charles Logan, Littlepage Sims, Saml. Newell Sr., Benjamin Tipton, William Reagan, Charles Reagan, John Reagan, Jacob Thomas, Henry Thomas, George Erving, William Lowery, F[?] McMurrey, Samuel McMurrey, Samuel McMurrey Jr., Robert McMurrey, John Caldwell, George Berry, Samuel Scott, John Lowry, George Caldwell, Thomas Waller, Samuel Weir, Hugh Weir,

****

North Carolina State Archives
General Assembly Sessions Records
November-December, 1789, Box #4
House Bills - Petition

General Assembly Sessions
1777 - 1789

To the honourable the General Assembly of the State of N. Carolina the petition of Sundry inhabitants on the unappropriated Taritory South of French Broad river humbly sheweth.

That your petitioners having seated themselves on the above taritory with Views to promote publick Oeconomy Equely with domestick advantage, desirous to Submit to laws and Conform to the requisitions of government, and to live in that Orderly manner that would Insure to us the Countenance and protection of Just and Equitable laws formed only to [Faded] [Faded] virtue and impress the [?]ieians. And your petitioners being feelingly senceable has [Faded] the [Faded] that has of late prevented this district has been to publick as well as private [Faded] to and how much we are both as a Community and individually exposed to the savages as well of [Faded] as [Faded] enemies, humbly implore the interposition of your honourable body that you would Commisserate our present distress and grant us Relief by extending to us the protection of government that we may with other Citizens participate of those Blessings common to all Christian and enlightened people Under the influence of Just laws and the Auspices of a well ragulated Commonwealth.

And whareas your petitioners has in the Cause of their settling and defending this taritory [Several lines missing] Numberless hardships and difficultys perticularly in a [Faded] Indian War by which they are much impoverished. It is their humble petition to your honourable body that when you in your Wisdom thinks proper to Open a land office for the taritory before mentioned that you would grant to each Actual Adventurer a pre-emtion of the land on which he lives, on as moderate terms as you may Judge Consistant with Justice and Sound polocy; Also reasonable time for each settler to raise the sums required of them by government for the purchase of their lands.

It is farther the earnest Prayer of your petitioners that an Entri taker be appointed amongst us to take in entrys of sd. lands which will save the poor inhabitants the enormous expence that will nasasarily Occur if they have to travil to the seat of Government or some interior part to enter their lands as thare is many who may posobly be able to enter a small tract on which they Could maintain a helpless family would nevertheless fail in raising money to support them to and from the entri takers office if it was to be fixed in some distant part of the State.

[Editor's note: The next paragraph has been marked through and crossed out. It was most likely meant to be omitted or ignored.]

General Assembly Sessions
1777 - 1789

[And Whareas thare is many who ware among the first adventurers to this Country and Continued during the [**Faded**] all the benefits and advantages of the Country that defended it at the braking out of the War refusing to defend it by which they might have rendered that Service to the Publick that could only entitle them to the benefits of a preemtion. It is our earnest request that none such must be allowed preemtions but that the land Clamed by such deserters may be liable to be held by the first that will actually Settle the same which will be an extensive mean to popolate and defend the Country.]

And your petitioners as in duty bound Shall ever Pray &C

Saml Newell, Jos. Black, Saml. Newell Senr., Benjamin Tipton, Jos Bogle, John McKain, Adam Dunlap, John Kerr, James Dunlap, John Dunlap, Page Sims, Mathew Houston, John Cusick, William Tipton, Oliver Alexander, John Dunkin, John Alexander, Ebin Alexander, James Maginly, George Tedford, James Cunningham, James Telfo[?], Barcly McGhee, Andrew Jackson, James [?], James McKenny, John Singelton, James Gillespie, John Thompson, Thos Brown, Calvin Johnson, James M Alester, Robert Hanna, William Massey, James Gillespy, John McCain, John Coats, Wm. Houston, Charles Logan, Charles Reagan, Henery Reagan, William Reagan, Jacob Thomas, Henry Thomas, George Erving, John Caldwell, William McMurrey, Samuel McMurrey Senr., Samuel McMurrey junr., Robert McMurrey, Thomas Waller, John Menis, Joseph McReynolds, E Bowman, Samuel Weir, Hugh Weir, James Houston, Matthew Russell, Joseph Tedfod, Samuel Jackson, John Tedford, James Houston, Matt Houston, Samuel Kennedy, Alexander McEwin, Patrick Young, Samuel Houston, John Houston, Robert Wilson, David Caldwell, John Kelley, Thomas Dickson, Thomas [**Faded**], James Beard, [**Name Faded**], John Cloid, Ezekiel Cloyd, William Russell.

****

North Carolina State Archives
General Assembly Sessions Records
November-December, 1789, Box #4
House Bills - Petition

North Carolina
    In House 24 Novr. 1789

General Assembly Sessions
1777 - 1789

Mr Speaker and Gentlemen
    We herewith send you the Petition of sundry the Inhabitants South of French Broad River which we prefer referring to the Committee on Indian Affairs and have added to this Comt. Mr Davie, Mr Stokes & Mr McDowell
S. Cabarrus S.H.C.
By Order J Hunt CHC

Message
Peto. From French Broad

    Petition of the Inhabitants South of French Broad River

    To the Honourable the Genl. Assembly of the State of No. Carolina the petition of Sundry inhabitants South of French Broad Humbly Sheweth,
    That your petitioners hath for some time past Experienced the utmost distress & greatest evils that a frontier can possibly be tested with Occationed by the want of the regular Administration of government as which gieves Opertunity to the wicked and desining to invent & carry on Schemes of the most Heinous Nature & attends with the most destructive Consequences to the peace & hapiness as well as the interest of our infant Settlements likewise the daly depredations Committed by the Cherokees is no less opressive & unjust which difficulties & many others we are Endevouring to bear with all the fortitude and patience we are possessed of with Ardent hopes that your Honourable body will take undar your wise Consideration the distressed Situation of your petitioners & grant us relief by Extending to us those Sociel blessings which we only Expect to feel undar the influence & Operation of your mild Constitution & laws -- Your petitioners begs leave to inform your honourable body the improvements on which we first claimd our lands was made undar Similar Circumstancis and at the same time with those for which pre-emtions was granted by the legislature of N. Carolina for lands inhabited N. of French Broad & also the laws of Franklin which at that time we put full faith in, not only Countenanced us in Setting Our Sd. Claims of land but ware urged on us undar a Severe penalty for [?] with the most flatering promises of protection & Security in possession of the same Your petitioners also begs leave to mention thay have Not in a disorderly forceable manner taken possession of the before mentioned land from the Indians, we have had

General Assembly Sessions
1777 - 1789

their consent for settling Sd. land [The rest of this sentence is faded and torn] & has uniformly Endeavoured to Cultivate [Torn] Strictest friendship and if at any time [Faded] have Appeared any thing unjustifyable on the side of the White people towards the Indians it has Neither been Countenanced of Nor approved by a large Majority of the Inhabitants South of French Broad Your petitioners further beg leave to mention to your Honourable body that the Cherokees have at all times been Reguardless of their Engagements to the State they have wantonly broke through the Stipulation of Treties & Violated the peace (in a manner) in the Verry instant of Ratifacation in the first place it was Stipulated by the Articles of the Treaty betwixt Virginia, NC and the Cherokee Indians in the Year 1777 that the Sd. Indians should Return or make Restitution for all the property taken in the War from the Whites the preceeding year, and continue to live in peace & friendship with the White Citizens of the United States which they have never comply'd with but on the contrary they have not only detained the property taken during the War above Mentioned but have ever since practiced the most inhuman unprovoked murdars & opresive Robberies on the Good Citizens of this & the Neighbouring States & ever since their most Solemn Engagements to the Commissioners of Congress at Swannanoa in June last they have not desisted in the least from their former practices but have continued their Robberies in all Quarters within their Reach on the western side of the mountains and some of our Citizens have fell Sacrifice to their Savage cruelty also some of those unhapy people that have fell into the hands of the Indians as Captives yet detained and can only be Redeemed by Extravigant Ransoms, Combinations of Speculators have also formed with intentions to deprive us of those lands in the defense of which we have had so many Sufferings & only at an immence expence of blood & [?]reasure holds possession of them, it is therefore the Humble prayer of your petitioners that your Honourable body would pass an Act fixing a line betwixt us & the Cherokees that will include Our Settlements undar the protection of your Govt. and Secure us Against the Barbarity and Opression of the heathen the su[?] Seemes of our more unnatural Enemies that called themselves Christians & the disordars that the want of a Regular Govrt. Expose us to on Every Side, it is likewise the prayer of your petitioners that at whatsoever time you may in your wisdom think proper to open an Office for the lands we reside on that you would grant to each Actual Setler a pre-emtion of the Cond. Has Settled undar such Regulations as your Honourable body may think most Just and Equitable and also allow Reasonable time for us to Raise the price of our land as

General Assembly Sessions
1777 - 1789

many of your petitioners are so impoverished by the last War that it will be with the Greatest Difficulty that we can comply with the most moderate terms of purchase. Yet many people [Faded] advantage Whatever [Faded] Naturely arise from proper Encouragements being given to emigrants from different Quarters of the Empire to settle in your State, the immence Sum that will be paid into your treasury for the purchase of lands &c will not Escape your penatration but which will leave the most lasting Sensations on Everry illustrous & generous mind is that of Relieving a multitude of their fellow Cittizens from the most distressing circumstancis & Communicating lasting blessings to them which will leave the most gratefull impressions on the harts of your petitioners who as in duty bound shall pray &cc.

[Faded], R. Gross, George Adams, Joseph White, Jonathan Wood, Nicholas Woodfin, John Evins, Henry Nave, John Brickey, [Name Faded], William Dun, Andrew McCain, William Clapton, Joseph Henery[?], [Name Faded], John Smith, John Wood, Daniel Luttrel, Elexander Ramsy, Elijah Wood, Charles Barney, [Name Faded], William Pryor, Francis Johnston, Thomas Going, Zekel Ray, Jos. Sarvay[?], Daniel Job, Joseph Pryor, Isaac Odell, [Name Faded], William McKissac, Jams Mackissac, Joshen Mackissac, Jamiah Odaal, Thomas Stephens, William Whitson, david Job, William Coleman, Solomon Coleman, Charles Dinney, John Coleman, John Denkin, Thos Heney, James Statel, William Sims, Dunken McKissak, John Nicols, Joseph Williams, Thos Williams, James Williams, David Nicols, Danl. Nicols, George Gross Junr., George Gross Senr., Peter Brickey, Jams Drimmer, Calep Odle, Moses McKay, Thomas [Faded], [Faded] Woodfin, William Henery, Henery Jones, George Henery, George [Faded], William Cumpton, Robt Taylor, Danl Adams, Wm Adams, James Seduscus[?], Jacob Seduscus, Wm Stanton, Hugh Doogan, Andrew Horn, Samuel Horn, Alexr. Ward, Alexr. Rodgers, Saml. Wilson, William Guinn, Moses Ashbrook, Thomas Moon, John McFarland, Benjamin McFarland, George McFarland, John Gilliland, R Douglas, Wm. Allen, Wm. Maberry, Frederick Mayberry, Mical Yokim, Thomas Beavers, John Beavers, John More, Benjamin Taylor, Craven Duncan, James Nickels, Samuel Littrel[?], Joseph Hough, Wesley White, James White, Alex Morrow, John McRoberts, Samuel McRoberts, William Winters, Zacceas Coplin, John Peery, Jos Sehorn, Ambrose Goare, Robt. Syfares[?], R[?]kits Copland, Jos. Copland, Jas. Cunningham, Wm. Cunningham, John Winters, Evan Lewis, Jas Ruddell, John Turnley, Wm. Cathey, Jacob Dobkins, Jos Davis, Adam Lowrey, Jas Lowrey, Amos

General Assembly Sessions
1777 - 1789

Lewis, Geo. Lewis, Jn Fulfer, Saml. Lowery, Wm. Russell, John Haley, Js. Carlock, Abrm. Carlock, Isaac Carlock, Coorod Good, Jn. Lewis, Jacob Lewis, [Name Faded], Samuel Jack, Geo. McNutt, Thos. Mogert[?], Seth Rogers, Isaac Rogers, William Thrift, Evin Morgan, John Calfee, Wm. Morgan, Henry Netherton, John Shaver, James Thurman[?], Jas. Adams, John Ceto, Wm Richeson, Able Richison Senr., Able Richison Junr., Wm. Isbell[?], Zachria Isbell, Wm. Bell, Matthew Bell, Richard Vernal Senr., Richard Vernal Junr., William Moon [Moore], James Wilson, Joseph Wilson, Alexr. Anderson, Jno. Dickson, Adam Wilson, Saml. Kerr, Jacob Boughman, Jacob Dieson, Saml. Hamilton, Saml. Henderson, Jas. Sims, Stephen Tence, Thos. Clark, Jas. Creton, Jos. Tinker[?], John Shields, Geor. Bush, Jas. Sterns, Pat Hamilton, Jas. Smith, Jesse Moon, Edmand Inge[?], Jno. Narr, Thos. Doget, Saml. Thomkins, Pat. Woods, Abram Manning, Jos. Moon, Stephen Sims, Jno. Jamison, Jas. Weeks, Jno. Wilson, Aduson Wilkins, Thos. Caldwell, Thos Dison, John McMahan, Thos. McCollock, Wm. Snead, Nicholas Barefeet[?], John Castiel, John Gillespy Senr., John Gillespy Junr., Wm Gillespy, Jas. Witherspoon, Jas. Gillespie, David Craig, James Craig Senr., James Craig Junr., John Craig, James McKenny, James Scott, Henry Ferguson, Joshua Hanna, Nicholas Hart, Wm Henry, John [Faded], John Caldwell, John Houston, Jas Houston, Saml. Houston, Matthew Houston, Lammis[?] McCartey, Jacob Thomas, Alexr. Kelley, John Witherspoon, David Caldwell, Matthew Russell, Robert Horn[?], William Garet, John Byrd, John McCollock, David Caldwell, John Hicklin, Firviros Conner, Humphreys Montgomery, William Gillespie, James Gillespie, Stephen Byrd, Amos Byrd Senr., Amos Byrd Junr., John Kelley, John Erving, Jas. McColock, Warren Martin, Andw. Griffin, Joseph Grant, Jas. Gillespy Junr., James Gillespy Senr., James Willis, James Ro[?], John Singleton, Spense Clack, David Cimmons, Rolley Clack, Joseph Beavours, James Beavours Senr., Samuel Thomson, John [?]allice, Cornelius Archer, John Fonsher, James Beavours Junr., Jesse Isbell, Joseah Rodgers, James Haney, Gorge Halmark, Richard Fonsher, James Majors, John Fonsher, John Mason, Donely Rusel, E[?] Montgomery, Elexander McLauglen, Frederick Jee[?], William Meller, Ohlayle[?] Jekele[?], John Wallace, William Hacher[?], David Walden, Joseph Taylor, Anthony Lovon, John Parker, And. Thompson, Thomas Wallace, Edmund Cancil, John Ominet, Robert Thompson, James Thompson, John Thompson, Alexander McCormick, Hearvey Rogers, Elijah Rogers, William Henderson Senr., William Henderson Junr., Robert Henderson, John Heanderson, Peter Every, Samuel Paxton, Barkley Magee, Matthew Wallis, Robert Hammel, John Telford, George Telford,

General Assembly Sessions
1777 - 1789

John Devil, David Egleton, Daniel McCinsay, John Clark, Alxr. Hooks, John Hooks, Robt. Hooks, James Guing, Wm Guing, Jacob Shul, John Jamison, Tobias Grimmit, Philaman Higgan, Thos. Millar Senr., Jos Millar, Thos Millar, [?] Millar, Charles Regin, Henry Regin, Wm. Regin, John Regin, Charles Regin, Thomas Waler, Wm Pohorn[?], William McMurry, Robert McMurry, Samuel McMurry, James Paul, Joseph [?]osson, Henry Tarewater, Lewis Tarewater, Jacob Iniman[?], Thos. Hardon, William Slackden, Michal Carter, Peter Douser, Isaac White, Phelty Thomas, Wm Overstreet, Adam Peek, Hugh Coor, Saml. Glass, Leonard Phouts, George Phouts, Saml. Newell, Benjamin Tipton, John Cusick, Jno Je[?] Cusick, Joseph Cusick, John McCain, John Williams, James Dunlap, James Dunlap, Ambress Legg, Adam Dunlap, Samuell Henery, Ismael Dor[?], James Houston, George Moss, Saml. Houston Senr., Joseph Bogle Junr., Samuel Newell Senr., John Coats, William Hines, Alexander Sloan, Robert Ferguson, William Sproul, Henry Frazier, Wm. Houston, John T[?]intey, George Erving, Stephen Graves, Jerimiah McCarter, Thomas Smith, Jas. Black, John Johnston.

****

North Carolina State Archives
General Assembly Sessions Records
November-December, 1789, Box #4
House Bills - Petition

To the Honourable The Commissioners in behalf of the United States to Treat with the Cherokee Indians, The Memorial of Sundry Inhabitants South of French Broad humbly representath, That your memorialists being induced by the laudable intention alone, of promoting publick as well as private interests & encouraged by the uniform liberal conduct of States (holding Vacant Teretory) towards the first adventurers takeing possession of the same, have emigrated from different quarters of the Empire & seated ourselves in the Teretory above mentioned (as we believe) not only with the Countenence & protection but even on the solicitations of Government so far as gives our settleing here (to us) every appearance of being strictly Legal (the salutary consequences of which has been felt by us & observed by wayfarers.) And as our Settlements had the Appearance of legality, so our conduct towards the Cherokees has been just & equitable We have had their consent for settling the land repeatedly. The price & purchase being by both partys refered to the future decisions[?] of Government. But as

General Assembly Sessions
1777 - 1789

events unforeseen by your Memorialists have taken place which Renders our lives & properties unsecure, & Government appears reather to frown the **[Faded]** frustration in our districts which has given us great alarm, , as fully sencible of our precarious -----

[Editor's Note: Several lines are missing from this document. They appear to have been cut away.]

line dividing the Citizens of the United States from the Cherokees. **[The rest of this line is missing.]** so as to include the Settlements by which means we will again become orderly Citizens & set in a Situation in which Government will take notice of us & give us the protection of those benign Laws under whose influence & operations alone we expect to be secure & happy. Your Memorialists beg leave to inform you that from your humane & patriotic character we have the most flattering hopes of relief from our present distresses, Well assured that no exertion on your part will be wanting in our favour, knowing that Virtue is its own receiver & no action is more meritorious than the releaveing of a multitude of the human family from distress & want, the purity of whose intentions (what ever may be their mistakes) will **[Faded]** plead for them. Your memorialists desire that you would do them the justice to rest assured that they repass an unbounded confidence in your integrity & attachment to their interest & as in duty bound shall ever pray
Solomon McCampbell, James Snodgrass, Joseph Shadon

Jno. Tharky[?], William Stockton, Joshua Ham[?], John McAlister, Jno. Clark, Jn. Burden, William Gillespy, James Gillespy, Matthew Russell, John Singleton, John Cloyd, Davis Stockton, James Stockton, Isaiah Hamilton, Samuel Stockton, Willm. Lee, George Ewing, Alex Ewing, John Kelley, Jas. Gillespy, Thos McCollock, Warner Martin, Saml Glass, John Gowan, Thomas Caldwell, David Cloyd, James Witherspoon, James Witherspoon, John Witherspoon, Hugh Cor, John McMahan, Nicholas Bartlet, Robert Perie, Adam Peek, James Mitchel, Benjamin Little, William Tipton, John Wheler, Nichodemus Keen, John Burden, John Therman, Edmund Calfteel, William Overstreet, Francis Cafteel, Morriss Mitchel, Jacob Meek, Phillip Tavill[?], Cunrode Hughson, James Willis, Patrick Statry, James Perie, Benjamin Burden, Leonard Phout, John Cafteel, William Burden, Anthony Buley, John Doyl, John Lashly, John Philips, John Dearmond Senr., John Dearmond Junr., Samuel Dearmond, James Dearmond, David Dearmond, Paul Dearmond, Calvin Johnston,

General Assembly Sessions
1777 - 1789

David Loveless, Micajah Carter, William Carter, James Anderson Senr., Thos Anderson, John Bayle, William Sneed, John Thomas, Thomas Wray, William Wray, John Wray, John Hitchcock, William Hitchcock, Lammas McCartey, John Gillespy Senr., John Gillespy Junr., William Gowan, Alexander Gillespy, John [Faded], Humphrey Montgomery, John Hook, John Clark, James Beard, Andrew Giffin, David Caldwell, Wm. Spe[?], Alexander Hooks, Sa[?] McCol[?], George Caldwell, Thos: Doxson[?], Wm Ewing, David Caldwell, John McCuleth, Wm Beard, John Hooks, Joseph Reynolds, Jas Ewing, Jas McCulath[?], James Carr, David Caldwell Senr., Jas. Gillespie Junr., John Walkes, Jas Gillespy, John [?], John Carson Senr., John Carson Junr., John McComb[?], Nicholas [?], David Sagleton, Daniel McKinzy, Charles Reagan Senr., William Reagan, James Ray, Page Sims, Benjamin Tipton, [Faded] Newell Senr., Jerimiah McCarter, James Dunlop, John [Faded], Adam Dunlop, John Lesly, William Hutson, David White, Benjamin Allen, William Upton, John Hyne, James Upton, John McCain, Jas. Bogle Senr., John Williams, Jonathan Cunningham, Jacob Cunnenhamm[?], David Linsey, John Reagan, Saml Bogle, Jos Black[?], John Cusick, John Caa[?], [Name Faded], Wm Houston, Henry Reagan, Ih[?] Stanton, Peter Avery, Wm Pohorn[?], Richard Williams, John Williams, John Dien[?], Robert Fergison, Henry Fergison, Hugh Fergison, Joseph McReynolds, John Hanna, Joseph Hart, Jos. Scott, Joseph McCorr[?], Saml. Henry, Bartley McGee, Oliver Alexander, John Dincan, Jas. McGinley, Ebenezer Alexander, John Alexander, John Craig, Jas. Craig, Jas. Craig Junr., Jas Roddey, John Nin[?], James McKerney, Jas. Tedford, John Tedford, George Tedford, John Lowrey, Moses Cunningham, John Der[?], Henry Ferguson, Robert Hamble, John Jackson, Andw. Jackson, Saml. Jackson, Wm Cavenieugh, David Craig, John Houston, Jas. Houston, Robert Pilson, Saml. Houston, Edward Eagins, Archibald Sloan, John Sloan, Alexr. Sloan, Jas. Sloan, James Cunningham.

****

North Carolina State Archives
General Assembly Sessions Records
November-December, 1789, Box #4
House Bills - Petition

To the Honourable the Commissioners appointed on behalf of the United States to treat With the Cherokee Indians.

General Assembly Sessions
1777 - 1789

The Memorial of the Inhabitants of French Broad humbly sheweth that Your Memorialists Being Induced By The Laudable Intention alone of promoting publick as well as private intrest and incouraged By the Uniform liberal Conduct of States holding vacant teretory toward the first adventurers taking possession of the same have Imigrated from different Quarters of the Empire and settleled our selves in the teretory above Mentioned as we believe not only with the Countenence and Protection But Even upon the Solicion of Government as farr as Gives our Setteling here to us Every apearince of Being Strictly Legal the salutary Efects of which has been felt by us and observed By foreners and as our Setterlers had the apearinces of Legality so our Conduct toward the Cherokees has been Just and Equatable we have had their Consent for Settling the land Repeatedly & the price and purchase Being By Both parties Refered to the future Determination of Government But as Events Unforseen By Your Memorialists have taken place Which Render our lives and properties insecure and government Rather seems to frown on us then to Extend protection In Distress which have given us a great alarm as fully Sensible of our precarious situation wee now Gentlemen turn our attention to you knowing you to be vested with ample power to Relieve us from our present Dificulties and Dangers that is to have this line Dividing the Citizens of the United States from the Cherokee Indians Extended so far as to take the Settlements by which means we will again Becom orderly Citizens and be set in a situation in which Government will take Notice of us and give us the protection of those Benign laws Under whose Influence and operation alone will Expect to Be secure and hapy Your Memorialists Beg leave to Inform you that from your Humane and Patriot Carecters We have the Mostt flattering hopes of relief from our present Distresses Well asure'd that no exertion on our part will be wanting in our favour knowing that Vertue is its own Rewarder and no action is more Meretorious then to Relieve a multitude of the humane family from Distress and Ruin the purity of whose Intentions Whatever May be their Mistakes will plead for Him. Your Memorialists Desire that you Would Do them the Justice to rest assured that the Repose on Unbounded Confidence in Your Integrity and attachment to their Intrest and as in Duty Bound Shall Ever Pray.

Spencer Clack, Jesse Isbell, Joseph Byrd, Jesse Byrd, John Blane, John Byrd, James Cameron, Lar[?] Rogers, Alexander Reed, James Cameron Senr., **[Faded]** Rogers, James Beavers, [?] Hamilton, Patric Hamilton, Patrick **[Faded]**, Joseph Woods, James Wood, John Woods, Tobius

General Assembly Sessions
1777 - 1789

Wierei[?], William Moon, Wm Price, John [?], Joseph Willson, Adam Willson, Alexander Anderson, James Willson, Joseph Dickson, Hugh Dickson, **[Name Faded]**, Wm Addam, Samuel Addam, Sam. Sisco, David **[Faded]**, Jos Te[?], Wm Millar Junr., Jams Ried, Jams [?], **[Name Faded]**, Wm Millar, Zacriah Jabol[?], Moses Renfra, Obediah Clack, Roland Clack, James Ransom, Abram Horn, James Daves, Soles Goor[?].

****

North Carolina State Archives
General Assembly Sessions Records
November-December, 1789, Box #4

[Editor's Note: The top part of this document is torn away]

Letter to **[Torn]** Gov. Do. Assy. & his [?] Seviers Mem. & Instructions from Govr. Martin
North Carolina

North Carolina
     In Senate 24 Nov 1789
Mr Speaker & Gentl.
We consent that the Petition **[Torn]** a number of of the people **[Torn]** living South of the French Broad River be referred us by your **[Torn]**, and have added **[Torn]** to the Committee on Indian Affairs.
Chas. Johnson Sp.

    Your Committee to whom, the case pf the people residing South of French Broad River was referred, Report,

    That previous to an Act of the General Assembly passed in 1783, reserving certain lands to the use of the Indians, near an hundred families were settled on the Territory South of French Broad.
    That by the above recited Act those families were left in that part reserved to the Indians, for hunting grounds. – That as early as 1782, His Excellency Governor Martin did appoint John Sevier, Charles McDowell and Waightsill Avery exquires, or any two of them Commissioners to hold a Treaty with the Cherokee Indians.

General Assembly Sessions
1777 - 1789

That on the 31st of May 1785 John Sevier did Treat with several of the headmen of the said Nation in a fair and open manner for all lands below Browns line south of Holston and low as the dividing Ridge between Tennessee and Little River, for which lands, the Indians were to receive a compensation, which compensation from unavoidable Accidents has not been yet paid, Your Committee therefore Report it advisable that a law be passed to comply with the said Treaty.

And upon the whole Your Committee are of opinion it would be expedient for this assembly to pass an Act for extending the boundary of Greene County so as to include these Settlers, and put them into a Separate and distinct Battalion of Militia, the officers of which shall be appointed in the usual mode, and also so many Justices of the Peace as may be necessary which Justices shall be considered as Members of the Court of Greene County.

Your Committee further recommends to this General Assembly that some person be appointed to pay the said Indians agreeably to the said Treaty who shall be furnished with a Sum of money not exceeding £600, to be laid out in goods which shall be paid down to the Indians or so much thereof as he shall find necessary to satisfy them for the purchase of said lands. – That an Entry Taker be appointed by this General Assembly for their District South of French Broad and the said Entry-Taker so appointed shall not enter upon the duties of his said Office until the Treaty herein Alluded to be complied with, and after such compliance the said Entry Taker shall proceed to take Entrys for the lands aforesaid, and shall take and receive for the use of the State the sum of eight shillings in the Current money of this State and Ten Pounds in Specie Certificates for each and every hundred Acres of land entered in his Office – And that each and every person in the said district who have made any improvements be intitled to a Right of Preemption, and shall be allowed twelve Months to enter the same.

Your Committee further Report that upon the lowest calculation upon the quantity of land eight shillings per hundred will produce the sum of £1200 which will fully reimburse the Treasury all the cash advanced for goods and expenditures with interest

All which is submitted

Wm. Lenoir, Chm.

North Carolina
In Senate 30th Novem. 1789

The foregoing Report was read and concurred with.

Chas. Johnson Sp.

General Assembly Sessions
1777 - 1789

By Order
J Haywood CS

In Hcom 5th Decr. 1789, read and concurred with
By Order
J Hunt CHC
S. Cabarrus S.P.C.

Report of the Comt. On Pet. Of Inhabitants South of French Broad

---

> The line the Inhabitants So. Of French Broad prays to be Established between themselves & Indians

Up the Tennessee as far as the Virga. War ford, thence a No. East course to the Top of the Ridge which divides the waters of Little River from Tennassee, and with that Ridge continuing the general course to the So. Carolina line.

A Bill for the relief of the Inhabitants on the South Side of French Broad River

In the House of Commons 12 December 1789, read the first time & passed
By Order, J Hunt CHC
Mr Beck & Mr Lassiter

In Senate 14th Decr. 1789 read the first time & passed.
H Haywood
T Blount

Genl. Sevier, Genl. McDowell
In the House of Commons 15 Decr. 1789, read the Second time & Rejected
By Order, J Hunt CHC

---

a bill for the Relief of the Inhabitants on the South Side of the French Broad River.

255

General Assembly Sessions
1777 - 1789

Whereas it hath been represented to this General Assembly that a number of Families did settle on the South Side of French Broad previous to the passing of the Act of Assembly in 1785, which reserves for the Cherokee Indians certain Lands therein described, And Whereas John Sevier Esquire One of the Commissioners appointed in the year 1782, by his Excellency Alexander Martin Esquire then Governor, to hold a Treaty with the said Indians, did in the Year 1785 in Consequence of his said Appointment (as circumstances prevented a Treaty to take place sooner) actually treat in a fair & open Manner with the principal Head Men & Warriors of the said Indian Nation for all the Lands situate below the Line commonly named Browns Line, South of Holston and as far as the dividing Ridge between Tennessee & Little Rivers, the Consideration of which purchase hath not yet been paid to the Indians by unavoidable accidents.

Be it therefore enacted by the General Assembly of the State of North Carolina, & it is hereby enacted by the Authority of the same, That **[Blank]** shall be and is hereby impowered to draw from the State Treasurer on his receipt the Sum of **[Blank]** to be by him applied to carry into Effect the above Treaty entered into between John Sevier Esquire and the Cherokee Indians, & to procure from the Said Nation, to the State of North Carolina a Grant for the territory bargained for by the said John Sevier.

Be it further Enacted that all the above Territory situate below Browns line, South of Holston and as far as the Dividing Ridge between Tennessee & Little River shall be & is hereby annexed to the County of Green, & all the Inhabitants of the Territory shall be & are hereby made part of the inhabitants of Green County, enjoying the same priviledges & Advantages as the Inhabitants of the said County, & subjects in every case to the Same Rules & Regulations – provided always that the Inhabitants of this annexed Territory to Green County, shall form a Separate Battallion of Militia by the Name of the Western Battallion of Green County; which Battallion shall be empowered & formed in the same manner as the Second Battallion of Rowan County; And the Said Battallion shall assemble together for a General Muster whenever called upon at **[Blank]** Any laws or Custom to the Contrary notwithstanding.

Be it further enacted that Every Head of Family of the said annexed Territory shall be entitled to a preemption of Six hundred & forty Acres of Land which if not already entered, they shall enter with the Entry taker of Green County, paying for the same, the purchase Money to the State, the Sum of Eight Shillings Current Money, & Sixty four pounds in Certificate of this State besides the Entry taker's fee; And the Surveyor of

General Assembly Sessions
1777 - 1789

the said County of Green is hereby directed to Survey all Such Entries in the manner prescribed by Law for all other public Surveys.

Be it further enacted, That **[Blank]** shall be & are hereby appointed Commissioners to Grant to every Head of family a Certificate of his being intitled to a preemption right as above, which Certificate shall be lodged by the party obtaining the Same in the Entry Taker's Office of Sd. County of Green, who shall not admit of any Entry without such Certificate being produced; and provided that No other Entry of Land within the said Territory shall be received by the Entry Taker, tho Such which may be made in Consequence of preemption Right.

Be it further enacted that all Laws or part of Laws which may come within the purview of this Act, are hereby repealed & made Null & void, to all interests & purposes, as if the same had never been made.

Appendix A
North Carolina Law

Appendix A
North Carolina Law

THE STATE RECORDS OF NORTH CAROLINA
VOLUME XXV., SUPPLEMENT, 1669-1771
EDITED BY: WALTER CLARK
NASH BROTHERS BOOK AND JOB PRINTERS
GOLDSBORO, N.C., 1906

LAWS OF NORTH CAROLINA - 1669
1669. An Act Prohibiting Strangers Tradeing With Indians. (Page 121).

Forasmuch as there is often recourse of Strangers from other parts into this County to truck and trade with the Indians which is conceived may prove very prejudiciall Wherefore be it enacted by the Pallatine and Lords Proprietors by and with the advice and consent of the Grand Assembly and the authority thereof that if any person or persons of what quallity or condition soever they shall be presume to come into this County to truck or trade with any of our neighboring Indians belonging to the County or that shall be found to have any Indian trade purchased from them or being found or appearing that they come to trade with any Indians as aforesaid Whether in their Townes or elsewhere within the County which is hereby left for the Magistrate to judge it shall bee lawfull for any person or persons to apprehend any such persons or Forreigners that shall be found amongst the Indians or elsewhere within the limitts of the County and him or them bring before the Governor or any one of the Councell who shall hereby have power to comitt them to prison there to abide till they have paid tenn thousand pounds of tobacco and caske otherwise to stand to the censure of the Vice Pallatine and Councell And it is further declared

Appendix A
North Carolina Law

that whatsoever Trade is found with the person apprehended One halfe thereof and one halfe of the fine shall belong to the Apprehendor and the other halfe to the Lords Proprietors.

****

THE STATE RECORDS Of NORTHCAROLINA
VOLUME XXIII., 1715-1776
EDITED BY: WALTER CLARK
NASH BROTHERS BOOK AND JOB PRINTERS
GOLDSBORO, NORTH CAROLINA, 1904

CHAPTER IV.
1715. An Act prohibiting Trading with the Indians. (Page 2).
    I.   Forasmuch as there is often recourse of strangers from other parts into this Country to truck & trade with the Indians which is conceived may prove prejudicial, wherefore.
    II.   Be it Enacted by the Palatin & Lords Proprietors by & with the advice & consent of the present Grand Assembly & the Authority thereof, that if any person or persons of what Quality or Condition soever they be, shall presume to come into this Country to Truck & Trade with any of our Neighbour Indians belonging to the Country, or shall be found to have any Indian Trade purchased from them, or being found or appearing that they come to trade with any Indians as aforesaid whether in their Town or Elsewhere within the Country, which is hereby left for the Majistrate to judge, It shall be lawful for any person or persons to apprehend any such person or Foreigner that shall be found amongst the Indians or elsewhere within the limits of the Country and him or them bring before the Governor or any one of the Council, who shall hereby have power to commit them to prison there to abide until they have paid Ten thousand pounds of Tobacco & Cask; otherwise to stand to the censure of the Governor.
    III.   And it is further declared that whatsoever Trade is found with the person apprehended one half thereof & one half of the Fine shall belong to the Apprehender & the other half to the Lords Proprietors.
Obsolete in 1791. [See Iredell's Laws, 1791, p. 9.]

****

THE STATE RECORDS OF NORTH CAROLINA

Appendix A
North Carolina Law

VOLUME XXIII., 1715-1776
EDITED BY: WALTER CLARK
NASH BROTHERS BOOK AND JOB PRINTERS
GOLDSBORO, NORTH CAROLINA, 1904

CHAPTER LXIX.
1715. An Act for Restraining the Indyans from molesting or Injureing the Inhabitants of this Government and for Secureing to the Indyans the right and property of their own lands. (Pages 87-88).

  I. Whereas (before ye late war) dayly and grievous Complaints of Depredations & Insults of ye Indyans were Exhibited against them by Divers persons bordering upon and residing near to ye Inhabitants of ye said Indyans for ye prevention of ye like Disorder for ye time to come and for Cultivating a better Understanding with ye said Indyans the want of which has been so Injurious to the Government.

  II. Be It Enacted by his Excellency the Pallatine, &c. And It Is Hereby Enacted that whoever shall Discover or find any Indyan or Indyans Killing, Hunting or in pursuit of any horses, Cattle or hogs the right and property whereof is in any white man Inhabitting within this Government every such person or persons on Discovery or Sight thereof may & he is hereby Impowered to apprehend every such Indyan or Indyans & him or them so apprehended & taken to Convey before Some one of the Commissioners to be appointed for Indyan affairs (& for want of such before ye nearest Magistrate) which said Commissioners or Magistrate together with the ruler or head man of the Town to which such Indyan Delinquent may belong is and are hereby Impowered to punish every such Delinquent in such manner as the nature of the offence may require and to award satisfaction to the party injured for all Damages by him Sustained (saving always the right of appeal to the Governor & Council) if either party shall think themselves agrieved or wronged thereby.

  III. And Be It Further Enacted by the Authority aforesaid that if any difference shall for the future Arise between any whyte man and Indyan concerning trade or otherwise howsoever, Every such Difference shall be heard, Tryed and Determined by such Commissioners as the Governor or Commander in Chief for the time being shall appoint together with the ruler or head man of the town to which the Indyan belongs (Saving only the right of appeal as is herein before Saved & Excepted).

  IV. And whereas we have too great reason to believe that disputes concerning land have already been of fatall Consequence to the peace and wellfare of this Collony.

Appendix A
North Carolina Law

V. Be It Further Enacted by the Authority Aforesaid that no whyte man shall for any Consideration whatsoever Purchase or buy any tract or Parcell of Land claimed or actually in possession of any Indyan without special liberty for so Doing from the Governor and Councill first had and obtained under the penalty of Twenty pounds for every hundred acres of Land so bargained for and purchased one halfe to the Informer & the other halfe to him or them which shall sue for the same to be recovered by Bill, Plaint or Information in any Court of Record within this Government wherein no Essoign, protection, Injunction nor Wager of Law shall be allowed or admitted of.

VI. And Be It Further Enacted by the Authority aforesaid that whatever whyte man shall Defraud or take from any of the Indyans his goods or shall beat or abuse or Injure his person each and every person so offending shall make full satisfaction to the party Injured and shall suffer such other punishment as he should or ought to have done had the offence been Committed to any Englishmen.

Edw'd Moseley, Speaker   Chas. Eden, N. Chevin, C. Gale, Fran. Foster, T. Knight

The acts below refer to the Meherrin and Tuscarora land claims.
See acts, Nov. 1729, ch. 2; Oct. 1748, ch. 3; April 1778, ch. 16; Aug. 1778, ch. 5; April 1780, ch. 23, ch. 25, s. 9; April 1783, ch. 21. [See Iredell's Laws, 1791, p. 31.]

****

THE STATE RECORDS OF NORTH CAROLINA
VOLUME XXV., SUPPLEMENT, 1669-1771
EDITED BY: WALTER L. CLARK
NASH BROTHERS BOOK AND JOB PRINTERS
GOLDSBORO, N.C., 1906

CHAPTER II.
1729. An Act for the More quiet settling the bounds of the Meherrin Indian Lands. (Page 211).

I. Whereas complaint is made by the Meherrin Indians, that the English people disturb them in their settlements, by coming to inhabit and send corn among them; and also, that their bounds allowed by order of council dated October the twenty sixth, one thousand seven hundred and twenty six did not extend high enough up from the forl of Meherrin neck: for remedy whereof,

Appendix A
North Carolina Law

II. Be it Enacted, by his Excellency the Palatine, and the rest of the true and absolute Lords Proprietors of Carolina, by and with the advice and consent of the rest of the members of the General Assembly now met at Edenton, for the North East Part of the said Province, and by the authority of the same, that the said order of council be vacated, and that the Indian bounds and limits shall be extended as followeth, viz. beginning at the mouth of Meherrin river, and so up the river to the mouth of Horse Pasture Creek formerly called Indian creek; then by the said creek up to the fork of it; then by the North East branch thereof to the head of the same; then by a straight line across to Chowan river, by the upper line of Mulberry old field survey, to Samuel Power's lands; then along the various courses of the river, to the first station.

III. And be it also enacted, by the authority aforesaid, that all English people, or any other, living in the said bounds, shall move off, and that no persons but the said Indians shall inhabit or cultivate any lands within the limits aforesaid, while the said Indians remain a nation, and live thereon: And if any person shall offend against this act, on complaint made to Mr. John Boude, who is hereby appointed a commissioner for the said Indians, he shall grant his warrant to the constable, requiring him with aid (if need be) to remove such person, at or before the twenty fifth of December next ensuing; and any person refusing to move, shall be brought before the said Commissioners, and upon his conviction of the same, shall forfeit for the first offence, five pounds: and if he still persist, and refuse to go off from the said lands, after warning from the commissioner, or by his order, for the second offence shall forfeit the sum of ten pounds, and for the third time of his so offending shall forfeit Twenty Pounds, and Two months Imprisonment, and give security for his or their good behaviour: to be recovered by bill, plaint or information, in any court of record in this government; wherein no essoin, protection, or wager of law, shall be allowed or admitted of.

IV. And be it further Enacted, by the authority aforesaid, that the said commissioner is hereby impowered and ordered to reinstate and settle the said Indians, in giving them peaceable possession of the said lands, and to turn off any other person or persons inhabiting within the said bounds, unless such person have special leave from the Governor and Council, for continuing thereon; provided that this act shall not invest the fee simple of the said lands in the Indians, but such as have patents for the same, or any part thereof, their title shall be good and valid; neither shall the said Indians have liberty or leave to rent, sell, or in anyways dispose of the said lands.

Appendix A
North Carolina Law

Considered as a Private Law in 1791. [See Iredell's Laws, 1791, p. 49.]

****

THE STATE RECORDS OF NORTH CAROLINA
VOLUME XXIII., 1715-1776
EDITED BY: WALTER L. CLARK
NASH BROTHERS BOOK AND JOB PRINTERS
GOLDSBORO, N.C., 1904

Page 333
1749. "An Act for restraining the Indians from molesting or injuring the Inhabitants of this Government: and for securing to the Indians the Right and Property of their own Lands."

****

THE STATE RECORDS OF NORTH CAROLINA
VOLUME XXV., SUPPLEMENT, 1669-1771
EDITED BY: WALTER L. CLARK
NASH BROTHERS BOOK AND JOB PRINTERS
GOLDSBORO, N.C., 1906

CHAPTER VIII.
1757. An Act for Preserving Peace and continuing a good Correspondence with the Indians in Alliance with his Majesty's Subjects. 9Pages 356-358).
    I. Whereas, nothing can contribute more to the welfare and security of the British Colonies in North America than the preserving a sincere Peace and friendly Correspondence with the several Nations or Tribes of Indians bordering thereon, And it hath been represented that many flagrant Frauds and Abuses have been too frequently committed in the commercial dealings of his Majesty's Subjects with the said Indians, which cannot but tend to alienate their Affections, and give the French the greater opportunity of insinuating themselves and carrying on their destructive Schemes against the British Colonies, and Whereas, his Majesty hath been pleased to appoint the Honorable Edmund Atkins, Esquire, to be Agent for and Superintendent of the Affairs of several Nations or Tribes of Indians inhabiting the Frontiers of Virginia, North and South Carolina, and Georgia, and their Confederates, in order therefore to

Appendix A
North Carolina Law

render the Execution of a Commission of so great importance to the welfare and security of his Majesty's Colonies the more Effectual to the good purposes for which it is intended, Be it Enacted by the Governor, Council and Assembly, and by the Authority of the same, That from and after the first day of May next no Person whatsoever shall presume to deal or Traffic with either the Catawbas or Cherokees or other Western Indians within the limits of this Province without having first obtained a License or Permission for such purpose from The Honorable Edmund Atkins, Esq., his Majesty's Agent for an Superintendent of Indian Affairs in Virginia, North and South Carolina and Georgia and given Bond with two sufficient Sureties in the Sum of two hundred Pounds Proclamation Money Payable to the said Edmund Atkins, or his Successor in Office, with Condition that he and those he shall employ shall demean themselves honestly and innoffensively to the Indians with whom he shall have License to deal and duly observe such Instructions and Orders in Writing as shall for the purposes aforesaid and for the better regulation of Trade be given to him from time to time by the said Edmund Atkins, or his Successor in Office.

II. And be it further Enacted by the Authority aforesaid, That if any Person whatever shall after the said first day of May next, Trade or Traffick with any of the said Indian Nations within the limits of this Province without having obtained a License or permission agreeable to the direction of this Act he shall forfeit the sum of two hundred Pounds to be recovered by such person as will sue for the same in any Court of Record, one half to his own use and the other half to the use of his Majesty towards defraying the Contingent charges of Government. And it shall and may be lawful for the said Edmund Atkins, or his Successor in Office, to cause the Person so offending to be Arrested and to seize his Goods and to cause the Goods so seized after Ten days notice by advertisement to be sold at Public Auction and the Money arising by such Sale to lay out for presents to be distributed among the said Indians in such manner as the said Edmund Atkins, or his Successor in Office, shall think most likely to fix and confirm the said Indians in Friendship and Amity with his Majesty's subjects. And to cause the Person so arrested to enter into Bond to the said Edmund Atkins, or his Successor in Office in the Sum of Two Hundred Pounds Proclamation Money with Conditions that he shall not thereafter deal with any of the said Indians contrary to the form and Effect of this Act. And in Case the person so offending shall fail or refuse to give Bond and Security as aforesaid, The said Edmund Atkins, or his Successor in Office, shall and may cause such Offender to be sent to the Public Gaol of the district wherein such Offence is committed till he shall before the

Appendix A
North Carolina Law

Supreme Court or the Chief Justice, or one other of the Justices of the said Supreme Court enter into recognizance with two sufficient Sureties in the Sum of Five Hundred Pounds Proclamation Money, for his good behaviour for one Year.

  III. And be it further Enacted by the Authority aforesaid, That if the said Edmund Atkins, or any other Person or Persons, shall be sued for by reason of any Act or thing by him or them done agreeable to the directions of this Act, he or they may plead the general Issue and give this Act in Evidence. And the Plaintiff, if he shall be cast on the Trial, shall pay double Costs.

  IV. And be it further Enacted, That this Act shall continue and be in force Two Years from the said first Day of May next and no longer.
This Act repealed by Act of 1758, chapter XIX., p. 501.

****

THE STATE RECORDS OF NORTH CAROLINA
VOLUME XXV., SUPPLEMENT, 1669-1771
EDITED BY: WALTER L. CLARK
NASH BROTHERS BOOK AND JOB PRINTERS
GOLDSBORO, N.C., 1906

CHAPTER I.
1759. An Act to Amend and Continue an Act, Intituled, an Act for the better Regulation of the Militia, and for other Purposes. (Page 393).
  I. Whereas, an Act Intitluled an Act for the better Regulation of the Militia, and other Purposes, is near expiring and the Power by the said Act for raising Militia and Marching them agains the Enemy, is limited to the Opposing Invasions and Supporting Expeditions within this Province only,
  II. And Whereas, it is absolutely necessary on this present Immergency that part of the Militia should march to joyn the Troops of South Carolina, now near our Frontier, and upon an Expedition to Obtain Satisfaction of the Cherokee Indians, for divers Murders and Depredations committed by them on our back Settlements, for remedy whereof,
  III. Be it Enacted by the Governor, Council and Assembly, and by the Authority of the same, That the Governor or Commander in Chief for the time being, by, and with the Advice and Consent of His Majesty's Council, may during the Continuance of this Act, Order to be raised and Marched out of this Province so many of the Militia as shall be judged

Appendix A
North Carolina Law

expedient to joyn the Forces of our Neighboring Provinces of South Carolina and Virginia in Opposing any Invasions or Supporting any Expedition against the Common Enemy, And the Several Officers and Soldiers so raised shall be under the same rules and regulations and lyable to the same pains and Punishments as are Provided in the before recited Act in case of Invasions within this Province.

CHAPTER II.
1759. An Act for Granting an Aid to His Majesty for paying and Subsisting the Forces and Militia now in the pay of this Province, and for other Purposes. (Pages 394-395).

    I. Whereas, the Cherokee Indians contrary to their Allegiance have lately committed several horrid Murders and Depredations on his Majesty's Subjects in this and the Neighbouring Provinces, and the present Assembly out of a desire of Satisfaction for the same, as well as to prevent future Injuries of the like kind, have by one Act of Assembly, Intituled, An Act to amend and continue an Act, Intituled, "An Act for the better Regulation of the Militia, and for other Purposes," Impowered his Excellency the Governor to March the Troops now in the Pay of this Province and so many of the Militia thereof, as he shall think necessary to Join the Forces of South Carolina in an Expedition intended against the said Cherokees.

    II. Be it therefore Enacted by the Governor, Council and Assembly, and it is hereby Enacted by the Authority of the same, That his Excellency the Governor, may and he is hereby Authorized and Impowered to Order the Troops now in the Pay of this Province, and so many of the Militia thereof as he shall think necessary to March and Join the Forces of South Carolina in an Expedition as aforesaid, and to continue on the said Duty until the tenth day of February next, if His Majesty's Service shall so long require it, and no longer.

****

THE STATE RECORDS OF NORTH CAROLINA
VOLUME XXIII., 1715-1776
EDITED BY: WALTER L. CLARK
NASH BROTHERS BOOK AND JOB PRINTERS
GOLDSBORO, N.C., 1904

CHAPTER I.

Appendix A
North Carolina Law

1760. An Act for granting an aid to his Majesty. (Pages 516-518).

XIII. And for the greater Encouragement of Persons as shall enlist voluntarily to serve in the said Companies, and other Inhabitants of this Province who shall undertake any Expedition against the Cherokees, and other Indians in Alliance with the French; Be it further Enacted, by the Authority aforesaid, That each of the said Indians who shall be taken a Captive during the present War by any Person as aforesaid, shall, and is hereby declared to be a Slave, and the Absolute Right and Property of who shall be the Captor of such Indian; and shall and may be possessed, pass, go and remain to such Captor, his Executors, Administrators, and Assigns, as a Chattel personal; And if any Person or Persons, inhabitant or Inhabitants of this province, not in actual Pay, shall kill an Enemy Indian or Indians, he or they, shall have and receive Ten Pounds for each and every Indian he or they shall so kill; and any Person or Persons who shall be in the actual Pay of this Province, shall have and receive Five Pounds for every Enemy, Indian or Indians he or they shall so kill, to be paid out of the Treasury; any Law, Usage or Custom, to the contrary, notwithstanding.

XIV. Provided always, That any Person claiming the said Reward, before he be allowed or paid the same, shall produce to the Assembly the Scalp of every Indian so killed, and make Oath, or otherwise prove that he was the Person who killed, or was present at the killing the Indian whose Scalp shall be so produced; and that he hath not before had or received any allowance from the Public for the same; And as a further Encouragement, shall also have, and keep to his or their own Use or Uses, all Plunder taken out of the Possession of any Enemy Indian or Indians, or within Twenty Miles of any of the Cherokee Towns, or any Indian Town at War with any of his Majesty's Subjects.

XV. And be it further Enacted, by the Authority aforesaid, That Two Thousand Pounds of the Remainder of the aforesaid Twelve Thousand Pounds, shall be, and is hereby appropriated, to and for the Payment of the aforesaid Rewards to such Person and Persons as, by killing any of the aforesaid Indians, shall be intitled to receive the same; but if a less Sum shall be found sufficient for the said Purpose, the Surplus shall be applied towards paying the several Creditors of the Public such Claims as already have been, or shall be allowed by the General Assembly, and to any other Purpose: And the Residue of the said Twelve Thousand Pounds is hereby appropriation to and for the Payment of the Debts of the Public, chargeable on the Contingent Fund, and shall not be otherwise applied.

Appendix A
North Carolina Law

****

THE STATE RECORDS OF NORTH CAROLINA
VOLUME XXIII., 1715-1776
EDITED BY: WALTER CLARK
NASH BROTHERS BOOK AND JOB PRINTERS
GOLDSBORO, NORTH CAROLINA, 1904

CHAPTER I.
1764. An Act for appointing a Militia. (Page 601).

    XXIV. And be it further Enacted, by the Authority aforesaid, For the Encouragement for any Person or Persons who shall range and reconnoitre the Frontiers of this Province as Volunteers at his or their Own Expence; it shall and may be lawful for such Ranger or Rangers, in Case of an Indian War, or an Invasion of this Province by Indians, to kill or take Prisoner any Enemy Indian of what Nation soever; and on producing such Indian or Indians, his, her, or their Scalp or Scalps before any two Justices of the Peace of this Province, that are most convenient to the Place where the said Indian or Indians shall be taken or Killed, and due Proof made thereof on Oath, of such Indian or Indians being taken or killed in this Province, and producing a Certificate thereof from the said two Justices, together with the Indian or Indians' Scalps to the Assembly; such Person or Persons shall be intitled to Thirty Pounds, Proclamation Money, for each and every Captive or Scalp so taken and produced as aforesaid; to be paid out of the Public Treasury of this Province.

    XXV. Provided nevertheless, That it shall not be lawful for any Party of Volunteers as aforesaid, to range or Reconnoitre the Frontiers of this Province, without leave first had from the Colonel or Commanding Officer of the Regiment to which they belong, and under the Command of an Officer appointed by Warrant from such Colonel or Commanding Officer.

    XXVI. And be it further Enacted, by the Authority aforesaid, That this Act shall be and continue in Force for and during Three Years, and no longer.

****

THE STATE RECORDS OF NORTH CAROLINA
VOLUME XXIV., 1777-1788
EDITED BY: WALTER L. CLARK

Appendix A
North Carolina Law

NASH BROTHERS BOOK AND JOB PRINTERS
GOLDSBORO, N.C., 1906

CHAPTER VII.
1777. An Act for the Encouragement of the Militia and Volunteers employed in prosecuting the present Indian War. (Page 15).
    I. Whereas the vigorous prosecution of the present Indian War may much sooner put an end to the same; On order therefore to encourage and stir up an enterprising spirit among the Militia and Volunteers employed in the said War.
    II. Be it Enacted by the General Assembly of the State of North Carolina, and by the authority of the same, that from and after the first day of June next, if peace shall not be made with the Cherokees before that time, and until peace shall be made, a Premium of fifteen Pounds for each Prisoner, and a premium of ten pounds for each scalp, shall be paid out of the Treasury to the Captor being in the service of the State, on producing a prisoner or scalp, and making oath that the prisoner was taken by him after the said first day of June, or that the scalp was taken and fleeced off the Head of an Indian Man slain by himself, after the said first day of June.
    III. And be it further enacted by the authority aforesaid, That a premium or reward of forty pounds for each scalp of an Indian Man, and a premium, or reward of Fifty Pounds, for producing an Indian Man Prisoner, be paid to any person in this State, not in the pay thereof who shall voluntarily undertake to make war upon the said Indians after the time aforesaid; Provided peace shall not before that time be made with the same Indians, and until peace shall be made, the Captors making oath as aforesaid, that such scalp or prisoner was taken by him after the said first day of June, and that the Indian so killed or taken was of the Nation of Indians commonly known by the name of Cherokees; and that the scalp produced was actually taken from an Indian killed by the person claiming the same.

CHAPTER XV.
1777. An Act to amend an Act, Intituled, An Act to establish a Militia in this State. (Page 118).
    XXIII. Whereas the Penalties incurred by some of the Militia, who refused to march on the late Expedition against the Cherokee Indians, and other Enemies, for the necessary Defence of this State, have been imposed agreeable to Act of Assembly, and the Resolves of Congress; and

Appendix A
North Carolina Law

whereas some of the said Penalties Incurred and imposed as aforesaid have not been collected, Be it therefore Enacted, by the Authority aforesaid, That the Colonel or Commanding Officer of every Regiment of Militia in this State shall, and he is hereby empowered and authorized to issue his Precept under his Hand and Seal, directed to the Sheriff of the County where the offender resides, to levy the said Fines by Distress and Sale of the Offenders Goods and Chattels, and the said Fines shall be applied in the same Manner as other Fines imposed by this Act; and the Sheriffs for this Service, shall out of the said Fines receive the Fees allowed by Law for levying Executions, and for every Neglect or Refusal shall forfeit and pay the Sum of Ten Pounds.

XXVI. And be it also Enacted, by the Authority aforesaid, That where any Invasion or Insurrection shall happen within this State, the nearest Militia Officer shall give immediate Notice thereof to his next superior Officer, who shall communicate the same to the next Superior, and so on to the Brigadier General, who shall convey the same to the Governor or Commander in Chief, and in the mean Time every such Officer shall use his utmost Endeavours to collect a Force sufficient to repel the Enemy, or suppress the Insurrection; and every Officer failing herein, shall be subject to such Punishment as shall be adjudged by a Court Martial.

CHAPTER V. 2ND SESSION
1778. An Act to prevent trading with the Cherokee Indians without license first had and obtained; and also to prevent Trespasses upon the Indian Hunting Grounds. (Pages 188-189).

I. Whereas, divers Avaricious and ill-disposed persons, have by Frauds in Traffick, or by Trespassing upon the Hunting Grounds of the Cherokee Indians, and divers other abuses, excited their Jealousies and Suspicions, which if not seasonably quieted, and such abuses in future prevented, may involve this and other of the United States in a bloody and expensive Indian War,

II. Be it therefore enacted by the Assembly of this State, and by the authority of the same, that no Person or Inhabitant of this State, shall trade, traffick, or barter with the Cherokee Indians within the Indian Country, unless he shall first obtain a License for so doing, from the Judges of the Superior Courts; and if any person shall trade, traffick, or barter contrary to the true Spirit and Intention of this Act, such person or persons so offending, shall, upon conviction thereof, duly had and obtained

Appendix A
North Carolina Law

in the Superior Court of the District nearest the place where such offence shall have been committed, forfeit and pay the sum of Five Hundred Pounds Current Money of this State, one half thereof to the use of the Informer, the other to the Governor of this State, to applied to defray the Contingent Charges of Government; to be recovered by action of Debt, Bill, Plaint or Indictment, wherein no Essoign, Excuse, or Plea in Abatement shall be admitted to the Jurisdiction of the said Court, nor shall Process be discontinued for or by reason of any Omission or Errors not substantially material; and in case such Offender or Offenders shall not within twenty four hours after conviction pay into the hands of the Sheriff of the County in which such District Court shall be held, the said sum of Five Hundred Pounds, and all Costs arising upon such prosecution, he shall stand in the Pillory two hours, and receive thirty nine lashes upon his bare back, and shall stand Committed to the Gaol of the District until such sums shall be compleatly discharged and paid.

   III. And be it further enacted by the authority aforesaid, That if any person shall hereafter be guilty of trespassing upon the Indian Hunting Grounds, knowing them to be such, he shall suffer the same Penalties, Fines, and forfeitures, to be prosecuted, sued for and recovered, and inflicted, as are by this act heretofore directed, with respect to Persons trafficking with the Cherokee Indians, and under the same Rules, Regulations, Latitude and Restrictions, prescribed to be had against the offenders specified in this Act heretofore, and all Fines and Forfeitures shall be applied in Manner as before directed.

      Allen Jones, S.S.
      Thomas Benbury, S.C.

CHAPTER XXIV. 1ST SESSION.
1780. An Act to amend an Act, intituled, "An Act to regulate and establish a Militia in this State." (Pages 335-336).
   VIII. And be it further enacted by the authority aforesaid, that no Frenchman, Spaniard, British deserter, Hessian deserter, Indian or slave, shall in the future be received by any militia officer as a substitute for any militia soldier or officer, under any pretence whatsoever.

CHAPTER I. 1ST SESSION.
1781. An Act for raising Troops out of the Militia of this State for the defence thereof, and for other purposes. (Page 386).

Appendix A
North Carolina Law

XIV. And be it further enacted, that no British deserter, Hessian deserter, apprentice, Indian, sailor, or negro slave, shall be received as a substitute for any volunteer or person drafted in consequence of this act; nor shall any such persons (apprentices excepted) be classed or admitted into the service, in order to exempt any of the said classed from a draft.

CHAPTER I. 1ST SESSION.
1782. An Act for Raising troops to compleat the Continental Battallions of this State, and other purposes. (Page 414).
IV. Provided always, That no British or Hessian deserter who hath not been a resident of this State twelve months, or orphan or apprentice under eighteen years of age, Indian, sailor or negro slave, shall be received as a substitute for any class volunteer or draft whatever: And provided further, That no militia officer shall take or receive any person offered as a substitute for any person, then being himself a substitute for any person or class under this Act, on pain of forfeiting for every such offence, the sum of fifty pounds specie, to be recovered by action of debt in any court of record in this State, by any person who will sue for the same, and applied one half to his own use, the other half to the use of the State, and becoming moreover liable to be removed from office.

CHAPTER XXI. 1ST SESSION.
1783. An Act for appointing an agent and holding a treaty with the Cherokee Indians, and for other purposes. (Pages 509-510).
I. Whereas, holding treaties and appointing one or more agents to keep up a continual friendly correspondence with the said Indians, may prevent future wars, and save expence of blood and treasure;
II. Be it therefore enacted by the General Assembly of the State of North Carolina, and it is hereby Enacted by the authority of the same, That his Excellency, the Governor, as soon as may be shall hold, or by such persons as he shall commissionate for that purpose, cause to be held a treaty with the Chickamawga and Over-Hill Cherokees, and also with the Cherokees of the Middle and Valley settlements, at the Long Island on Holston River; and his Excellency the Governor is hereby impowered to cause the musket powder belonging to this State, or so much thereof as he shall think necessary, not exceeding one thousand weight, to be removed to the frontiers convenient to the place where the said treaty shall be held, and to give the said powder, or cause the same to be given in presents to the

Appendix A
North Carolina Law

said Indians; and his Excellency the Governor is hereby impowered to issue warrants on the treasury for any sum not exceeding two thousand five hundred pounds specie, and cause the same to be laid out in the purchase of goods suitable for the said Indians, and the same goods to give or cause to be given in consideration of the lands by the said Indians to be ceded to the State, and also to issue warrants on the treasury for the sum of one thousand pounds specie, to defray the expences of removing the said powder and goods, and the purchase of necessary provisions for the support of the said Indians, attending the treaty, and other expences thereof: And a full and accurate account of all expenditures, articles, stipulations, cessions, agreements and proceedings of the said treaty, wherein this State is or may be interested, shall be laid before the next General Assembly.

  III. And be it further Enacted by the authority aforesaid, That Joseph Martin be, and he is hereby appointed agent in behalf of this State for the Chickamawga and Over-Hill Cherokees, and for the Cherokees of the Middle settlements and Valley towns; and the said agent shall visit the Indians under his agency in their own country once in six months, shall deliver to them messages from the Governor, receive their talks, record them in his journal, record in the like manner such public talks as he without order may deliver them, and send copies of both to the Governor.

  IV. And in order that all the dealings and intercourses with the said Indians may be carried on in the most friendly and upright manner, and every fraud and imposition as far as possible prevented, Be it therefore Enacted by the authority aforesaid, That no person whatsoever shall deal or traffic with the said Indians within the limits of this State, without license first had and obtained from the Governor for the same, and that these licenses shall be granted only to men of the most upright and unexceptional honest characters, and shall not authorize any person obtaining them to trade with the said Indians for any longer time than one year, and those be annually received and obtained.

  V. And be it further Enacted by the authority aforesaid, That every person obtaining such licence, shall pay for the same to the Governor the sum of five pounds specie: And if any person shall without such licence presume to deal with the said Indians within the limits of this State, he shall forfeit and pay fifty pounds specie for the first offence, and one hundred pounds specie for every subsequent offence, one half to the use of the public, the other half to him or them that shall prosecute for the same, to be recovered by action of debt, bill, plaint, or information, in any court of record.

Appendix A
North Carolina Law

VI. And be it Enacted by the authority aforesaid, That the said agent shall be allowed one hundred pounds specie per annum for all services.

****

THE STATE RECORDS OF NORTH CAROLINA
VOLUME XXV., SUPPLEMENT, 1669-1771
EDITED BY: WALTER CLARK
NASH BROTHERS BOOK AND JOB PRINTERS
GOLDSBORO, N.C., 1906

CHAPTER XXXV
1789. An Act to Emancipate Certain Negroes Therein Mentioned.
(Page 37).

Whereas, it hath been represented to this General Assembly, that Robert Shaw, in his life-time, did receive a valuable consideration for the further services of a certain negro woman named Amelia, and has certified the same and declared her to be free: And by petition of Thomas Lovick, it appears to be his desire that a certain negro woman by the name of Betty, belonging to him, should be set free; also a petition of Monsieur Chaponel, desiring to have set free a mulatto slave belonging to him, by the name of Lucy, of three and half years old: And whereas, it appears by the petition of Ephraim Knight, of Halifax County, that he is desirous to emancipate two young mulatto men, called Richard and Alexander, the property of said Ephraim: And it hath also been represented to this Assembly by John Alderson, of Hyde County, that it is his desire to set free a mulatto boy belonging to him, called Sam: And whereas, it hath been made appear to this Assembly by the petition of Thomas Newman, of Fayetteville, that he hath a mulatto boy belonging to him, which he is desirous to emancipate, and known by the name of Thomas:

I. Be it enacted by the General Assembly of the State of North Carolina, and it is hereby enacted by the authority of the same, That the said negro women called Amelia and Betty, and the mulatto girl called Lucy, and the said mulatto men Richard and Alexander, and the mulatto boy called Sam, and the negro boy named Thomas Clinch, shall be, and each of them are hereby emancipated and declared free; and the said Richard and Alexander shall take and use the surname of Day, and the mulatto boy Sam shall be known and called by the name of Samuel Johnson; and the said slaves so liberated, and each of them, are hereby

Appendix A
North Carolina Law

declared to be able and capable in law to posses and enjoy every right, privelege and immunity, in as full and ample manner as they could or might have done if they had been born free.

CHAPTER LXIII.
1789. An Act for the Relief of Such Persons Who May Bee Wounded by the Indians Within the District of Mero, and for Other Purposes. (Pages 58-59).

Whereas, it hath been represented to the General Assembly, that several persons within the district of Mero being wounded by the Indians, had it not in their power to employ physicians, surgeons, nurser, or to provide themselves with the necessary medicines and attendance, by which means their lives have been much endangered: And whereas, it is probable that several persons under the said circumstances have died for want of proper care: For remedy thereof,

I. Be it therefor enacted by the General Assembly of the State of North Carolina, and it is hereby enacted by the authority of the same, That from and after the passing of this Act, the county courts of Davidson, Sumner, and Tennessee shall be and they are hereby empowered and authorised, whenever it may appear to their satisfaction that the person wounded by the Indians is not able to defray the expences of his treatment and cure, to pass the accounts of physicians, surgeons and nurses, and those for the necessary medicines, provisions and attendance, the same being properly attested and proven on oath; which accounts thus passed by the said courts shall be received in payment of all public taxes by the collectors, sheriff or other officers in said district; any law or custom to the contrary notwithstanding.

And whereas, it is good policy to keep up a friendly intercourse with the Indian tribes in amity with the good people of this State:

II. Be it therefore enacted by the authority aforesaid, That all accounts of provisions furnished to Indians within the district of Mero by any of the inhabitants thereof, being duly proven upon oath, and the same being exhibited in the court of the county wherein such persons reside, the said court shall be and is hereby empowered to pass all such accounts, and to fix the price of such provisions furnished to the Indians; which accounts thus passed by the court as aforesaid, shall be received in payment of any of the public taxes in said district; any law or custom to the contrary notwithstanding.

III. Be it further enacted, That on account of the scarcity of physicians and surgeons within the district of Mero, that all practising

Appendix A
North Carolina Law

physicians and surgeons within the said district shall be exempt from all militia duty, except in the case of actual invasion or insurrection.

IV. Be it further enacted, That all Acts of Assembly, or parts of Acts, which come within the purview of this Act, are hereby repealed and made null and void, to all intents and purposes, as if the same had never been made.

CHAPTER LXV.
1789. An Act to Repeal Part of an Act, Entitled, "An Act for Appointing an Agent, and Holding a Treaty With the Cherokee Indians, and for Other Purposes." (Page 59).

I. Be it enacted by the General Assembly of the State of North Carolina, and it is hereby enacted by the authority of the same, That so much of the before recited Act as relates to the Appointment of an Indian Agent, his duty and pay, be and the same is hereby repealed and made void.

CHAPTER LXXI.
1789. An Act to Prescribe the Mode of Paying the Militia Officers and Soldiers for Their Services on an Expedition Carried on Against the Chicamoga Indians by Brigadier General Joseph Martin, in the Year One Thousand Seven Hundred and Eighty-Eight. (Pages 62-63).

Whereas, the militia of Washington district were called out on actual service by order and under command of Brigadier General Joseph Martin, against the Chicamoga Indians, who at that time were plundering and killing the inhabitants of said district:

I. Be it therefore enacted by the General Assembly of the State of North Carolina, and it is hereby enacted by the authority of the same, That the commanding officer of the said expedition shall, any time after the passing of this Act, exhibit into the comptroller's office of this State, attested pay-rolls on oath for the service of the said militia, stating therein the true number and names of the officers and soldiers in each company, proportioning the officers to the number of soldiers so called out; also a roll with the names of the field and staff officers who served on the said expedition, reporting in each roll the exact time of service of the said militia respectively, on the exhibiting whereof, the comptroller is hereby directed and required to examine the same, and pursuant thereto make out and issue according to the law unto and in the name of each officer and soldier respectively, who were ordered out as aforesaid, certificates of such service; which certificates shall be received by the several sheriffs of the

Appendix A
North Carolina Law

said district, and by the treasurer of this State from the said sheriffs, in payment of the public money tax that is or may become due within the said district of Washington, and no other until all such certificates be paid. Provided, That those who have no such certificates shall pay their taxes as otherwise provided by law.

And for the intent and purpose that the above specified certificates shall and may be received for taxes as above mentioned, due or which may become due in the district of Washington:

II. Be it enacted by the authority aforesaid, That the collectors of public money tax in the said district in their respective counties, are hereby required to delay the collection of taxes due in said district for the term of three months after the passing of this Act.

III. And be it further enacted by the authority aforesaid, That so much of an Act passed at Fayetteville, in the year one thousand seven hundred and eighty-eight, as relates to raising men for the purpose of fixing a garrison on the north side of Tennessee river, be and the same is hereby repealed and made void; and the men raised by virtue thereof, shall be and they are hereby discharged from service.

IV. And be it enacted by the authority aforesaid, That the comptroller shall liquidate and adjust, on exhibiting the same to him, the commissary's accounts of the expedition, and issue certificates for the same; which shall be received and paid as above mentioned, such accounts being supported by proper vouchers and the oath of the said commissary.

Read three times and ratified in General Assembly, the 22d day of December, 1789, except Chap. I., which was ratified the 18th of December, and Chap. XXXVIII. which was ratified the 18th of November, 1789.

Charles Johnson,
Speaker of the Senate.
Stephen Cabarrus,
Speaker of the House of Commons
(Copy Test.) J. Glasgow, Secretary.

Appendix B
Early Tribes

Croatan Indians
Secotan, a Chiefdom
Chowanoc, a Chiefdom
Moratoc, a Chiefdom
Bay River or Bear River
Yawpim
Waccamaw
Occaneechi
Matchapungo
Maherrin
Currituck
Chowan
Tuscarora

Weapemeoc, a Chiefdom
Pomouik, a Chiefdom
Neusiok, a Chiefdom
Poteskites
Neuse River Indians
Waccon
Saponi
Mattamuskeet
Pasquotank
Hatteras
Coree
Cape Fear
Sara or Cheraw

Mohawks & Senecas show up in North Carolina's early Court records; mostly as instigators in the Tuscarora War.

Other tribes mentioned in North Carolina records are the Creeks, Choctaws, Chickasaws, Appalachees, Cherokees, Catawbas, Shawanesa, Putestamies, Chippowas, Trevas, Twightwees and Hossew.

Index

Index

A

Act to Pardon and to consign to Oblivion the Offences &c of certain Persons in the Counties of Washington, Sullivan, Green and Hawkins, 235
Adams
  Danl., 247
  George, 247
  Jas., 248
  Wm., 247
Addam
  Samuel, 253
  Wm., 253
Africa, 49
Akehurst
  Daniel, 22, 30
  Mr., 20
Alderson
  Mr, 240
Alexander
  Alin, 241
  Colo. Nathl., 90
  Colonel Nathl., 85
  Ebenezer, 251
  Ebin, 241, 244
  John, 241, 244, 251
  Moses, 85
  Nathl., 74
  Oliver, 244, 251
Allen
  Benjamin, 251
  Wm., 247
Allison
  Thomas, 85
America
  Trade and Traffic of, 35
Ameys
  Mr, 20
Amy
  Mr., 19
  Mr. Thomas, 19
  Mr. Thos., 19
  Thomas, Esqr., 21
Anderson
  Alexander, 253
  Alexr., 248
  James, Senr., 251
  John, Deputy Surveyor, 16
  John, Surveyor, 27
  Mr, 240
  Thos, 251
Appalachian Mountains, viii, 123, 229
Aransjon
  Barefoot, 241
Archdell
  Governor, 14
Archer
  Cornelius, 248
Ash
  John B., Sp., 238
  Saml., 103
Ashbrook
  Moses, 247
Ashe
  J, 76
  John, 84
  John B., 133, 163
  John B., Sp., 233
Ashton
  John, 2
Asia, 49
Atkins
  Edmund, 75, 76, 77
  Edmund Esqr., 76
  Edmund Esqr., Superintendant of Indian Affairs, 75
  Mr., 78
Augustine
  Castle of, 35
Avery
  Peter, 251
  Waightshill, 99
  Waightsill, 100, 253
Axon
  Wm., 1

B

Badham

Index

Mr., 25
Baker
  Mr, 238
Barefeet
  Nicholas, 248
Barney
  Charles, 247
Barrow
  John, 84
  Mr. Wm., 21
  Wm., 19
Bartlet
  Nicholas, 250
Bartram
  Willm., 84
Bashford
  Thomas, 89
Batchlear
  Richard, 24
Battallions
  Second, 256
  Western, 256
Bayle
  John, 251
Beard
  James, 244, 251
  Wm., 251
Beavers
  James, 252
  John, 242, 247
  Joseph, 241
  Thomas, 247
Beavours
  James, Junr., 248
  James, Senr., 248
  Joseph, 248
Beck
  Mr., 255

Bell
  Matthew, 248
  Wm., 248
Benbury
  M, 100
  Tho, 112, 113, 114, 115
  Thos., 102, 103, 110
Bennet
  James, 2
Bennett
  James, 3, 4
Berry
  George, 242
Bevers
  James, 242
Biswell
  James, 175
Black
  Jas., 249
  Jos, 251
  Jos., 242, 244
Blacknall
  Jno., 29
  Mr. Jno, Revd., 29
Blanchard
  Andrew, 101
Blane
  John, 252
Blanshard
  Benjamin, 26
Blansherds
  Capt. Aron, 3
Bledsoe
  Anthony, 175
  Mr, 108
  Mr., 108
Bloodworth

Mr., 160
Blount
  Charles, 90
  Col. William, 120
  Colo. Blount, 120
  Colo. William, 121
  Colo. William, Agent, 122
  Colonel William, 125
  Cpt., 20
  Mr, 102, 112, 113, 159
  Mr James, 101
  Mr., 160
  T., 255
  Tho., 132, 162
  Thomas, 22
  William, 125, 131, 132, 161, 162
  William Esqr., 122
  Wm, 159
  Wm., 130
  Wm. Esqr., 121
  Wm., Agent to attend Treaties, 121
Blounts
  Mr, 159
Body
  Col., 230
Bogle
  Jas., Senr., 251
  Joesph, Junr., 249

Index

Jos, 244
Saml., 251
Boughman
  Jacob, 248
Boundary Line
  Between
    Indians and
    White people,
    100
Bowie
  Majr., 159
Bowman
  E, 244
  Enos, 241
  Mrs., 175
Branches
  Gum, 3
  Jeneper, 3
  Tarkill, 3
Brian
  John, 241
Brickey
  John, 247
  Peter, 247
Bridges
  Bonners, 4
  Cashy, 4
  Jeneper, 3
Britt
  John, 24
  Wm., 13
Broughton
  Andrew, 8
  Tho., 41
Brown
  Capt., 88
  Mr., 78
  Thos, 241, 244
Browns Line, 254, 256

Bryan
  Capt. Morgan, 86, 88
  John, 101
  Nathan, 101
  William, 101
Bryant
  James, 109
Buckanan
  John, 175
Buley
  Anthony, 250
Bullen
  Capt., 73
Bullock
  Leonard Henly, 106
Burden
  Benjamin, 250
  Jn., 250
  John, 250
  William, 250
Burke
  Thomas, 99
Bush
  Abner, 175
  Geor., 248
  Wm., 175
Bushears
  Capt., 167
Buttler
  James, 109
Byrd
  Amos, Junr., 248
  Amos, Senr., 248
  Jesse, 252
  John, 248, 252
  Joseph, 252

  Stephen, 248

C

Cabarrus
  S, SHC, 235
  S., SHC, 231, 236, 238, 245
  S., SPC, 255
Cafteel
  Francis, 250
  John, 250
Cage
  Wm., 124
Cain
  Robert, 109
Caintucky, 164
Caldwell
  David, 241, 244, 248, 251
  David, Senr., 251
  George, 242, 251
  John, 242, 244, 248
  Thomas, 241, 250
  Thos., 248
Calfee
  John, 248
Calfteel
  Edmund, 250
Callaway
  Caleb, 22
Calloway
  Mr., 20
Cameron
  James, 252

Index

James, Senr., 252
Campbell
  John, 26
  Robert, 84
Canada, 51
Cancil
  Edmund, 248
Carel
  Martha, a Mulatto, 29
Carlock
  Abrm., 248
  Isaac, 248
  Js., 248
Carman
  Thos, 2
  Thos., 2
Carr
  James, 251
  Robert, 241
Carson
  John, Junr., 251
  John, Senr., 251
Carter
  Landon, 124
  Micajah, 251
  Michal, 249
  William, 251
Cary
  James, 84
Cashy, 4
Castiel
  John, 248
Caswell
  Governor, 134, 135
  Governor Richard, 99
  Govr., 115, 119

R., 100, 113, 115, 121, 122, 123
Rd., 108, 110, 111, 120
Richard, 84, 99
Richard Esquire, 130
Richard Esquire, Governor, 100, 125
Richard, Grand Master Mason, 99
Richd. Esqr, 115
Catawbas, ix
  Commissioners to treat with, 68
Cathey
  Alexr., 74
  Wm., 247
Cavenieugh
  Wm., 251
Cession Act
  Repealing of, 124
Ceto
  John, 248
Chapman
  Thomas, 124
Cheek
  James, 109
Cherokee
  Warriors, 256
Cherokees, viii, ix

Commissioners to treat with, 68
Cherokees, Expedition against to compel them to give up their lands., 230
Chevin
  Nath., Esqr., 9
Chickasaws, viii
Choctaws, viii
  Warlike Nation, 36
Chowan Precinct, 1
Church of England, 29
Churton
  Mr. William, 16
  Wm., 17
Cimmons
  David, 248
Cities & Towns
  Galphinton, 120
Cities and towns
  New Orleans, 35
Cities and Towns
  Charles Town, 39
  Charleston, South Carolina, 119, 120, 130, 131, 132, 161
  Golphinston, Georgia, 121

284

Index

Keowee, South Carolina, 122
Kinston, North Carolina, 119, 120, 121, 122
Mobile, 167
Moville, 36
New Bern, North Carolina, 84, 99
Philadelphia, Pennsylvania, 99, 132, 133, 162, 163
Wilmington. NC, 78
Citizens and Indians Understanding between, 163
Clack
  John, 241
  Obediah, 253
  Roland, 253
  Rolley, 248
  Spencer, 252
  Spense, 248
Clapton
  William, 247
Clark
  Jno., 250
  John, 249, 251
  Thos., 248
Clay
  Mr, 238
Cloid
  John, 241, 244
Cloyd
  David, 250
  Ezekiel, 241, 244
  John, 250
Coale
  James, 29
Coats
  John, 241, 244, 249
Cogdell
  Charles, 89
Coleman
  John, 247
  Solomon, 247
  William, 247
Collet
  Abraham, 109
Colyears
  William, 175
Commisaries to provide necessaries for Indian allies, 69
Commissioners meeting with Cherokees, 161
To treat with Indians, 121
To treat with the Indians, 99
Waightsill Avery, William Sharpe, Robert Lanier, & Joseph Winston, 100
William Blount and Joseph Martin, 125
Committee on Indian Affairs, 231, 238, 245, 253
Companies
  Stuart and Barr, 162
  Stuart and Barr of Philadelphia, 132
Conner
  Firviros, 248
Cooke
  John, Attorney, 101
  Mr, 102
  Wm., Special Agent, 123
Coor
  Hugh, 249
  Mr, 108
  Mr., 108
Coors
  Jam., 133
Copland
  Jos., 247
Coplin
  Zacceas, 247
Cor
  Hugh, 250
Coroner
  Jos, Coroner, 5
Courts
  Supreme Court of Justice,

Index

Oyer & Terminer, 5
Cox
  Mr. Perrigan, 84
Craig
  David, 248, 251
  James, Junr., 248
  James, Senr., 248
  Jas, 251
  Jas., Junr., 251
  John, 251
  John, Junr., 248
Crecy
  Mr., 234
Creeks, viii
  Bennets, 26
  Carets, 26
  Grasey creek, 82
  Grassey Creek, 110
  Homney, 94
  Richland, 94
Creton
  Jas., 248
Crook
  Zepheniah, 110
Cullan
  A., 176
Cummins
  Mr. William, 87
Cumpton
  William, 247
Cunnenhamm
  Jacob, 251
Cunningham
  James, 244, 251
  Jas., 247
  Jonathan, 251
  Moses, 251
  Wm., 247
Cusick
  John, 244, 249, 251
  Joseph, 249

D

Daniel
  Robert, Deputy Governor, 23
  Robt., Esqr., Landgrave, 13
Daniell
  Robert, Esqr., Landgrave, 11
Daves
  James, 253
Davidson
  Anne, 109
  Capt., 96
  John, 109
  Samuel, 109
Davie
  Mr, 112, 113, 245
  Mr., 236
Davis
  Jos, 247
Daw
  Capt. Rich, 21
  Capt. Rich., 21
  Nicholas, 24
Dawe
  Nicolas, 11
Dawson
  John, 84
Dearmond
  David, 250
  James, 250
  John, Junr., 250
  John, Senr., 250
  Paul, 250
  Samuel, 250
Denkin
  John, 247
Dereham
  Tho., 13
Devenport
  Capt., killed by Indians, 164
Devil
  John, 249
Devis
  John, 41
Dickey
  Capt. George, 109
Dickson
  Hugh, 253
  Jno., 248
  Joseph, 253
  Thomas, 241, 244
Dien
  John, 251
Dieson
  Jacob, 248
Dills
  Thos., 109
Dincan
  John, 251
Dinney
  Charles, 247
Dinwiddie
  Mr., 68

Index

Robert Esquire, 47
Dison
 Thos., 248
District South of French Broad, 254
Dobbin
 Leiut. Alexr., 86
Dobbs
 Arthur, 69, 72, 78, 79, 82
Dobkins
 Jacob, 247
Doget
 Thos., 248
Doogan
 Hugh, 247
Douglas
 R., 247
Douser
 Peter, 249
Dove
 Capt. William, 12
Downs
 Henry junr., 89
Doxson
 Thos., 251
Doyl
 John, 250
Drimmer
 Jams, 247
Dromegoole
 Mr. Alexander, 231
Dromgoole
 Alexander, 230
Droughan
 Walter, 8

Dudley
 Christopher, 17
Duke University, viii
Dun
 William, 247
Duncan
 Craven, 247
Dunkin
 John, 241, 244
Dunlap
 Adam, 244, 249
 James, 244, 249
 John, 244
Dunlop
 Adam, 251
 James, 251
Dunn
 John, 88

E

Eagins
 Edward, 251
Earl of Halifax
 Letters, 47
Earthquake, 96
Eborn
 Henry, 24
Eden
 Charles, 11, 12, 16
 Charles, Governor, 16
Egleton
 David, 249
Ellis
 Capt. Evan, 87
 Capt. Willis, 87
 Willis, 89

Emmens
 David, 241
Entry Taker
 duties of, 256
Erving
 George, 242, 244, 249
 John, 248
Europe
 War in, 35
Every
 Peter, 248
Evins
 John, 247
 Nathaniel, 176
Ewing
 Alex., 250
 Alexander, 241
 George, 250
 Jas, 251
 Robert, 175
 Wm., 251

F

Fanshire
 Benjamin, 241
 David, 241
 Richard, 241
Fergison
 Henry, 251
 Hugh, 251
 Robert, 251
Ferguson
 Henry, 248, 251
 Robert, 249
Ffosens
 Simon[?], 24
Fleming
 Mr. James, 17

Index

Flemings
  James, 17
Florida
  West part of, 104
Floyd
  Lieut. Matthew, 87
  Nichols, 241
Fonsher
  John, 248
  Richard, 248
Fords
  War ford in Virginia, 255
Foreman
  Anthony, 230
Forts
  Alabama, 36
  Albama, 37
  In upper Cherokee Country, 50
  Lewis, 36
  Niagara, 51
  Taken by the French, 50
  Thoulouse, 35
Foster
  Thomas, 88
Franklin
  Lost State of, 245
Freeman
  John, 8
French
  Acquainted with the Indian way., 36
  Defense against, 35
  Forts built by, 49
  Forts on the Ohio, 51
  in alliance with Cherokees, 83
  Incroachments of, 48
  Lieut. Samuel, 89
  Natives of Canada, 36
  Their Indian allies, 37
French & Indians Expedition against, 41
French and Indian War, viii
French Enemies, 43
French Europeans Missionaries encourage them to take Indian wives, 36
Frohock
  John, 84
  Mr. John, iii, 83, 89
Fry
  William, 4, 6, 7
Fulfer
  Jn., 248
Fulford
  Joseph, exempt from taxes, 91
  Mr. Joseph, 91

G

Gale
  Christopher, Esqr., Chief Justice, 29
  CJ, 29
  Majr., 15
Gardner
  John, 109
Garet
  William, 248
Garrett
  Tho, 18
  Thomas, 2, 3
  Thos., 2
Gaston
  Alexander, 100, 101, 102
  Mr, 101
  Mr., 101, 102
Gatlin
  Edward, 13
General Assembly Sessions Records, vii
George
  Capt., 73
Giffin
  Andrew, 251
Giles
  Ensign William, 87
Gillespie

Index

James, 241,
  244, 248
Jas., 248
Jas., Junr., 251
William, 248
Gillespy
  Alexander, 251
  James, 244, 250
  James, Senr.,
    248
  Jas, 251
  Jas., 241, 250
  Jas., Junr., 248
  John, Junr., 248,
    251
  John, Senr.,
    248, 251
  William, 250
  Wm., 248
Gilliland
  John, 247
Glasgow
  J., 100
Glass
  Saml., 249, 250
Glen
  Mr., 50
Glover
  John, 8, 9
  Mr. William, 15
Goare
  Ambrose, 247
Going
  Thomas, 247
Good
  Coorod, 248
Goor
  Soles, 253
Governor Hyde,
  viii

Gowan
  John, 250
  William, 251
Grant
  Elizabeth, 109
  Joseph, 248
  William, 109
Graves
  Stephen, 249
Gray
  John, 109
Great Britain, 38
Great Brittain, 7
  Colonies of, 48
Griffin
  Andw., 248
Grimmit
  Tobias, 249
Gross
  George, Junr.,
    247
  George, Senr.,
    247
  R., 247
Grove
  Mr., 234, 238
Guing
  James, 249
  Wm., 249
Guinn
  William, 247

H

Hacher
  William, 248
Haldim[?]
  Maj. Gen., 91
Haley
  John, 248

Hall
  James, 175
  Major Wm., 175
  Richard, 175
Hallmark
  George, 241
Halmark
  Gorge, 248
Halsey
  Daniel, 17
  Wm., 90
Hamble
  Robert, 251
Hamilton
  Isaiah, 250
  Mr, 237
  Mr., 236
  Pat, 248
  Patric, 252
  Saml., 248
Hammel
  Robert, 248
Hanby
  James, 241
Haney
  James, 248
Hanna
  John, 251
  Joshua, 241,
    248
  Robert, 241,
    244
Hannah
  Widow, 109
Hanry[?]
  John, 110
Harden
  Capt., 94
  Mr., 108
Hardin

Index

Col., 176
Hardon
  Thos., 249
Hardy
  Jos., Coroner, 4, 7
  Joseph, Coroner, 6
Harling
  Mr. Ellis, Superintendant of Indian Affairs, 103
Harmon
  Henry, iii, 83
Harnett
  Cornelius Esqr., 83
Harris
  Charles, 85
  Mr. Robert, 69
Harritage
  Wm., 69
Hart
  David, 106
  Joseph, 251
  Nathaniel, 106
  Nicholas, 248
  Thomas, 106
Hatch
  Mr. Anthony, 10, 12
Hawkins
  Ben, 119, 122
  Ben, Appointed by Congress as Commissioner, 122

Benjamin, 119, 123
Mr, 112
Mr., 108, 113, 236
Mr. John, 16, 27
Hayes
  Robert, 175
  Wm., 175
Haywood
  H., 255
  J, 111, 112, 113, 114, 115, 236
  J, CS, 230, 234, 236, 237, 238, 240, 255
  J.. *See* J., CS, 231, 233, 234
  Jno, 110
  Jno., 110
  John, 108
Heanderson
  John, 248
Heard
  Stephen Esqr., 105
Hecklefield
  Capt John, 9
  Capt. John, 16
  Captn John, 27
Hecklefields
  Major John, 17
Henderson
  John, 241
  Jos, 28
  Richard, 106, 111
  Richd., 111

Robert, 241, 248
Saml., 248
Thomas, 241
William, Junr., 248
William, Senr., 248
Wm., Junr., 241
Wm., Senr., 241
Henery
  George, 247
  Joseph, 247
  Samuel, 241
  Samuell, 249
  William, 247
Heney
  Thos, 247
Henry
  Saml., 251
  Wm., 248
Henson
  Elisabeth, 109
Herritage
  Wm., 41
Hicklin
  John, 248
Hickman
  Thomas, 175
  Thos., 168
Hicks
  Robert, 80, 81, 82
  Robert Esqr., 80, 81
Higgan
  Philaman, 249
Hill
  Benjamin, 28
  Henry, 3

Index

Hines
  William, 249
Hinson
  Allin, 109
Hinten
  James, 2
Hintens
  Jacob, 1
Hinton
  James, 1
Hiser
  John, 241
Hitchcock
  John, 251
  William, 251
Hitter
  Thomas, 3
Hogg
  James, 106, 107, 108
Holmes
  Archibald, 15
  Robert, 24
Holston, 256
Hook
  John, 251
Hooks
  Alexander, 251
  Alxr., 249
  John, 249, 251
  Robt., 249
Hooper
  Mr, 112, 113
Hopewell, 161
Horn
  Abram, 253
  Andrew, 247
  Robert, 248
  Samuel, 247
Horton

David, 241
Hough
  Joseph, 247
House Gleebs, 42
Houston
  James, 241, 244, 249
  James:, 241
  Jas, 248
  Jas., 251
  John, 241, 244, 248, 251
  Matt, 241, 244
  Matthew, 242, 244, 248
  Saml., 248, 251
  Saml., Senr., 249
  Samuel, 244
  Samuell, 241
  Wm., 242, 244, 251
Howard
  Ensign Philip, 87
Hubbard
  Major, 117
Hubbert
  James, 176
Hugen
  Thomas Junior, 82
Hugens
  Aughter, 81, 82
  Thomas, 80
  Thomas Senior, 80
  Thos. Junior, 82
  Thos. Senior, 82
Hughson

Cunrode, 250
Humphreys
  Names not given, 109
Hunt
  Capt. Jonathan, 86
  J, 111, 112, 113, 114, 115, 133
  J, CHC, 229, 234, 235, 236, 237, 238, 240, 245, 255
  J., 110, 163
  J., CHC, 231, 234
  John, 103
Hurricanes, 39
Hutchins
  Anthony, 84
  Capt. Anthony, 89
Hutson
  William, 251
Hyne
  John, 251

I

Indian
  Indian Camps, 95
  Indian Squaws, 96
  Regulation of Indian trade, 43
  Indian Slavery

Index

Cherokees and other Indians, 83
Cyrus, an Indian Slave from South Carolina, 8
Indian boy held as slave, 103
Indian held in bondage, 101
Prisoners for Slaves, 96
Indian Slaves, ix
Indian Trade
Adam Tate, 104
Bond required of Traders, 76
Frauds and irregularities, 74, 76
Traders to obtain Licence, 77
Traders to obtain Licence or Permission, 75
Indians, 245
a survey to lay out lands for the Yawpim Indians, 27
Accused of Murder, 5
Accused of stealing horses, 242

Agent to the Chickasaw Nation, 227
Apelatchicolas, 134
Appellachys, 35
Appointment of Agent, 236
Articles of a Treaty betwixt Virginia, NC & the Cherokee Indians, 246
Attempt to enslave Indians, 19
Bad behaviour, 4
Bare River Indians, 9, 12
Bay River Indians, 20
Bear River Indians, 19, 21
Canadees, 40
Capt Gibbs, a Bear River Indian, 22
Captives held by the Indians, 246
Catawba Nation, 78, 85
Catawba Towns, 78

Catawbas, 75, 76, 89
Cattabo, 74
Ceeding of Western Lands to the United States, 113
Charles Beasley, a Chowan Indian, 1, 2, 7
Charles Beazley, a Chowan Indian, 2, 3
Charles Besly, a Chowan Indian, 8
Cherokee, 99, 232
Cherokee Corner, 134
Cherokee hunting grounds, 253
Cherokee lands, 256
Cherokee Nation, 38, 103, 107, 227
Cherokee town of Chota, 228
Cherokee Towns, 228
Cherokee Warriors and headmen, 231
Cherokees, 37, 38, 75, 76,

292

Index

82, 85, 86, 88, 89, 106, 111, 114, 120, 161, 174, 230, 237, 242, 249 Build Forts among, 38
Cherokees against the French, 73
Cherokees dissatisfied, 132, 162
Cherokees, conduct toward, 249
Cherokees, Depredations of, 245
Cherokees, lands of, 256
Cherokees, line dividing settlers from the Indians., 250
Cherokees, Purhase of land from, 106
Cherokees, raiding Whites, 174
Chicamoga, 239
Chickamaga, 176
Chickasaw Nation, 166, 174
Chickasaw Nations of Indians, 227
Chickasaws, 133, 161, 163
Chief Chaldo, of Eastenora, 166
Chief Clanose, from high wasse, 166
Chief Draging Canoe, 166
Chief Escholato, of Niccoracke, 166
Chief Little Turkey, 166
Chief Taquatche, from Lookout Mountain, 166
Chief Tonoya, of the Spring, 166
Chief Tossels, 166
Chief Wilskunney, from Chote, 166
Chiefs murdered, 116
ChiefsTokenlisky and Morter, 166
Chil Howe, 176
Choctaws, 36, 37
Chowan Indians, 7
Chowan Indians, 2
Commissioners to Treat with Cherokees, 251
Committee on Indian Affairs., 229
Creek Ingon, Interpertor, 74
Creek Nation, 104, 105, 230
Creeks, 37, 134, 164, 167, 174
Creeks, raiding Whites, 174
Creeks, White people amongst, 120
Dark Night, killing of, 176
Depredations, 43, 82
Depredations of, 175
Dividing the Citizens of the United States from the Cherokee Indians, 252

293

Index

Duke of Chatenoga, 166
Edmund, a Bear River Indian, 22
Encroachments by Whites, 174
Expedition against, 94, 233
Expedition against the Cherokees, 239
Expedition against the Chicomogas, 239
Fanny Mingo, 168
Felony against Cherokee Indian, 80
Geo Ffisher, a Bear River Indian, 23
Green Corn Busk, 164
Hair Lip King, 167, 168
Hatteras Indians, 10
High wassey, 176
Hostilities committed by the Chowan Indians, 26
Illegal settlement of Cherokee Lands, 93
Impudent in killing stock, 13
in Friendship and Amity, 75
Indian captives belonging to the Town of Bare River, iii, 9
Indian Deed, 7
Indian scalps taken, iii, 83, 84
Indian Slaves, 10
Indian Town, 111
Indians, 4
Indians set fire to mountain, 95
Indignities against colonists, 20
James Bennet, a Chowan Indian, 1, 8
James Bennett, a Chowan Indian, 2
James Bennett, a Chowan Indian, 1, 3, 7
James Bennett, Thos. Hiter, Charles Beazley, Jeremiah Pushin, John Robins, John Reding, & Nuce Will, 2
James Strawberry, an Indian, 6
James Strawberry, an Indian, 5, 6
Jemiah Pushing, a Chowan Indian, 1
Jereme Pushen, a Chowan Indian, 7
Jereme Pushing, a Chowan Indian, 8
Jeremiah Pushen, a Chowan Indian, 2
Jeremiah Pushing, a Chowan Indian, 1, 2, 3
Jno. Reding, a Chowan Indian, 3
John Hoyter, a Chowan Indian, 13

Index

John Hoyter, Chief of Chowan Indians, 14
John Reading, a Chowan Indian, 8
John Reding, a Chowan Indian, 2, 7
John Robins, a Chowan Indian, 2, 3
Killing of a half breed by Whites, 117
King Charles, King of the Matchapungo Indians, 23
King hagler of Catawbas, 73
King Sothell, a Bear River Indian, 22
land surveyed for Chowan Indians, 13
Lands allotted to, 131
Lay out lands for the Yawpim Indians, 16
Long Town, 165
Lower Creeks, 38
Macklassawtuskau, 168
Marramuskite Indians, 12
Matchapungo Indians, 23
Matchepungo Indians, 19
Mathews, a Bear River Indian, 22
Meahearin Town, 18
Meherrin Indians, 18
Middle Settlements, 95
Mountain Leader, 167
Mountain Leader, Chickasaw Nation, 165
Murder of two Cherokees, 91
Nations of, 35
New town, 166
Northern Indians, 132
Northern Tribes, 163
Nuce Will, a Chowan Indian, 2, 3
old abraham, killing of, 176
Panticough (Pamlico), Indians, 15
Payment to, 254
Petition to move Chowan Indians from their lands, 26
Provocations against, 116
Pyomingo, 167
Pyomingo,, 167
Raven of Chota, 103
Rogue Indians, 14
Rum given to, 20
Sales of Indian lands, 7
Sales of Indian Lands, 3
Scalping of Indians, 94
Scouting parties against, 90
Sothell, King of the Bear River Indians, 22
Southwell, King of the Bay River Indians, 20
Spiritous Liquors being sold, 78
Swannanoa, 246
Taking of Indian scalps, 89

295

Index

Talk delivered by the Old Corn Tassle, 160
Talk from King Hagler, 78
Tasel, killing of, 176
the Red King, 167
Thomas Hiter, a Chowan Indian, 1, 2
Thomas Hittor, a Chowan Indian, 7
Thomas Pushen, a Chowan Indian, 7
Thos. Hiter, a Chowan Indian, 2, 3
To be moved off their land, 18
to extinguish their Claims, 163
to receive compensation, 254
Tom King, a Woccon Indian, 11
Town of too Cowee, 95
Trade in skins, 37

Treating with Southern Indians, 119
Treaty with Cherokees, 121, 125, 232, 236, 242, 253
Treaty with the Bear River Indians, 22
Treaty with the Cherokee, 229
Treaty with the Cherokees, 256
Tuscarora Indians, 12
Tuskau Potapo, 168
Upper Creeks, 36
War with, 243
Warriors and Cheifs of the Cherokee Nation, 229
Western Indians, 75, 76, 174
White killed by Indians, 110
Whites living on Indian lands, 161
Whites settling on Indian lands, 167

Wm. Glover, 168
Woccon Indians, 11
Indians Slavery
Indian Man belonging to James Coale, 29
Indians Atrocities by the Matchapungo Indians, 23
Inge Edmand, 248
Inhabitants of French Broad, 252
Inhabitants South of French Broad, 246, 249, 255
Iniman Jacob, 249
Insurrections, 39
Isaacs Mr., 110
Isbell Jesse, 248, 252
Wm., 248
Zachria, 248
Island, on Holsten, 100
Islands Seviers, 184

J

Jabol Zacriah, 253

Index

Jack
  Samuel, 248
Jackson
  Andrew, 244
  Andw., 251
  John, 241, 251
  Saml., 251
  Samuel, 241, 244
Jamaica, 40
Jamison
  Jno., 248
  John, 249
Jasper
  Richard, 24
Jenkins
  Lewis, 109
Jenys
  Paul, 41
Job
  Daniel, 247
  David, 247
Johnson
  Calvin, 241, 244
  Chas, Sp., 253
  Chas., Sp., 230, 231, 236, 254
  Hugh, 241
  Robert, 41
Johnston
  Calvin, 250
  Francis, 247
  John, 249
  Saml., 231
  W., 108
  William, 106, 107, 108
  Wm., 107
Jones
  Allen, 103
  Edward, 105
  Henery, 247
  Mr, 112, 114
Justes
  James, 109

K

Keen
  Nichodemus, 250
Kelley
  Alexr., 248
  John, 244, 248, 250
Kelly
  John, 241
Kennedy
  Samuel, 244
Kerr
  Capt. Kerr, 85
  John, 242, 244
  Saml., 248
Kersey
  Thomas, 84
Kimsey
  Thos, 6
Kindell
  William, 109
Kingman
  Mr., 15
  Robt., 15
Knott
  Elizabeth, 4, 6
  Elizabeth, assaulted by an Indian, 6
  Elizabeth, death of, 7
  Mrs., 4
Knowling
  Thomas, 168
Knox
  Andrew, 84
  Wm., 227, 228
  Wm., Secretary at War, 227
Kuykendal
  Capt. John, 85

L

Lacitar
  Robert, 26
Laciter
  George, 26
  Robert, 26
Lanier
  Robert, 99, 100
Lashly
  John, 250
Lassiter
  Mr., 255
Laws
  Inspection Law, 43
  Laws to be passed in the Colonies, 65
Lawson
  Anthony, 241
  John, 20
Ledbetter
  Richard, 109
Lee
  John, 110
  Willm., 250
Legg
  Ambress, 249
Legge

Index

Hum., 13
Lenoir
  Wm., 254
Lesly
  John, 251
Lewis
  Amos, 248
  Evan, 247
  Geo., 248
  Jacob, 248
  Jn., 248
  Samuel, 175
Linsey
  David, 251
Liscomb
  John, 4, 5, 6, 7
Little
  Benjamin, 250
  Capt. William, 89
Littrel
  Samuel, 247
Logan
  Charles, 242, 244
Long
  John, 88
Long Island
  in Holston, 106
Loveless
  David, 251
Lovon
  Anthony, 248
Lowery
  Saml., 248
  William, 242
Lowgan
  Jas., 109
Lowrey
  Adam, 247

Jas, 247
John, 251
Lowry
  John, 242
Luckie
  Lieut. William, 87
Luton
  Capt., iii, 13
  Capt. Thos., 19
Lutrell
  John, Heirs of, 106
Luttrel
  Daniel, 247
Lyttleton
  Governor, of South Carolina, 82

M

M Alester
  James, 241, 244
Mabary
  John, 241
Maberry
  Wm., 247
Mackissac
  Jams, 247
  Joshen, 247
Maclaine
  A, 133
  M, 100
  Mr., 160
Macon
  Mr, 112, 114
Magee
  Barkley, 248
Magers

James, 241
Magills
  Scott, 241
Maginly
  James, 241, 244
Majors
  James, 248
Maloogen
  John, 168
Manning
  Abram, 248
Martin
  Alex., 112, 114
  Alexander Esqr., 134
  Alexander, Governor, 229, 256
  Alexr., 134
  Col. Joseph, 120, 121
  Colo. Joseph, 227
  Colonel Joseph, 125
  General Joseph, 239
  Genl. Joseph, 239
  Governor, 116, 117, 118, 253
  Govr., 253
  Jesse, 168
  Jos, 134, 158
  Joseph, 119, 123, 125, 134, 160, 227
  Joseph, Agent for the

Index

Cherokee Nation, 227
Joseph, Agent for the Chickasaw Nation, 227
Warner, 250
Warren, 248
Mason
  John, 248
Massey
  William, 244
Mayberry
  Frederick, 247
McAlister
  John, 250
McCain
  Andrew, 247
  John, 241, 244, 249, 251
McCampbell
  Solomon, 250
McCarbeneys
  Mr., 176
McCarter
  Jeremiah, 249
  Jerimiah, 251
McCartey, 248
  Lammas, 251
McCinsay
  Daniel, 249
McClelan
  Samuel, 241
McCollock
  John, 248
  Thos, 250
  Thos., 248
McColock
  Jas., 248
McComb
  John, 251
McCormick
  Alexander, 248
McCowan
  Mr, 234
  Mr., 234
McCulath
  Jas, 251
McCuleth
  John, 251
McDowell
  C., 108
  Capt., 110
  Charles, 253
  Col., 96
  Genl., 255
  Joseph, 110
  Mr, 234, 245
McEwen
  Alexander, 241
McEwin
  Alexander, 244
Mcfadden
  Capt., 95, 96
McFaden
  Elias, 109
McFadine
  Capt. Jos, 109
McFalls
  Mery, 110
McFarland
  Benjamin, 247
  George, 247
  John, 247
McGee
  Bartley, 251
McGhee
  Barcly, 241, 244
McGillivray
Alexander, Chief of the Creek Nation, 231
  Alexr., 230
  Danl., 230
McGilvary
  Alexr., 230
McGinley
  Jas., 251
McGlalin
  Alexr., 241
McKain
  John, 244
McKay
  Moses, 247
McKenny
  James, 241, 244, 248
McKenzie
  Mr., 160
McKerney
  James, 251
McKinzy
  Daniel, 251
McKissac
  William, 247
McKissak
  Dunken, 247
McLauglen
  Elexander, 248
McLellan
  John, 241
McMahan
  John, 248, 250
McManus
  Capt. James, 86
McMurrey
  Robert, 242, 244

Index

Samuel, 242
Samuel, Jr., 242
Samuel, Junr., 244
Samuel, Senr., 244
William, 244
McMurry
  Robert, 249
  Samuel, 249
  William, 249
McNutt
  Geo., 248
McReynolds
  Joseph, 241, 244, 251
McRoberts
  John, 247
  Samuel, 247
McWhorter
  Lieut. John, 87
Meek
  Jacob, 250
Meglalin
  Alexr., Jr., 241
Meller
  William, 248
Menis
  John, 241, 244
Michael
  Capt. Conrad, 86
  Capt. Conrod, 86
  Conrod, 88
Militia Battalion, 232
Millar
  Jos, 249
  Thos, 249

Thos., Senr., 249
Wm., 253
Wm., Junr., 253
Miller
  James, 103, 109
  Lieut. John, 87
  Wm., 241
Mills
  Neley, 109
Misconduct of Certain Persons in the Counties of Washington, Sullivan, Greene & Hawkins, 234
Missisippi Company, 36
Mitchel
  James, 250
  Morriss, 250
Mitchell
  David, 81
  James, 80, 81
  Mr., 81
Mkennie
  Mr, 234
Mogert
  Thos., 248
Monntaug
  Roger, 24
Montfort
  Jos., 90
Montgomery
  Hugh, 88
  Humphrey, 251
  Humphreys, 248
  J., Attorney, 9
  Jno., 102

John, Esqr., Chief Justice, 28
Moon
  Jesse, 248
  John, 241
  Jos., 248
  Thomas, 247
  William, 248, 253
Moor
  Mr., 109
Moore
  Capt. Wm., 94
  Maurice, 84
  Mr, 108
  Mr., 108
Moors, viii
More
  Edward, 80, 81
  John, 247
  Mr., 81
Morgan
  Evin, 248
  Mr. Robert, 16
  Robert, 27
  Wm., 248
Morrow
  Alex, 247
Moseley
  E., 10
Moss
  George, 249
Moultrie
  Govr., 160
Mountains
  Powel's, 106
  Richland Creek Mountain, 96
Mt. Gomery

Index

Alexr., 241
Murray
  J, 76
  Ja, 41

N

Nail
  Edward, 84
Nanderhorst
  A., 131, 161
  Colo., 131, 132, 162
Narr
  Jno., 248
Nave
  Henry, 247
NC Counties
  Granville County, 80
NC Counties
  Albemarle, 2, 17
  Anson County, 69, 74
  Bertie, 5, 28
  Burke, 110, 232
  Burke County, 108, 110
  Carteret County, 91
  Chowan, 2, 29
  Chowan Precinct, 3, 12, 16
  Craven County, 102
  Curratuck, 29
  Davidson, 163, 174, 175

Davidson County, 133
Gilford County, 134
Granville County, 80
Granville County, 69
Green, 176, 256, 257
Greene, 123, 232, 235
Guilford County, 134
Hawkins, 235
Orange County, 69
Pamlico, 12
Rowan, 232, 256
Rowan County, 69, 89
Rutherford, 110
Rutherford County, 108, 109
Sullivan, 123, 134, 235
Sumner, 174, 175
Washington, 123, 233, 235, 239
NC Towns
  Edenton, 5, 7, 29, 236
  Fayette Ville, 231
  Greene, 232

Hillsborough, 227
Morganton, 232
Neele
  Capt., 110
Negroes
  Great number of, 39
Netherton
  Henry, 248
Nevels
  Capt. William, 109
Nevill
  James, 21
  James, Deputy Marshall, 21
Newell
  Saml, 242
  Saml., 244, 249
  Saml., Senr., 244
  Saml., Sr., 242
  Samuel, Senr., 249
Newels Station, 232
Nickels
  James, 247
Nicols
  Danl., 247
  David, 247
  John, 247
Nowlin
  Thomas, 175

O

Odaal
  Jamiah, 247

Index

Odell
  Isaac, 247
Odle
  Calep, 247
Ogg
  George, 132, 162
  Mr, 160
  Mr., 132
  Mr. George, 132, 162
Oglesby
  Mr., 25
Oglethorpe
  James Esqr., 38
Ohio
  Territoty of, 49
Oldam
  James, 241
Olliphant
  John, 88
Ominet
  John, 248
Oneale
  Capt. John, 10
  John, 11
Osburn
  Colonel Alexander, 86
Outlaw
  Colo., 160, 230
  Mr., 176
Outlaws
  Mr., 233
Overstreet
  William, 250
  Wm., 249

P

Paine
  Capt., 89
Palmer
  Thomas, 15
Palock
  Thomas, 18
Parish Clerks, 42
Parishes
  Society, 5, 6
Parker
  John, 241, 248
  Jos, 241
  Thomas, 88
Patihes
  William, 241
Paul
  James, 249
Paxton
  Samuel, 248
Payne
  Mr, 238
Peek
  Adam, 249, 250
Peery
  John, 247
Perie
  James, 250
  Robert, 250
Person
  Mr, 101
  Mr., 108, 234, 236
Phelps
  Capt. Aventon, 88
phifar
  Martin, 74
Phifer
  Capt. Martin, 85
Martian, 73
Martin,
  Commissary, 84
  Mr., 108
Philips
  John, 250
Phout
  Leonard, 250
Phouts
  George, 249
  Leonard, 249
Pickens
  Andrew, 119, 123
Pifer
  Martain, 73
Pilson
  Robert, 251
Piper
  Mr. Martin, 69
Pohorn
  Wm., 249, 251
Polk
  M., 160
Portuguese
  Menasses a Portagees, 83
Powell
  Wm., 13
Price
  Burlen, 241
  Mrs., 175
  Wm., 175, 253
Pride
  Mr., 237
Privateers, 40
Pryor
  Joseph, 247

Index

William, 247
Pushing
  Jeremiah, 3, 4

Q

Queen Ann's War, 35

R

Ramsey
  Thomas, 175
Ramsy
  Elexander, 247
Randall
  William, 101
Ransom
  James, 253
Ray
  James, 251
  Zekel, 247
Reading
  Lyonel, 24
  Lyonell, 13
Reagan
  Charles, 242, 244
  Charles, Senr., 251
  Henery, 244
  Henry, 251
  John, 242, 251
  William, 242, 244, 251
Reding
  John, 3
Reed
  Alexander, 252
  Coll. Wm., 10

Wm., Esqr., 9
Regin
  Charles, 249
  Henry, 249
  John, 249
  Wm., 249
Relfe
  Captn. Tho., 16, 27
  Mr. John, 16, 27
Religion
  Civil and religious rights, 42
Renfra
  Moses, 253
Renfro
  Josiah, 175
Reprehensible conduct of settlers, 235
Revision of Laws, 44
Reynolds
  Joseph, 251
Rhea
  Mr, 234
Richardson
  Dan, 25
  Danl., 17
Richeson
  Wm., 248
Richison
  Able, Junr., 248
  Able, Senr., 248
Ridle
  Cornelius, 175
Ried
  Jams., 253
River

French Broad, 232
Tennessee, 232
Rivers
  Ashly, 20
  Bare, iii, 9
  Big Baron, 168
  Big Pigeon, 232
  Clynch, 106
  Cumberland, 106
  Duck, 168
  French Broad, 242
  French Broad, 176, 229, 230, 231, 233, 237, 238, 240, 245, 249, 253, 255, 256
  French Broad, Inhabitants south of, 243
  French Broad, South Side Inhabitants, 255
  Holeson, 229
  Holstein, 237, 238
  Holston, 106, 176, 254, 256
  Little, 9, 10, 12, 16, 17, 27, 229, 232, 254, 255, 256
  Missisippee, 163
  Mississippi, 133

Index

Mississippi, 35, 36
Moville, 35
Ohio, 47
Pascotank, 30
Powell's, 106
Powels, 111
Tenasee, 229
Tennesee, 133, 163
Tennessee, 256
Tuckysiege, 95
Roanoake, 20
Roberson
  Colo. Jas., 166
Robertson
  James, Superintendant of Indian Affairs, 103
  Jas., 175
  Mark, 175
Robins
  Jno., 4
  John, 3
Robinson
  Michael, 88
Roddey
  Jas, 251
Rodgers
  Alexr., 247
  Elige, 242
  Henery, 241
  James, 241
  Joseah, 248
Rogers
  Elijah, 248
  Hearvey, 248
  Isaac, 248
  Seth, 248

Rountre
  ffrancis, 26
  Robert, 26
Rountree
  ffrancis, 26
  Robert, 26
Rowan
  Matt., 69
Ruddell
  Jas, 247
Rusel
  Donely, 248
Russell
  George, 109
  Matthew, 241, 244, 248, 250
  William, 244
  Wm., 248
Rutherford
  Brigadier General, 94
  Capt., 86
  Genl., 112, 114
  Jno., 90
  John, 90
  John Esq., 90
Ryall
  John, 88

S

Sagleton
  David, 251
Sales of Indian Lands, 1
Sanders
  Jas., 175
Sarvay
  Jos., 247
Savages

  Nations of, 35
Scollay
  Samuel, 28
Scots Place, 94
Scott
  Doctor Andrew, 89
  James, 248
  Jos., 251
  Samuel, 242
Secretary at War, 228
Seduscus
  Jacob, 247
  James, 247
Sehorn
  Jos, 247
Sevier
  Genl., 115, 255
  John, 119, 229, 230, 232, 235, 253, 254, 256
  John Esquire, 256
  John, accused of hostilities committed against the Indians, 228
  John, Esquire, 231, 235
  John, Pardon Granted, 234
  Mr., 230
Shadon
  Joseph, 250
Sharp
  Mr., 108
Sharpe

Index

William, 99, 100
Shaver
  John, 248
Shelby
  Col. Evan, 134, 135
  Mr., 108
Shields
  John, 248
Shipley
  Nathen, 109
Shul
  Jacob, 249
Simmons
  Emanuel, 101
Sims
  Jas., 248
  Littlepage, 242
  Page, 244, 251
  Stephen, 248
  William, 247
Singelton
  John, 241, 244
Singleton
  John, 248, 250
Sisco
  Sam, 253
Skilman
  Isaac, 241
Slackden
  William, 249
Slade
  henry, 22
  Mr., 20
Slaid
  Henry, 24
Slaves
  Scipio, 28
  Suke, 110

Sloakum
  Samuel, 24
Sloan
  Alexander, 249
  Alexr., 251
  Archibald, 251
  Jas., 251
  John, 251
Slockum
  Samuel, 24
Smallwood
  William, 241
Smith
  Charles, 24
  Jas., 248
  Jn., 69
  Jno, 76, 77
  John, 247
  Lieut. Andrew, 87
  Mr, 234
  Mr., 81
  Mr. George, 69
  Richard, 13, 73, 80, 81
  Thomas, 249
  William, 4
  Wm. Smith, 2
Smothers
  Wm., 175
Snead
  Wm., 248
Sneed
  William, 251
Snodgrass
  James, 250
Sothell
  Governor, 14
Spaniards, viii

Defense against, 35
  of Florida, 38
Spencer
  Thomas, 29
Spenser
  William, 110
Spiller
  Mr., 236
Spivey
  Thomas, 26
Spradling
  Alderson, 110
Springs
  Roaring, 168
Sproul
  William, 249
Stallings
  Nicholas, 26
Stanton
  Wm., 247
Starkey
  Edward, 111
  Mr. John, 84
Starky
  John, 84
Statel
  James, 247
States
  Colony of
    Georgia, 35
  Florida, 38
  Georgia, 35, 37, 38, 40, 75, 76, 91, 104, 120, 130, 134, 135
  Georgia, Richmond County, 105

Index

New York, 37
North Carolina, 120
North Carolina, 39, 49, 75, 76, 104, 123, 124, 129
South Carolina, 8, 34, 35, 40, 75, 76, 78, 99, 100, 255
State of Franklin, 116
State of Franklin, Washington County, 116
Virginia, 4, 49, 65, 69, 73, 74, 75, 76, 99, 100, 106, 228, 246
Stations
  Bledsoes, 168
Staton
  Mr., 175
Statry
  Patrick, 250
Step
  Mary, scalped by Indians, 109
Stephens
  Thomas, 247
Sterns
  Jas., 248
Stirks[?]
  Saml., 104, 105
Stockton
  David, 250
  James, 250
  Samuel, 250
  William, 250
Stokes
  Mr, 234, 245
Stores
  Franklin Store, 132
Sugar Islands, 40
Survier
  John, 176
Swann
  John, 84
  Sam, 41
Swanson
  Mr., 134, 135
Swiss
  Settlement at Purysburgh, 35
Syfares
  Robt., 247

T

Tage[?]
  Captn., iii, 83
Tailler
  Thomas, 7
Taillor
  Thomas, 7
Tailor
  Thomas, 7
Tait
  David, 104, 105
Talbot
  Thomas, 124
Tarewater
  Henry, 249
  Lewis, 249
Tate
  Adam, 104, 105
  David, British Commisary, 104
  Mr. Adam, Indian Trader, 104
Tavill
  Phillip, 250
Taxes
  Increase of, 39
Tayeler
  Joseph, 241
Tayler
  Mr. Thomas, 16, 27
Taylor
  Benjamin, 247
  Joseph, 248
  Robt., 247
Teague
  Capt. Elijah, 86, 87
Tedfod
  Joseph, 244
Tedford
  George, 244, 251
  James, 241
  Jas., 251
  John, 241, 244, 251
  Joseph, 241
Telford
  George, 248
  John, 248
Tence
  Stephen, 248
Territory

Index

Ohio, 41
Territory South of French Broad, 253
Terry
  Capt. William, 89
Terrys
  Capt., 85
Tharky
  Jno., 250
Therman
  John, 250
Thomas
  Eneas, 175
  Henry, 242, 244
  Jacob, 242, 244, 248
  James, 175
  John, 2, 251
  Phelty, 249
Thomkins
  Saml., 248
Thompson
  And., 248
  Capt. Laurance, 87
  James, 242, 248
  John, 241, 244, 248
  Lieut. John, 87
  Robert, 242, 248
  Saml., 241
Thomson
  Chas., 159, 227
  Chas., Secy., 227, 228
  Samuel, 248
Thrift

William, 248
Thurman
  James, 248
Tilor
  Mr. Nich, 21
  Mr. Nich., 21
Tinker
  Jos., 248
Tipton
  Benjamin, 242, 244, 249, 251
  Meshak, 241
  William, 244, 250
Tisdale
  Mr, 101
  Mr., 101, 102
  William, 100, 101, 102
Tomlinson
  Edge, 100
  John Edge, 100
  M, 101
  Mr, 101
  Mr., 101
Tranthaw[?]
  Ann, 91
Treaties
  At Hopewell and Golphinton, 130
  Cherokees, Choctaws, and Chickasaws, 129
  Chicasaw Treaty, 159

Hopewell on Keeowee, 129
Injurious to the citizens, 163
North Carolina to seek disavowal of the Treaties, 131
Papers respecting Indian Affairs, 131, 161
Treaties with the Shawanoes & Cherokees, 160
Treaty with Cherokees, 99
Treaty with the Cherokee, 112
Treaty with the Cherokees, 159
With Cherokees & other Southern Indians, 119
with the Cherokee Indians, 114, 161
With the Chicasaws &

307

Index

Choctaws, 160
Indians, 256
Truewhitt
  Levi, 13
Turnley
  John, 247
Tuscarora War, viii
Tylor
  Mr. Nicho, 19
  Nicholas, 13

U

Unfair Trade Practices, viii
University of North Carolina, viii
University of Virginia, viii
Upton
  James, 251
  William, 251
  Wm., 242

V

Va Towns
  Suffolk, 78
Valleys
  Powells, 111
Vanderhorst
  Col., 159
Vanois
  Edmund, 241
Vernal
  Richard, Junr., 248

Richard, Senr., 248
Virginia
  Militia of, 49
  Province of, 48

W

Waddell
  Capt., 89
  Captain Hugh, 69
  Colo., 82, 90
  Colo. Hugh Waddell, 89
  Hugh, 84
Wade
  Mr., 110
Walden
  David, 248
Waler
  Thomas, 249
Walker
  Capt., 14
  Henderson, 19
  Henderson, Esqr., 21
  Hendsn., 21
  Jas., 241
Walkes
  John, 251
Wallace
  J, Senr., 242
  Joel, 242
  John, 241, 248
  Ollipher, 241
  Thomas, 248
  W., 241
Waller

Thomas, 242, 244
Wallis
  Calep, 175
  Matthew, 248
Ward
  Alexr., 247
  Bryan, 132, 162
  Michael, 3
  Mr., 132, 163
  William, 17
Watson
  G, 110
  Mr. James, 69
Watsons
  Capt. James, 109
Watts
  John, 73
Weatherford
  Martin, 105
  Mr. Martin, 104
Weeks
  Jas., 248
Weir
  Hugh, 242, 244
  Samuel, 242, 244
Welch
  James, 24
West
  Mr. Thomas, Treasurer, 16
  Tho., 17
West Florida, 104, 105
Western Battalion, 232
Western Frontier
  Defense of, 79

Index

Western Revolt, 116
Western Waters, 107
Westward Expansion, viii
Wheler
  John, 250
White
  David, 251
  Isaac, 249
  James, 109, 247
  James Esqr., Superintendant of India Affairs, 158
  Joseph, 247
  Mr., 160
  Mr. James, 159
  Mr., Superintendant, 160
  Wesly, 247
Whitmill
  Mr., 69
Whitson
  William, 247
Wilkins
  Aduson, 248
Will
  Nuce, 3
Williams
  Curtions, 109
  James, 247
  John, 106, 249, 251
  Joseph, 247
  Lewis, 18
  Mr John, 108
  Mr., 108
  Richard, 251
  Thos, 247
  Willm., 84
Willis
  James, 248, 250
  Mr., 234
Willson
  Adam, 253
  James, 253
  Joseph, 253
Wilson
  Adam, 248
  James, 248
  Jno., 248
  Joseph, 248
  Robert, 244
  Robt., 241
  Saml., 109, 247
Win
  William, 24
Winston
  Joseph, 99, 100
Winters
  John, 247
  William, 247
Witherspoon
  James, 250
  Jas., 248
  John, 248, 250
Wood
  Capt., 110
  Elijah, 247
  James, 252
  John, 247
  Jonathan, 247
Wood Rangers, 36
Woodfin
  Nicholas, 247
Woods
  John, 252
  Joseph, 252
  Lieut., 94
  Pat, 248
Wray
  John, 251
  Thomas, 251
  William, 251
Wyatt
  John, 4

Y

Yokim
  Mical, 247
Young
  Patrick, 241, 244

About The Author:

William L. Byrd III has been involved in genealogical and historical research for more than thirty years. His primary areas of interest are Native Americans, African Americans, West Indians, East Indians and Moors in Virginia, North Carolina, and South Carolina.

He has been published by the *North Carolina Genealogical Society Journal*, the *Magazine of Virginia Genealogy*, *The Rowan County Register*, and *The South Carolina Magazine of Ancestral Research*. He has also co-authored articles with Sheila Stover in the *North Carolina Genealogical Society Journal*, *The Augustan Society Omnibus*, the *Pan-American Indian Association News*, and the *Eagle: New England's American Indian Journal*. He has received an "**Award of Special Recognition**" from **The North Carolina Society of Historians** in the category of "**The History Article Award**" for preserving North Carolina history.

He is a U.S. Army Veteran from the Vietnam era, and served with the U.S. Armed Forces Overseas. He is currently retired, and resides with his family in Hickory, North Carolina.

Other Heritage Books by William L. Byrd, III:

Against the Peace and Dignity of the State: North Carolina Laws Regarding Slaves, Free Persons of Color, and Indians

Bladen County, North Carolina Tax Lists: 1768 through 1774, Volume I

Bladen County, North Carolina Tax Lists: 1775 through 1789, Volume II

For So Long as the Sun and Moon Endure: Indian Records from the North Carolina General Assembly Sessions, & Other Sources

In Full Force and Virtue: North Carolina Emancipation Records, 1713–1860

North Carolina General Assembly Sessions Records: Slaves and Free Persons of Color, 1709–1789

North Carolina Slaves and Free Persons of Color: Chowan County, Volume One

North Carolina Slaves and Free Persons of Color: Chowan County, Volume Two

North Carolina Slaves and Free Persons of Color: Pasquotank County

North Carolina Slaves and Free Persons of Color: Perquimans County

Villainy Often Goes Unpunished: Indian Records from the North Carolina General Assembly Sessions, 1675–1789

Other Heritage Books by William L. Byrd, III and John H. Smith:

North Carolina Slaves and Free Persons of Color: Burke, Lincoln, and Rowan Counties

North Carolina Slaves and Free Persons of Color: Hyde and Beaufort Counties

North Carolina Slaves and Free Persons of Color: Iredell County

North Carolina Slaves and Free Persons of Color: Mecklenburg, Gaston, and Union Counties

North Carolina Slaves and Free Persons of Color: McDowell County

North Carolina Slaves and Free Persons of Color: Stokes and Yadkin Counties

www.ingramcontent.com/pod-product-compliance
Lightning Source LLC
Chambersburg PA
CBHW060553230426
43670CB00011B/1804